THE ENEMY WITHIN

THE ENEMY WITHIN

The McClellan Committee's Crusade
Against Jimmy Hoffa and
Corrupt Labor Unions

by Robert F. Kennedy

New introduction by Edwin Guthman

Foreword by Arthur Krock

DA CAPO PRESS • NEW YORK

Library of Congress Cataloging in Publication Data

Kennedy, Robert F., 1925–1968.
  The enemy within: the McClellan Committee's crusade against Jimmy Hoffa and corrupt labor unions / by Robert F. Kennedy; new introduction by Edwin Guthman; foreword by Arthur Krock.—1st Da Capo Press ed.
    p.   cm.
  Originally published: New York: Harper & Row, [1960].
  Includes index.
  ISBN 0-306-80590-1
  1. Trade-unions—Corrupt practices—United States. 2. United States. Congress. Senate. Committee on Improper Activities in the Labor or Management Field. I. Title.
HD6490.C642U544   1994   94-15807
364.1′68—dc20   CIP

All profits coming to the author for this book will be given to help retarded children.

First Da Capo Press edition 1994

This Da Capo Press paperback edition of *The Enemy Within* is an unabridged republication of the edition originally published in New York in 1960, here supplemented with a new introduction by Edwin Guthman. It is reprinted by arrangement with HarperCollins Publishers.

Published by Da Capo Press, Inc.
A Subsidiary of Plenum Publishing Corporation
233 Spring Street, New York, N.Y. 10013

Manufactured in the United States of America

To my wife—whose love through this long struggle made the difficult easy, the impossible possible— this book is dedicated

I have sworn upon the altar of God, eternal hostility against every form of tyranny over the mind of man.

THOMAS JEFFERSON, September 23, 1800

CONTENTS

CONTENTS

Eight pages of photographs
will be found following p. 114

This book is a report on the work of the Select Committee on Improper Activities in the Labor or Management Field, highlighting some of the typical problems and abuses that were discovered. It is based on the record of the investigations conducted by the Committee's professional staff, the sworn testimony taken before the Committee, and the official reports of the Committee to the United States Senate.

INTRODUCTION

Robert Kennedy is remembered for his pursuit of justice and his concern for the downtrodden and disadvantaged, but his most enduring legacy to the nation may well be that he mobilized all federal law enforcement agencies in a coordinated effort against organized crime.

On February 22, 1961, two days after being sworn in as Attorney General in his brother's cabinet, Kennedy acted to convince all 27 agencies—from the Federal Bureau of Investigation and the Internal Revenue Service to the Civil Aeronautics Board and the Atomic Energy Commission—to pool information on the nation's top gangsters and to coordinate their racketeering investigations. Essentially, that set the stage for a federal effort to combat organized crime which, despite shifting degrees of motivation and effectiveness, continues today.

The Enemy Within, a detailed account of a Senate Committee's exposure of crime and corruption in labor unions and corporations in the late 1950s, is the basic document for exploring and understanding what Kennedy accomplished prior to becoming Attorney General. The book lays out the threat that the mob posed and explains the responses of Congress, the committee, and Kennedy. With 34 years of hindsight, we can see how they made a positive difference, and continue to do so.

The investigation began in the fall of 1956, a few weeks before Kennedy celebrated his 30th birthday. He was only dimly aware of the extent to which corrupt union leaders were in league with crime syndicate chieftains, and that they often were being helped in more ways than one by lawyers, business executives, and financiers.

Kennedy was chief counsel of the Senate Permanent Subcommittee on Investigations, which was spinning its wheels until Clark Mollenhoff, a relentless investigative reporter for the Des Moines Iowa *Register-Tribune*, convinced Kennedy and the subcommittee's chairman, Sen. John L. McClellan (D., Arkansas), that racketeering, especially in the Teamsters Union, deserved the subcommittee's attention. When the early probing by Kennedy and his small staff indicated that corruption in the Teamsters Union was far worse than suspected, pressure mounted to head off the investigation. The Senate responded by creating the Select Committee on Improper Activities in the Labor or Management Field with McClellan and Kennedy as chairman and chief counsel respectively.

What happened next fills the book's pages. Through two-and-a-half years the committee heard more than 1,500 witnesses, exposed sordid dishonesty and abuse of power, and won enactment of tough labor reform legislation.

It is, as Joseph A. Loftus, who covered the hearings for *The New York Times*, noted in his review of *The Enemy Within*, "an exciting, valuable and honest" report. But there's more. Kennedy included many of his personal experiences and his characteristically candid opinions, including his views of the committee members, how Congressional investigating committees should operate, and—most importantly—how organized crime's increasing power threatened our system of self-government.

Kennedy acknowledged that when the investigation got underway in 1956, "I had only a vague impression of the Teamsters Union— some notion that it was big and tough...." Eighteen months later he was telling his staff that the mobsters' power was such that "either we are going to be successful, or they are going to have the country." That was not hyperbole—as the record of convictions and organized crime action in this country, in Central and South America, in Asia and Europe would show. But no one prominent in law enforcement or politics had put it quite that way before. "The point I want to make," Kennedy wrote, "is this: If we do not on a national scale attack organized criminals with weapons and techniques as effective as their own, they will destroy us."

However, when Kennedy wrote that and later, when he became Attorney General, there was substantial doubt in law enforcement and in the country that the threat was real. The nation's Number One crime fighter, FBI Director J. Edgar Hoover, did not believe there was a national crime syndicate and said so—often—despite mounting evidence that there was. The Internal Revenue Service thought investigating organized crime was a wasteful use of its manpower and failed to do anything. Only at the Bureau of Narcotics was the threat taken seriously.

Being the President's brother, as well as the nation's chief law enforcement officer, gave Kennedy the power to push Hoover into the battle, "beyond the point of no return," as Victor Navasky noted in his book *Kennedy Justice*. Hoover was reluctant as first. The FBI had never shared intelligence information with other agencies. But Kennedy persuaded the FBI and the other agencies to talk to each other and devote resources to the effort. No one had done that before.

Within a year of implementing Kennedy's policy a break of the greatest significance occurred. Joseph M. Valachi, a close associate of Vito Genovese, one of New York City's five gangster chieftains, broke the mob's code of silence. He was the first.

Valachi, serving time in the Federal Penitentiary in Atlanta for trafficking in heroin, feared that the mob would kill him in prison and turned in desperation to the Bureau of Narcotics. Later, with the FBI in charge, Valachi revealed in amazing detail the full story of his 33 years in the Genovese crime family with names and inner secrets of what he called "La Cosa Nostra" (Our Thing).

When Valachi set forth his story in testimony before an investigating subcommittee of the Senate in 1963, doubt that there was a national crime syndicate disappeared. The FBI, along with the rest of law enforcement, was committed irrevocably to battling it and Kennedy's basic objective in writing *The Enemy Within* was achieved. So this book is more than an account of the labor rackets investigation, which was one of the most sensational and productive that Congress ever undertook. It is, in effect, a call to arms and a warning of the consequences inherent in our blindness and unwillingness to fortify our country against the enemies within—corruption and greed. Kennedy's rationale for leading an unprecedented, effective effort to curb organized crime comes through with force and clarity and his message rings down through the years.

When spreading corruption is linked inseparably with organized crime, the combination of power, he said, is a threat to every person as well as to the foundation of our democracy, and every person who wishes to remain free must be doubly wary and vigilant.

Edwin Guthman
Pacific Palisades, California
January 1994

FOREWORD

"Wine that is salable and good needeth no bush or garland of yew to be hanged before" is a proverb which has lost none of its common sense in the 420 years since Richard Taverner included it in his compendium of folk wisdom derived from centuries of experience.

Never did the saying better apply than to a foreword to this book. It is an account of dramatic and sordid crime against organized labor's rank and file, and generally the people of the United States, committed by gangsters in trades unions and the cowardly or mercenary employers and lawyers who on occasion criminally conspired with them.

It is also an account of the calm, dedicated and ceaseless toil of those public servants who exposed this crime before the committee of the United States Senate of which John L. McClellan of Arkansas is the chairman. And because this crushing task of exposure was entrusted by the committee to its young counsel, Robert F. Kennedy, this thrilling, depressing, but still encouraging, history of a model Congressional inquiry could adequately have been presented by him alone.

Publishers and authors elect to begin books with a foreword for the reason, I assume, that the doors of wineshops of old were garlanded with bush or yew. Or maybe for the reason that a maître d'hôtel advances with a menu to flourish before a guest uncertain of what will agree with both his pocketbook and his palate. But I think the convention might be altered in a book apparent by a glance at its jacket to be an authoritative narrative of one of the most famous episodes in modern Congressional history. For I suspect that many, hurriedly turning the early pages to get at the absorbing tale Bob Kennedy has to tell, will read this commentary, if at all, as an epilogue (which most forewords ought to be).

Congressional investigations are essential to the intelligent fulfillment of at least three duties of citizens under a government of freedom. Even if these inquiries are pursued without regard for the rights of individuals, at the expense of fair play and the spirit of the American Constitution, they are likely to inform the people of some official infractions of their trust that otherwise would never be known. But when they are conducted as the McClellan inquiry has been, the proceedings not only uncover abuses of government and of the people: they supply the material for corrective legislation; and they reveal to voters, as no other process can, the basic characteristics of members of Congress who have been elected on the superficial showing of campaign oratory and public personality.

In this book, a rare combination of the *roman policier* with an autobiography of a zealous prosecutor who still served the Christian ethic of compassion, and is imbued with the humor which seems to be transmitted unbroken through the Irish genes, Bob Kennedy has supplied materials for the fulfillment of all three of these duties by those Americans who view their liberties as imposing a serious obligation of citizenship.

To them particularly I commend the following portions of *The Enemy Within,* lest they be hastily passed over in the rush and tumult of this absorbing story of organized crime:

The recommendation for a National Crime Commission. The structure proposed is unusual because this would not be just another Federal commission, making and issuing dull "studies" of what already is known; creating an expanding system of jobs; providing a forum for speeches of its members as dull as the studies of its staff. This establishment would be a center, disseminating information on the movements of gangsters to the Federal and local enforcement officers who otherwise would not know that a big crime syndicate, for example, had moved from one city to another until the gang (as in Miami) had bought into hotels, race tracks and real-estate projects.

The formula for a model Congressional inquiry: A committee which takes "full responsibility for the testimony of its witnesses"; makes "a painstaking effort to confirm privately and in advance everything you think he will include in his testimony"; forbids the circulation of mere hearsay; gives every witness the right to have counsel in executive as well as open hearings; and equips him with "full knowledge of the purpose of a hearing and why he is being called as a witness."

And though, as the author concedes, no formula of procedure can "prevent a Representative or Senator or counsel from asking an unfair question . . . or from yelling at or browbeating a witness," these basic rules when scrupulously enforced by a resolute chairman will produce the model hearing which McClellan and Kennedy sought to conduct and largely succeeded in doing. Also: "because of limited jurisdiction our Committee could not go into improper activities of business per se . . . only when there was some direct connection with labor. . . . But even thus restricted . . . we exposed improper activities on the part of at least fifteen attorneys and fifty companies and corporations . . . [yet] no management group or bar association (except for the bar association in Tennessee) has taken any steps to clean house."

Bob Kennedy is so much impressed with the policing of internal fiscal corruption by the AFL-CIO that I do not find him sufficiently repelled by the organized violence employed in strikes by a number of unions, which is a corrupt use of their power. He does take the position that union officials must be held responsible for the beatings and other intimidations to which their members readily resort to gain strike objectives, even when there is no evidence that these officials are privy in any way to this crooked use of organized labor's legalized right to strike. This union corruption, frequently compounded by authorities sworn to maintain law and order, seems to me as reprehensible as some of the financial criminality exposed by Kennedy. But this flaw (or I for one find it so) is a minor one in this objective and thrilling account of a national criminal activity which Bob Kennedy had already played a major part in disclosing and arraigning for due punishment before the bar of justice, and the even more punitive process of outraged public opinion.

ARTHUR KROCK

ACKNOWLEDGMENTS

I AM NOT AN EXPERT on labor-management affairs, particularly proficient in the field of labor legislation, nor am I an authority on labor union practices in the United States. Many witnesses who appeared before the Committee, including some of the most corrupt, have forgotten more in some of these fields than perhaps I shall ever know. However, this has not been my field of endeavor.

My work over the past three years has dealt with tyranny, corruption and dishonesty in the operations of certain labor unions and in labor-management affairs. This is an area I have studied and I know and it is mainly with this subject, plus the internal operations of a Congressional investigating committee, that this book is concerned.

To Senator McClellan, the Chairman of the Senate Select Committee on Improper Activities in the Labor or Management Field, for whom I have worked for seven years and for whom I have the greatest affection and admiration, I am extremely grateful. For his courage, understanding, perseverance and patience under the most trying circumstances, the people of this country owe him a great debt.

I am deeply obligated to the Staff of the Committee. It was their loyalty, intelligence and devotion to duty that made the Committee a success. My one regret in writing this book is that space precluded me from mentioning each staff member and the manner of his contribution to the work of the Committee. My deepest thanks, however, to:

Jerome S. Adlerman
John A. Aporta
Jack S. Balaban
Carmine S. Bellino
Alphonse F. Calabrese
John Cye Cheasty
Edgar S. Clark
John P. Constandy
Joseph Corrigan
LaVern J. Duffy
Robert E. Dunne
John P. Findlay
Robert Greene
Walter Henson
Edward M. Jones
Cy Jordan
James H. Joy
Paul E. Kamerick
Arthur Kaplan
James P. Kelly
George Kopecky
Irwin Langenbacher
Michael J. McInerney
James J. P. McShane
Joseph F. Maher
George H. Martin
Walter R. May
Ralph W. Mills
James Mooney
James F. Mundie
Leo C. Nulty
Thomas O'Brien
Kenneth O'Donnell
Francis X. Plant
Levin Poole
Harold Ranstad

Peter Reese
Pierre Salinger
Carl Schultz
Walter J. Sheridan
Richard G. Sinclair
John A. Terry
Paul J. Tierney
Martin S. Uhlmann
Sherman S. Willse

Susan S. Becker
Marie Brucas
Mary L. Casey
Dorothy H. Davies
Alice Dearborn
Margaret W. Ducketh
Dorothy E. Frey
Lena K. Heck
Diana Hirsh
Verna Mae Kaylor
Mary C. Kuhn
Rosemary K. Kennedy
Mary F. Kenney
Margaret Mason
Lillian Mates
Barbara Maxwell
Margaret Mobley
Angela M. Novello
Mary Powers
Rita Rowlett
Hannah H. Stokes
Elizabeth K. Sullivan
Sara L. Vollett
Ruth Young Watt
Georgia H. Wilber
Ruth B. Young

My particular thanks to Mrs. Ruth Young Watt, the Chief Clerk of the Committee, and her husband Walter; and to Mrs. Alice Dearborn, the Committee's Chief File Clerk—who always seemed to be able to find the missing document.

My special thanks to: J. Edgar Hoover, Director of the Federal Bureau of Investigation, for his advice and assistance, as well as Courtney Evans of his office; Joseph Campbell of the General Accounting Office; Harry J. Anslinger of the Bureau of Narcotics; many District Attorneys around the country but particularly Frank Hogan and his office in New York City; various Police Departments, but most particularly New York's and Commissioner Stephen Kennedy, St. Louis's and Captains John Doherty and Tom Moran, and Los Angeles's and Chief Parker and my friends Captain Hamilton and Lieutenant Stephens; the Crime Commissions around the country, and especially to **Dan Sullivan, Aaron Cohen, Virgil Peterson, Maurice** Corcoran, Jim Connor, and Dan Canfield.

I am indebted to those witnesses who at great risk to themselves furnished information to the staff and testified before the Committee. They met the true test of citizenship.

In the preparation and in the organization of this book, I wish to express my particular and heartfelt thanks to John Seigenthaler of the Nashville *Tennessean;* for his assistance, his judgment, guidance and advice I am most grateful.

I am also indebted to Dave Hackett, my school friend, for his encouragement and ideas.

My thanks also to Evan Thomas and Marguerite Munson of Harper's, whose criticisms and editorial help on the manuscript and whose patience with the author were absolutely indispensable.

To Miss Angela Novello and Miss Dorothy E. Frey, for typing and retyping this work all day and often long into the night and yet always remaining cheerful, I am most grateful. To Angie, who has been my secretary for the three long years of this Committee, I can never adequately express my thanks.

Whatever contribution I have made would not have been possible without the help and guidance of my mother and father.

ROBERT F. KENNEDY

PART I

Chapter 1 / THE TIP-OFF

A BLUSTERING SNOWSTORM blanketed Chicago on December 20, 1956. Dark, heavy clouds draped low over the city, and the cold was biting. The Christmas rush and the mounting banks of snow clogged the streets.

At a glance Carmine Bellino and I, our arms burdened with bundles, might have been mistaken for gift-laden Christmas shoppers as we hurried from Chicago's Boulevard National Bank into a waiting taxicab. But we were Senate investigators, not shoppers, and "the gifts" were the subpoenaed records of a labor-relations consultant and close associate of Dave Beck, named Nathan W. Shefferman.

From the bank we went directly to our room in the Palmer House, and began an immediate study of the documents that we had been tipped off might contain interesting information on the activities of the powerful head of the Teamsters Union. They did. In an hour we had come to the startling but inescapable conclusion that Dave Beck, the president of America's largest and most powerful labor union, the Teamsters, was a crook.

Today, looking back over more than three years, this seems somewhat less than a startling discovery. Dave Beck has been convicted. The world knows he was dishonest. But in December, 1956, he was a respected national figure; he had been photographed with President Eisenhower; he traveled widely; he was a university trustee; and by

3

virtue of his position with the Teamsters an authoritative force in the economy of the United States.

And yet the evidence was unmistakable as Carmine Bellino and I reviewed it. He had grossly misused union funds. The amount would run into hundreds of thousands of dollars.

Carmine Bellino was the experienced chief accountant-consultant for the Senate Permanent Subcommittee on Investigations, for which I was chief counsel; on a matter such as this he would not be mistaken.

We had planned to fly home from Chicago that day to spend the holidays with our families, but the storm grounded all flights. We packed up our stack of subpoenaed files and left the city by train. Carmine was bound for his home in Washington; I for Hyannis, Massachusetts, where my family was spending Christmas.

As we left Chicago we knew that Dave Beck was through as a labor leader and as a national figure. It was just a matter of time. The documents we had just been reading provided the evidence that would finish him.

It was also the evidence that led to the establishment of the McClellan Committee and its full-scale investigation of labor-management corruption. But it hadn't started like this. We hadn't been after Dave Beck. It hadn't even started as an investigation of the Teamsters. In fact, at the outset, I had only a vague impression of the Teamsters Union—some notion that it was big and tough, and that Dan Tobin, Beck's immediate predecessor as president, had come from my home state of Massachusetts. I didn't know much more about it than that.

Ironically enough, I first came to know something about the Teamsters through Edward Bennett Williams, the Washington criminal attorney who later was to represent Dave Beck and Jimmy Hoffa and to serve as general counsel for the Teamsters Union. We had met in 1954 and become friends. We lunched frequently in those days and on several occasions he visited me at home. Through him I met his law associate, Eddie Cheyfitz, who was the public relations man and attorney for Beck, and who later joined with Williams in representing Jimmy Hoffa. On several occasions they spoke to me about leaving the Government and coming into their law firm. I told them I thought that I would stay in the Government a few years longer.

One day early in 1956, before our labor investigation was even contemplated, Eddie Cheyfitz had invited me to come and inspect the new Teamsters Building in Washington. It was to become known as "the marble palace"—perhaps it was called by that name then. Dave Beck had just built "the palace" with some five million dollars of Teamster funds—and, as the investigation was later to disclose, had conspired with Nathan Shefferman to defraud the Teamsters Union in connection with the purchase of the land.

I didn't meet Dave Beck on my first visit—I had to wait for that pleasure until January of 1957. I met his secretary though, and she took me on a tour of his office. It was as big as it possibly could have been without being an auditorium. I genuinely admired the view from the big bay windows across the park to the Capitol. It was all very friendly. My brother's book, *Profiles in Courage,* had just been published. Eddie Cheyfitz suggested that Dave Beck would like to have an autographed copy. His secretary thought that an excellent idea. So did I.

Then Cheyfitz introduced me to John English, a tall, slim man who is secretary-treasurer of the union, and to Einar Mohn, the middle-aged, relatively nondescript-looking executive assistant to Dave Beck and a Teamster vice president. No question has ever been raised about John English's integrity. He is one of the oldest of the Teamsters, and for a long time it was the hope of the honest elements in organized labor that he would be in the forefront of the attempt to clean up his union. I was later to discover, however, that although he appeared to hate corruption and dishonesty, it was primarily a hatred of Dave Beck. He liked and accepted Jimmy Hoffa.

Einar Mohn is first and foremost an organization man. As we learned during the course of our investigations, he did what he was told—nothing more, nothing less. His foremost interest was and is keeping his job and not offending the boss. Nevertheless, he is an honest man, and if he had shown courage at the right time, he could have made a major difference with the Teamster movement.

Over lunch in the Teamster cafeteria, we talked about Walter Reuther. Cheyfitz told about having seen Reuther in Russia in 1933. He said that he (Cheyfitz) had broken with the Communist party some years ago—but he was not sure of the Reuther brothers.

When I returned to the Senate Office Building, my brother wasn't in his office, so I asked his secretary to have him autograph a copy of his book and send it to Dave Beck at the Teamster headquarters. I don't know if he ever did. I have never dared inquire.

It was a long step—and several months of frustrating but fascinating work—from Dave Beck's office in "the marble palace" that day to the bank vaults where Nathan Shefferman's records were kept. I suppose you could say the story of how we came by those records really began back in January, 1955, when the Democrats took control of the Senate, and Senator McClellan became chairman and I counsel of the Senate Permanent Subcommittee on Investigations. By 1956 we were investigating dishonesty and corruption among contractors and subordinate government officials in the clothing-procurement program of the Military Services. We had handled a number of other cases of considerable importance, such as trade with Red China, the conflict-of-interest cases which brought about such resignations from the Government as that of Harold Talbott as Secretary of the Air Force and Robert Tripp Ross as Assistant Secretary of the Army.

As we continued our investigative work, we found that some of the leading East Coast gangsters, Albert Anastasia, Johnny Dio and his brother Tommy, and others, were involved directly or indirectly in the manufacturing or trucking of uniforms. We found corruption, violence, extortions permeated all their activities.

We had heard Johnny Dio in executive session[1] in May of 1956 and knew from information furnished us by District Attorney Frank Hogan in New York that Dio and other racketeers had muscled into the labor movement in that area.

[1] Perhaps I should explain that executive sessions are closed meetings at which neither the public nor the press is allowed. They are ordinarily called either when a witness has refused to talk to the investigator on the case but has indicated that he will talk to the members of the Committee, or when the investigators or counsel feel it would be helpful to have certain testimony under oath before proceeding further with the investigation.

Clark Mollenhoff, Washington correspondent for the Cowles Publications and perhaps the nation's best-informed reporter in the field of labor-management corruption, told me racketeers had moved into the Teamsters Union in the Midwest and elsewhere in the country. I pointed out that two previous Congressional investigations had been made of the Teamsters and that there was a question whether our Committee had jurisdiction to conduct such an inquiry.

"Those other two Congressional investigations were fixed because of political pressure,"[2] he said, "and you do have jurisdiction because these unions are tax exempt and are misusing their funds."

After consulting the Chairman, I decided to conduct a nationwide survey of the labor scene and sent investigators into cities in the East and Midwest in an effort to develop a complete picture. In the second week of November Carmine Bellino and I set out for the West Coast to see what the situation was there.

Before leaving for Los Angeles, I talked with Eddie Cheyfitz again. He offered some "leads." Frank Brewster, head of the Western Conference of Teamsters, was the corrupt union figure on the West Coast, he said. He gave me the name of a Teamsters Union official who would be able to tell me "the whole story." That man was Dutch Woxberg of Los Angeles, whom, as it happened, we never saw, but who I later learned was Jimmy Hoffa's representative on the West Coast and the focal point of the opposition to Brewster.

Even then we weren't investigating the Teamsters. I had no idea at this juncture that Dave Beck was corrupt. In my naïveté, I called Einar Mohn at Teamster headquarters in Washington to notify the union's officials I was making this trip. I asked if there was any help Dave Beck could give me, or if there was anyone else on the West Coast who would be of assistance.

I told Mohn that I wanted to be completely fair. To my surprise he was not only gruff and unresponsive, he was distinctly unfriendly. I detected in his clipped tones a note of discontent—as if all was not sweetness and light; as if President Beck and the union would not be happy about such an investigation. He made it clear that they would give me no assistance.

[2] See Chapter 4.

We arrived in Los Angeles on November 14, 1956, and got in touch with Captain James Hamilton of the Intelligence Division of the Police Department, and Lieutenant Joseph Stephens, chief of the Police Labor Squad. We interviewed union officials, employers and employees and several confidential informants. We talked to dissident members of the Sailors Union of the Pacific; we learned of officers and organizers of the Retail Clerks in San Diego who had been beaten by goons; we learned of the attempt by gangsters and hoodlums to take over a local union of the Plumbers and Steamfitters with resulting shakedowns on new building projects.

Through these same people we came upon evidence of a garbage racket in Los Angeles—a collusive arrangement between the Teamsters Union and an employer association of "selected membership."

We received reports of unsolved murders which appeared to be traceable to gangsters' muscling in on labor affairs. We studied reports of goons moving into the garment field.

We interviewed Anthony Doria, gangster Johnny Dio's friend and mentor. He could talk as fast and as long and say as little as any man on earth.

Some cases cried out for an investigation. There was the union organizer from Los Angeles who had traveled to San Diego to organize juke-box operators. He was told to stay out of San Diego or he would be killed. But he returned to San Diego. He was knocked unconscious. When he regained consciousness the next morning he was covered with blood and had terrible pains in his stomach. The pains were so intense that he was unable to drive back to his home in Los Angeles and stopped at a hospital. There was an emergency operation. The doctors removed from his backside a large cucumber. Later he was told that if he ever returned to San Diego it would be a watermelon. He never went back.

Captain Hamilton suggested that I go to Portland, Oregon. There, two newspapermen, Wally Turner and Bill Lambert, had uncovered a web of vice and corruption involving Teamster officials, the underworld and public office holders. I was interested, naturally, and determined to go into it later. At the moment, however, I was anxious to move on to Seattle, where I wanted to go into the activities of Frank Brewster—the man Eddie Cheyfitz had told me was the source of West Coast labor union corruption—and examine the records of his Western Conference of Teamsters.

In this ambition I was disappointed. When I called on Sam Bassett, the Seattle lawyer for the Western Conference, he told me Brewster was out of town.

"No one knows when he will return to Seattle," he said. Then he added, "You can't look at the records until he returns."

Where was he? How could he be reached?

The answer: "No one knows."

Though I was convinced Sam Bassett knew, it was obvious I wasn't going to get anything out of him. Nevertheless I determined to make what contacts I could while I was there. Ed Guthman, a reporter for the Seattle *Times* and a Pulitzer Prize winner, put me in touch with a group of Teamsters from Brewster's Local 174. They had evidence—several invoices—indicating that Brewster had spent union funds for the upkeep of his race horses.

Then we made a contact that changed the course of the entire investigation—perhaps the course of the entire labor movement in the United States.

Before I had left Washington, a friend had suggested that I look up an old acquaintance of his who was working in Seattle. Now, after failing to find Brewster, and with a free afternoon before going to Portland to help get under way the investigation of vice there, I telephoned this "friend of a friend." I made an appointment, then went by to visit him at his office.

We exchanged pleasantries; he asked about things in Washington; about his friend; about my work. Then he wanted to know what had brought me to Seattle. I told him.

Again and again during the course of our investigations a lesson was brought home to me. Worth-while information may come from the most unexpected sources: an anonymous telephone call; a seemingly crank letter; an offhand remark dropped at lunch; or from a "friend of a friend."

This man—call him Mr. X—had concrete information on the

9

Teamsters Union—and on Dave Beck. He said that contrary to what I had been told in Washington, Beck was the man whose affairs were shot with corruption. Beck, not Brewster, he said, was the real evil in the Teamsters Union. He then gave me the name of a friend of Dave Beck who ran a labor relations firm in Chicago. This Chicago man turned out to be a key to Beck's empire of crookedness. The Chicago man was Nathan W. Shefferman. Mr. X told me that Shefferman, through the firms he represented, made purchases for Beck, who paid him for these purchases out of Union funds.

He told me a contractor in Seattle, whose name was John Lindsay, had built a Teamsters building—but had also done a considerable amount of construction work on Beck's Seattle estate, all of which was paid for out of union funds.

Knowing Dave Beck had sold his house to the union a couple of years before for $163,000, I was skeptical. I asked: "Do you mean that the union paid for it in the first place and then bought the house from him for $163,000?"

Mr. X said he had seen evidence indicating that this was true.

The afternoon had flown by. I called Carmine Bellino to come up from Los Angeles to help me develop leads which would confirm or disprove this information. We registered at Seattle's Olympic Hotel—he under the name "Basilio," I under the name "Rogers." It was not out of any flair for the dramatic that we used fictitious names. Nor was it even with the idea that at this point in our work anyone would care much that we were there. We simply felt that with the important new information we had received, it might be more convenient for us if it was not widely known that we were in town.

The following day we returned to see Mr. X. He furnished us with additional information of the same general nature, but necessarily the details were somewhat sketchy.

We interviewed many people in the next two days, but we were still unable to locate the two men we most wanted to see in Seattle: Frank Brewster and the contractor named Lindsay who, as the Senate hearings were to prove, had been paid with union funds for the work he had done on Beck's home. We went to Lindsay's house on the lake outside Seattle, and waited for hours, but he did not appear. As in the case of Brewster, we could find no one who knew where he was or when he was expected.

We wanted to talk to Frank Brewster more than ever. We were interested in learning now not only about his own activities—but also what he knew about Beck's relationship with Nathan Shefferman. We wanted to know what services Shefferman had performed for the money we had heard he received from the Teamsters.

Then on December 9, I received a telephone call from one of our staff members in Los Angeles. Frank Brewster was registered at a hotel there. Los Angeles police had located him for us. If I came at once there was a chance to see and interview him. Carmine and I flew down that night. By the time we arrived, he had disappeared again.

I was tired of being given the run-around by Brewster. Delay is a favorite—and sometimes successful—strategy of people under investigation. Apparently they feel that if they can draw out the investigation for long enough you will grow impatient and disappear. We were not going to disappear.

I called Sam Bassett, the Teamster attorney, at his home in Seattle. I told him that before I left the West Coast I wanted to see Brewster. If I didn't get a definite appointment to see him within the next ten days, I assured him, our investigators would conduct an intensive search and, once he was found, he would be subpoenaed to Washington. I advised Mr. Bassett to get in touch with Mr. Brewster and tell him it would be more practical for him to see me now in a preliminary interview.

A short time later I heard from Bassett. He had found Frank Brewster and he would see us Saturday morning, December 15, in Seattle.

Sam Bassett was the first of a long line of Teamster attorneys I was to encounter who, though paid out of union funds, represent, the Senate Committee found, not the best interests of the union membership but the leadership, which often was corrupt. Some of them will resort to anything from delay and obstructionist tactics to misleading statements to keep dishonest union officials in power.

Sam Bassett gave me my "baptism" in dealing with this sort. He was a good teacher and we learned quickly.

Strangely, I found Frank Brewster a likable man. He is husky and handsome and dresses well. (As it turned out, the union was largely responsible for his attire.) His office in the Seattle Teamsters headquarters was attractive but about a quarter of the size of Dave Beck's in Washington.

During that first talk he was not friendly. But before we concluded our Washington hearings on his affairs—and even after I testified against him at his contempt trial—we got along well. I think he took the attitude that we were simply doing our job—and that he had been caught making some embarrassing mistakes.

I never felt Frank Brewster was an evil man, that he was a gangster or a hoodlum, or wanted such people under him in the Teamsters Union. He was not of the stripe of Jimmy Hoffa and his pals. His weakness was that he enjoyed living too well, and in the process of so doing, had inherited some of the bad habits of Dave Beck, his predecessor as president of the Western Conference.

When later we were able to examine what records of the Western Conference of Teamsters were still intact, we found clear evidence that Brewster had used the union's funds to live a life of luxury. He transported his jockey and trainer around the country; he bought tailor-made clothes for his trainer; he repaired his horse van; he maintained a box at the race track—all at the expense of the Teamsters Union.

He had a business agent for the Teamsters whose chores included walking Brewster's horses in the early morning and driving them to the various race tracks. On one occasion this business agent stayed at the El Rancho Hotel at Millbrae, which was only a short distance from two of California's major race tracks. His expenses there were paid by the Teamsters.

(On that one Brewster had an explanation: "There's a highway close to them that he checks on trucks that run up and down the highway.")

Under Brewster's administration the financing was generally loose. There was a "Local 174 Fund"—which was Brewster's own local—

for which there were no books or records, or even a bank account. Ninety-nine thousand dollars' worth of checks had been made out from Local 174's regular bank account to this special account. Only $4,000 was traceable. That $4,000 had been used as a down payment on Frank Brewster's new home in Palm Springs—but it was charged to organizational expenses.

He loaned Teamster funds to cronies and friends, and he had a special financial arrangement with George Newell, who was the insurance broker for the Western Conference of Teamsters. From this deal Brewster received $5,000 a year for three years. He said it was for getting up early and walking Newell's horses; Newell charged the money off to "commissions." The two were in a horse stable venture together, and when they sold out Brewster made a $40,000 profit and Newell took a $40,000 loss. The Committee was highly critical of this entire relationship, particularly since Newell got exceedingly high commissions for handling the West Coast Conference of Teamsters insurance business.

During our first meeting there in Seattle that Saturday morning, I asked Brewster about Nathan Shefferman. He said Shefferman had never worked for the Teamsters. In the days when Beck was president and he himself secretary-treasurer of the Western Conference, he said, he had signed Teamster checks in blank for Beck. He did not know where the money went. It could have been paid to Shefferman. He did know that Nathan Shefferman had never done work of any sort for the Western Conference of Teamsters for which he had received compensation. While our interview with Brewster covered a wide area of pertinent subjects, this was most important. It meant that if Beck was paying money to Nathan Shefferman from Western Conference funds, as our information indicated, it was not apparently for any legitimate work Shefferman did for the union.

By the end of our conversation Brewster had become highly irritated; he was indignant that we were investigating him and maintained that he was completely innocent of any wrongdoing. I said I would be far more impressed if I did not know that on several points he had lied to us. This was a flat statement of fact, made without anger, and he seemed to accept it as such.

In parting, I handed him a subpoena for all records of the Western Conference of Teamsters as well as for his own Local 174; and before we left Seattle we also served subpoenas on the Seattle National Bank and Trust Co. for the Teamster accounts.

Following that first face-to-face session with Frank Brewster, we set out for Chicago and a meeting with Nathan Shefferman. We wanted to talk with him, and we wanted to examine his records. We believed now that he was getting large amounts of money from Dave Beck. We wanted to know why.

When we had first attempted to arrange a meeting with him he had been as reluctant as Brewster. He said he would discuss his labor relations business only with Mike Bernstein, the Republican counsel for the Senate Labor and Public Welfare Committee. When I told him we were coming anyway, he protested. He did not want to see me. I pressed the point and finally we had agreed on an appointment for December 18.

Just before we left for Chicago I had a conversation with an ex-law enforcement officer—a man with innumerable contacts, and a man, whom, under normal circumstances, I would have considered the best possible source of information.

He told me: "Dave Beck has cut corners, but there is nothing on him. Frank Brewster is the one."

I thought how difficult it is even for "informed sources" to be informed.

Nathan Shefferman was an elderly man, affable and smiling throughout our first conversation. I was interested to observe hanging around the walls of his office patriotic and philosophical quotations from the speeches of Abraham Lincoln. Shefferman talked about his role as a labor relations consultant, told me of the many speeches he had made, all stressing "labor and management working together for a better America," and presented me with copies of them.

His approach to labor-management problems, he told me, made it possible for him to be friendly with many labor union officials.

Dave Beck, he said, was one of them. He described his relationship with the Teamsters president as a very unusual one; they had been on opposite sides of the fence many times.

I wasn't impressed. I asked, "Have you made any purchases for Dave Beck?"

He readily admitted that he had. He didn't remember how many, or what they were, didn't know the amounts of money involved. He kept insisting that he, Shefferman, was a fine fellow and never knowingly had done anything wrong in his life. If there was anything improper in this whole relationship, he implied that it was all due to Dave Beck. He, Shefferman, was an innocent bystander.

"If Beck wanted things wholesale, why shouldn't I buy them for him?" he said.

Did he get paid out of union funds for the purchases?

"I never bothered to look," he replied.

We asked for his records. His son, Shelton Shefferman, had all his books and records, he said. And Shelton was out of town that day. We could talk with him when he returned. Shelton would be able to furnish us with information regarding the transactions he had made for Beck.

We arranged to return two days later—when his son would be in town—and study the records of the Shefferman firm. Nathan Shefferman that day seemed confident that his affable, friendly manner would see him through any problems he might have with us.

On the day of the first Shefferman interview I visited the office of Adlai Stevenson in Chicago to pay my respects to him and members of his staff with whom I had traveled during the 1956 campaign. Carmine Bellino was with me. While we were there we finally reached John Lindsay, the Seattle contractor who had been paid Teamster money for major construction work on Dave Beck's palatial home. Over the telephone I asked him if he had done work on Dave Beck's estate. He admitted that he had. I asked if he had been paid for that work out of union funds. Again, he said he had. Next to Shefferman's records, this was the most important evidence we were to receive during our trip.

And two days later, that snowy, bitter December 20, we got the Shefferman records.

Shelton Shefferman met us in his father's office. He was abusive, contrary and petty—but to his father, not to us. We had some preliminary discussions and then we were dodging the Christmas shoppers, wading through the slush and the cold to the Boulevard Bank and those voluminous files that were to spell out Dave Beck's downfall.

Chapter 2 / THE FALL OF DAVE BECK

BACK IN WASHINGTON, two days after Christmas, Carmine and I went to see Senator McClellan in his apartment and outlined for him the evidence that we had uncovered. He was enthusiastic, but recognized as we did that for a full investigation in this field the jurisdiction of the Permanent Subcommittee would have to be broadened or else a new committee with broad powers would have to be established.

Later that day, Einan Mohn and J. Albert Woll, the Teamster attorney, came to my office. They looked grim and angry. They had heard about my visits to Seattle and Chicago. From the moment they sat down I knew what line they were going to take—and they did: Who did I think I was; who did the Committee think they were? They would not tolerate what we had been doing. I must be out of my mind. If I stopped right now, though they would still be annoyed with me, I would be far better off than if I tried to continue with this silly business. No one shouted, but their air of superiority was galling.

Mohn did most of the talking and he was plain in his criticism, making no bones about how he felt. He said the investigation had been completely unjustified; he knew we hadn't found anything to warrant it, and I had simply been conducting a "fishing expedition" in serving the subpoenas.

Their attitude angered me, and I informed them that we had developed considerable material on some of the highest-ranking officials in the Teamsters Union. I told them that there was a disgraceful situation in their union, which they were interested only in covering up. I told them that we planned to go ahead with our investigation of them, and instead of coming to tell me what to do they should go back and clean up their union.

Mohn and Woll contended that we had no jurisdiction to subpoena their bank accounts and records and added that they planned to take legal steps to keep us from getting them. They said neither Brewster nor any West Coast Teamster official would honor our subpoena.

I felt that we had jurisdiction because I believed their financial reports, which various unions were required to file with the Secretary of Labor, were inaccurate or false and the Federal Government was doing nothing about it.

The conversation lasted twenty minutes or so. They left grimmer than when they came.

Sam Bassett, the West Coast Teamster attorney, filed suit in a state court in Seattle to enjoin us from obtaining any records from either the bank or the Teamsters Union. It seemed unlikely that a state court judge would determine that a committee of Congress in Washington, D.C., did not have jurisdiction in such a matter. But this state judge granted the Teamsters the injunction they wanted. We were barred from the records while we appealed.

Meanwhile reports were coming in from our staff of investigators. From New York we were learning more about Johnny Dio's phony locals and how some of them had operated. We had found a Teamsters local whose officials were making out checks to fictitious people, forging the endorsements on the back and pocketing the money. In Los Angeles we learned more about the cartage racket and the use of the union as an enforcement arm for the employers rather than as a representative of the employees. In Chicago we had some people doing more work on Shefferman; in Seattle, we had started working on the records of Frank Brewster; in Portland, we were following up leads given us by the man who was to be our key witness in the vice rackets hearing.

18

In short, a major fight was brewing with the Teamsters, and I wanted to be prepared for it.

On January 4, I went to see Secretary of Labor Mitchell and discussed what we had been doing. He felt that a full-scale investigation should be made, and pledged the co-operation of his department. This, by the way, we invariably received.

The next step necessarily was an interview with Dave Beck. Albert Woll told me that at the appropriate time President Beck would be available. He said it was not necessary to subpoena him. He would see us when the time came.

Beck, of course, knew that we were moving in. He knew we had subpoenaed the files from the bank and from Brewster. Perhaps he knew that we had seen Shefferman and been in touch with Lindsay. At any rate, on the day I visited Secretary of Labor Mitchell, I learned that Beck was leaving the country.

We subpoenaed the airline records in Seattle and found that he was scheduled to leave the city that same night and was to be in New York the next day, January 5. I felt that once Beck was out of the country he might refuse to return in view of the evidence we had against him. The "appropriate time" to talk to him seemed at hand. I telephoned Albert Woll and told him we had received word that Mr. Beck was getting ready to travel abroad. I informed him that we were going to have an investigator meet Mr. Beck when he got off the airplane in New York and hand him a subpoena, unless Woll would assure me that Beck would see me voluntarily.

Woll seemed surprised and shocked, genuinely, I believe, to hear about the trip. He called me back within a short time and proposed that we meet Beck at 9 P.M. the following night, Saturday, January 5, at the Waldorf-Astoria in New York.

We were dealing with a ticklish, difficult and extremely sensitive subject. We were investigating the International president of the largest, richest and most powerful union in the United States. Investigating labor union officials had not been a popular "sport" around Washington, D.C.

I took with me to New York a letter from Senator McClellan informing Beck that our Committee was going to develop in public hearings some information regarding his activities that would be derogatory. The Senator's letter invited him to attend and answer the charges.

In the hotel Carmine Bellino and I were met at the reception desk by Woll, who took us directly to Beck's room. With the Teamster president was Simon Wampold, a lawyer who was his financial adviser and partner from Seattle.

What struck me about Beck on that first visit, and subsequently when he testified, were his eyes. At first they appeared to be lost in his large oval face; but soon you realized it was Dave Beck's eyes more than anything else that attracted your attention. They seemed like tiny pinpoints of light that were constantly moving back and forth.

Woll introduced us, and we sat down to talk. For an hour or so we discussed the subject of racketeering within the labor movement. Beck spoke out forcefully against racketeering. He said he was anxious to clean the gangsters out of the Teamsters Union. He knew there were racketeers in the union in New York, but with time, he said, he could clean it up.

As he continued to talk about racketeering, it almost developed into a speech that he might have memorized. He warmed to the task of convincing us. His face grew red and florid and his voice began to climb to a higher pitch until he was almost shouting. He seemed to feel that he could yell us into believing in the righteousness and good intentions of his cause.

Then I asked him questions about his personal activities, specifically relating to Nathan Shefferman. This he knew was coming. He was almost patronizing and his tone was completely relaxed as he announced that he could not possibly answer any of my questions about this particular matter. He said he had nothing to hide. But his own personal tax attorney was not present and so naturally he would not indulge in a discussion of personal matters. His manner suggested that we could better spend our time talking about more important subjects.

I asked whether any work done on his home had been paid for by Teamster Union funds. As he answered, his voice started to climb again. It was a personal matter.

I suggested that since he had nothing to hide there should be no problem about answering the question; after all, he had two lawyers with him already.

I presented him with the letter from Senator McClellan. He took it from my hand, opened the envelope and put on his glasses. He walked to a corner of the room and read it under the light of a table lamp.

Finally he looked up.

"You'll hear from me," he said.

And he would hear from us.

Early the following week I paid a visit to the National Labor Relations Board. Reports from our investigators indicated a misuse or misappropriation of union funds in Teamster locals in New York and Portland, Oregon, as well as in Seattle. As I had earlier reminded Mohn and Woll, the law requires that unions with access to the NLRB file annual financial statements with the Labor Department. I wanted to determine how they were reporting the funds that were being misused—and how close a check the Board or Labor Department made to discover fraud.

I was shocked to find that only in rare cases were these reports examined by anyone. They were considered secret information and were not available to the public or to the press. Furthermore, I learned that the Secretary of Labor and the Chairman of the National Labor Relations Board held that, because of a Supreme Court decision, as far as their departments were concerned, the reports did not even have to be true. It was necessary only that they be filed each year, regardless of their accuracy.[1]

A visit to the United States Treasury Department revealed that their agents seldom examined the books of any labor unions, because unions are tax exempt! We were told that they examined only the records of entities from which the Department might obtain additional taxes.

Certainly the jurisdiction of the Committee was now clear. The

[1] In the so-called Gold decision the Supreme Court held that even if Gold filed a false affidavit with the NLRB that he was not a Communist, his union could not for that reason be denied access to the Board. It was the interpretation of the Secretary of Labor and the Chairman of the NLRB that this ruling should apply also to financial reports.

Federal Government was not functioning efficiently if thousands of reports, filed each year, were never looked at—much less examined—and served only to take up space in government buildings. (The Senate Permanent Subcommittee on Investigations has jurisdiction over inefficiency, waste and malpractices in all departments of the Executive Branch of the Government.)

By this time it was well known that our Committee was investigating labor-management relations. Newspapers were reporting developments and public interest was increasing. Hearings had begun, my own schedule was loaded, and the workload at our office was appalling. Eddie Cheyfitz was in constant touch with me during this whole period of investigation. He was a constant source of information, furnishing data on Beck and Brewster—and suggesting throughout that James Hoffa was a reformed and able leader who should be given a chance. By now he had left Dave Beck and was no longer working for the union. He wasn't actually working for Hoffa either, though he was formally retained later. But even now it was obvious that he was extremely interested in having Jimmy Hoffa made International president and regarded Brewster as his main competition.

One day I was preparing to go to a subcommittee hearing when Cheyfitz telephoned to say that Einar Mohn had sent out a telegram to all Teamster vice presidents. It notified them that if called on to answer questions about their affairs they should refuse to do so, and that they could take the Fifth Amendment without fear of disciplinary action by the union.

I subpoenaed the telegram from Western Union. It was bound to be resented deeply by the members of the Congress.

And I went to Teamsters headquarters and handed a subpoena to Einar Mohn. He showed up as scheduled on the morning of January 17 but was excused by Senator McClellan because he had not been able to locate Albert Woll, his attorney. When he and Woll arrived the following day, he refused to answer all questions concerning the telegram on the ground that the Committee had no jurisdiction, thus no right to inquire.

Frank Brewster was called in from the West Coast. He refused to answer on the same grounds.

During the hearing we put into the record some of the material we had gathered showing the misappropriations of union funds in Seattle and New York, and outlined the activities of Dave Beck and his payment of union funds to Lindsay for the construction work at his home.

The hearing aroused interest throughout the country and there was a public demand that some action be taken to correct such abuses.

Dave Beck now let it be known that he was not accepting Senator McClellan's invitation to appear and answer charges. He was back in Seattle from Europe and his doctors now told us he was too ill to travel to Washington.

At this point politics came into the picture. An attempt was made to have the investigation channeled to another committee. Some of those we were investigating felt that they could handle the situation better if the probe were conducted by a committee staff proficient in legislation rather than in investigations.

Then other labor unions, in addition to the Teamsters, including ones against whom no charges of corruption had been made or were ever made, began actively trying to stop us.

A great deal of the opposition was based on the fear that the death of one Democratic Senator at that time might shift the balance of the Senate and make Senator McCarthy chairman of our Committee. The labor leaders and a considerable segment of the Senate were disturbed at the possibility that this investigation might fall under his direction.

Toward the end of January a move developed to create a "select bipartisan committee,"[2] with four Senators from the Labor Committee and four from our Committee. There was considerable interest in who the members would be. Senator McCarthy, as the senior Republican on the Permanent Subcommittee, would naturally be one of those selected. An attempt to bypass him failed when Senator McClellan and Senator Ervin stated that unless Senator McCarthy was a member, they would not serve. The previous two years, while Senator Mc-

---

[2] A select committee is one appointed by the United States Senate to perform a particular task. The McClellan Committee was specifically given jurisdiction to look into matters involving corrupt influences in labor-management relations. A select committee is set up for a specific period of time; it goes out of existence after it has performed its function, whereas a regular committee continues year after year.

Clellan had been chairman of the investigating committee, he had received more assistance from Senator McCarthy than from either of the other two Republicans, and he felt it would be manifestly unfair to pass him over at this juncture. It was therefore agreed that McCarthy should be made a member.

Senator McCarthy, realizing there was some hesitation about even establishing the select committee because of the possibility that he might become chairman, agreed that Senator Ives of the Labor Committee should be the vice chairman. This solved the last major problem. It was then simply a question of the make-up of the rest of the Committee.

Very few of the Democrats on the Labor Committee were willing to accept a position on it. My brother and Senator McNamara agreed to serve. My brother did so reluctantly, feeling that one Kennedy connected with the Committee was enough. Senator Goldwater joined Senator Ives as the other Republican from the Labor Committee. Senators Mundt and McCarthy agreed to represent the Republicans from the Permanent Subcommittee on Investigations. Senator McClellan, of course, accepted and was made chairman. Senator Ervin of North Carolina was appointed when the other two Democratic members, with more seniority, declined.

The Select Committee was established and went into operation on the thirty-first of January, 1957. The original members were McClellan, Ives, Kennedy, McNamara, McCarthy, Ervin, Mundt and Goldwater.

Our efforts to set up the Committee and get it functioning ran concurrently with the game of tag we were having with Dave Beck. He remained out of reach.

One morning Eddie Cheyfitz called me. At this point Beck was in Miami attending a convention of the Teamsters Union. But Cheyfitz said he had heard from James Hoffa; Hoffa had had an appointment with Beck for breakfast that morning, but Beck never arrived. Cheyfitz said Hoffa had checked at Beck's hotel, found he was still registered and his clothes were still in his room. But Hoffa had heard that he had left the country.

We checked and learned that this was exactly what had happened.

Beck was scared. We next heard of him when his picture was snapped in the West Indies, where he told reporters that he was traveling for his wife's health. The last we had heard it had been his own health, which was too bad for him to travel to Washington. I did not believe he would ever come back to this country.

On the assurances of Albert Woll, I had not subpoenaed Beck. Now that he was out of the United States we had no power to subpoena him.

Actually, the last man we wanted as a witness in early February was Dave Beck. We still didn't have all of the documentation that I felt we needed for a complete case. Because of the union's resistance, we had not been able to get Teamster files and records until the Select Committee was set up, when the Teamster argument over jurisdiction collapsed. But it then turned out that many of the Teamster records that would show Beck's operations had been destroyed. It was explained that they had been stored in the union headquarters basement and someone must have thrown them out, because they could no longer be found. This was to become the familiar pattern.

Thus, Beck's financial manipulations had to be reconstructed from independent records. We had to list all checks or disbursements and trace them through. Often we could do this only through bank records. Innocent-looking transactions frequently reveal something of tremendous significance. Through the accounting and investigative genius of Carmine Bellino, the Committee was able to prove that Beck had taken, not borrowed, some $370,000 from the Western Conference of Teamsters.

He had been busy with his union's funds. Among other things, as the hearings showed, he had given Shefferman $85,000 of Teamster money to pay for personal purchases for himself and his family. On his estate in Seattle he had built a swimming pool, improved his own house, built a house for his son, and had other repair work done. This cost approximately $150,000—and of course he used union funds to pay contractor John Lindsay for the work.

Perhaps the worst of Dave Beck's troubles had started in 1953 when the Internal Revenue wanted to ask him some routine questions. He wouldn't talk to them. The Revenue agents are curious men and when Beck refused to answer their questions they started checking on him.

25

The interest of the tax authorities spurred him into action. At that time he had already dug deep into the treasury of the Western Conference of Teamsters. He now sought to return his takings.

In August, 1954, when he returned $200,000 to the union, he indicated that he owed more, though how much more he did not know. He wrote the Teamsters that his accountants had already spent over seven hundred hours on his books and still couldn't arrive at an exact figure. He said he had been "borrowing" this money and was now going to pay it back. A little later he returned another $50,000, and after our investigation, another $120,000, making a total of $370,000.

But Beck in his panic compounded his sins. He borrowed the first $200,000 from the Fruehauf Trailer Company, one of the major trucking companies in the country. The loan was effected in an elaborate, complicated way. Those involved—Roy Fruehauf, Bert Seymour of the Associated Transport Company, which also participated in the loan, and Beck—have since been indicted by the Federal Government under the provision of the Taft-Hartley Act making it a misdemeanor for an employer "to pay or deliver any money or other thing of value" to an employee representative. The indictment was dismissed by a Federal District Court in New York and the Government has appealed the dismissal to the United States Supreme Court.

In order to repay Fruehauf, who, in turn, needed to repay Associated Transport Company, Dave Beck, union president, in April of 1955 bought citizen Dave Beck's Seattle home for $163,000. The Teamsters Union then gave Beck the use of the house rent free.

Beck had long been friendly with Fruehauf and Seymour. In fact, he had prevailed upon them to give $14,000 to buy toy trucks which they testified they understood were to be used for industry promotion. The money went to start a company operated by Dave Beck, Jr. and Shelton Shefferman which sold toy trucks to Teamster locals around the country. Dave Beck told subordinate union officials, "Buy or you'll answer to me." Profit for Beck, Jr. and young Shefferman—$84,000.

Beck, Sr. established a beer distributing company and granted unusual favors to the Anheuser-Busch Company of St. Louis. In return he was treated with unusual deference—outwardly, at least; in inter-office memos, he was referred to as "His Majesty, the Wheel." Beck, Sr. had Beck, Jr. made president of the distributing company by having the Teamsters refuse to handle the beer until his partner in the firm agreed to that arrangement.

We would have liked another month to work on his affairs, but his running battle with the Committee had aroused so much public speculation about whether he would ever return that when he did come back in March we had no choice but to call him immediately.

Frank Brewster, however, was an important witness before Beck testified. When he appeared before our Committee about the middle of March I asked him about Beck in the midst of his testimony regarding his own misuse of funds.

He said: "Please don't get into Beck now, I have enough trouble myself."

On the very last day that he testified, I had a talk with him while we waited for the hearings to start. I was going to ask some direct questions about Beck and I told him so. He had handled himself well during the hearings. There was no reason for him to take the rap for Dave Beck, I told him.

It was apparent by this time that Beck was going to maintain that he had "borrowed" the money he had taken from the Western Conference. There was no better way to disprove Beck's claim than to have Frank Brewster refute it under oath. He had been the secretary-treasurer of the West Coast Teamsters when Beck took the cash. If Brewster pretended that he had known all along that Beck was "borrowing" money he would give credence to Beck's fraud. I told him that when I put the questions to him I hoped he would give a straightforward answer.

This was a crucial point in our hearings, when Brewster had to decide whether to perjure himself for Dave Beck. It was one of the rare occasions when I wrote out the questions that I intended to ask.

MR. KENNEDY: Do you know of any checks made payable to Dave Beck which were considered loans for any year from 1949 through 1952 inclusive?

MR. BREWSTER: I could not identify and remember any checks that were made out to Dave Beck as a loan. As I explained before, I signed checks in blank, but as far as my memory serves me, I do not remember any of the checks being made out when I signed them.

MR. KENNEDY: I have another question. Did you consider any of the money that went to the Public Relations account in Los Angeles as loans to Dave Beck?

MR. BREWSTER: I did not.

MR. KENNEDY: I have another question I want to ask you. Did you consider moneys that went to Mr. Nathan Shefferman as loans to Dave Beck?

MR. BREWSTER: I have no knowledge to the best of my memory of that transaction whatsoever. That was strictly between Dave Beck and Shefferman. As I testified, I had very little business with Shefferman, practically nil. Anything between Dave Beck and Shefferman I had no knowledge of whatsoever.

MR. KENNEDY: Were you ever told by Mr. Dave Beck that the moneys that were being given or sent to Mr. Lindsay were in effect loans to Dave Beck?

MR. BREWSTER: I was not.

These questions, as I have said, looked forward to the time Beck would appear. None of the spectators and few of the reporters present that day realized the significance of Brewster's answers.

When Frank Brewster had finished his testimony before our Committee, though he had been exposed as a labor leader who had played fast and loose with union funds, he was far better equipped for his job than he had been the first day we met. There was no law to prohibit what he had done—although there obviously should have been one. He admitted there was loose financing in his union, but he promised to reorganize financial procedures and he promised to repay any money the Committee found that he owed to his union.

The Committee's information is that he has kept his word.

When Brewster was leaving the hearing room after his testimony was completed, I said to him: "If I come back to Seattle to visit, how will you treat me?"

He looked me straight in the eye, but then with a smile said: "Just like an employer, Bob, just like an employer."

Subsequently, at the International Convention in Miami, Frank Brewster was one of the few who stood up to Hoffa. He couldn't stomach having the International Brotherhood of Teamsters turned over to the underworld of the country and he fought hard, even though it would have been easier to make his peace with Hoffa, who could not lose the election. After the convention was over, a number of newspapermen who had attended it spoke to me admiringly of Brewster's opposition. I wrote him a congratulatory note telling him I understood he had shown courage.

In early 1959, my brother went to speak in Seattle. Because of his stand on the need for corrective legislation and because of the work of the Committee, labor leaders generally boycotted the meeting. Only one major labor leader showed up. That was Frank Brewster. Jack went out of his way to shake hands with him.

I must confess that when Dave Beck first took the stand, and before he started to testify, I felt sorry for him. Why I should have had that feeling for someone who had so grossly betrayed the union membership, had taken $370,000 of union members' dues money, had answered to no one, and had not been brought to justice, is difficult to explain. But I looked at him, and realized that here was a major public figure about to be utterly and completely destroyed before our eyes. I knew the evidence we had uncovered would be overwhelming. It would make him an object of disgust and ridicule. I knew from what we had and from my conference with him in New York that he would have no choice but to plead the Fifth Amendment against self-incrimination. It was no contest now. He couldn't or wouldn't fight back.

Within five minutes of the start of the hearing this feeling left me. Dave Beck, expecting in some way to influence the Committee, had retained ex-Senator James Duff as his attorney, and he was taking the Fifth Amendment. But the way he took it made it seem that Duff —not Dave Beck—was taking the Fifth. For some reason, Senator Duff could not attend the hearing, and sent his assistants in his place.

On every pertinent question that we put to Beck, he gave protracted, wordy answers and finally got around to the Fifth Amendment. His demeanor seemed to suggest that he, personally, was reluctant to mention the Fifth Amendment but that he was doing it in order to help Senator Duff. It was exasperating and, once during the morning session, Senator McClellan brought out the fact that the Teamster president must have mentioned Senator Duff's name over a hundred times. Beck was pleased.

Then there were long, rambling, philosophical questions by some

members of the Committee and longer and more rambling philosophical answers. Even by the time the morning session was over we
had not got down to any of the hard facts. In the afternoon there was
more of the same thing, and Dave Beck seemed to be coming out of
the hearing reasonably well. He stopped talking about Senator Duff
but he seized on very general questions by Senator Mundt and
Senator Goldwater and continued to give general answers, which for
the most part were pointless.

I could hardly contain myself when in answer to Senator Mundt
on whether there should be a Federal law to control union funds,
Beck said: "I am very happy to put into the record . . . in my official
position as president of this international union, the largest in the
world. . . . But I want to make it very definite and clear that you
will, in this Committee and Congress itself, render a distinct service
to the country as a whole for the long pull and for labor and for its
individual membership, if you write into Congressional law, absolute
compulsion for accounting of funds, if possible by certified public
accountants."

At this point he seemed to be enjoying himself. A few minutes later
he came out personally in favor of a Federal law to prevent the
destruction of union documents and by inference was critical of the
way Frank Brewster had handled the finances and books of the
Western Conference of Teamsters.

By then it was almost the end of the hearing and Beck had completely dominated it. The Chairman asked the indulgence of members
of the Committee while the staff placed the material we had available
in the record. He suggested "that we give counsel some time now
to cover some of these matters which will be very helpful to the
Committee, if we can get answers."

I began: "Can you tell the Committee what your relationship has
been with Mr. Nathan Shefferman?"

Then for the next half-hour I asked Beck specific questions about
the manipulations, the misuse, the misappropriation of large sums of
union funds. This was the reason he was here; the reason we were
here. On each question he declined to answer—and by this time, not
so confidently.

MR. KENNEDY: Were Union funds used, Mr. Beck, to pay for gardening at your home?

MR. BECK: I must decline to answer the question because this Committee lacks jurisdiction or authority under Articles 1, 2 and 3 of the Constitution; further I decline to answer because I refuse to give testimony against myself and invoke the Fourth and Fifth Amendments; further because the question is not relevant or pertinent to the investigation.

MR. KENNEDY: Did you take some $320,000 of Union funds?

Mr. Beck declined to answer, in the same words that he used before.

MR. KENNEDY: Do you feel that if you gave a truthful answer to this Committee on your taking of $320,000 of Union funds that that might tend to incriminate you?

MR. BECK: It might.

MR. KENNEDY: Is that right?

MR. BECK: It might.

MR. KENNEDY: You feel that yourself?

MR. BECK: It might.

MR. KENNEDY: I feel the same way.

CHAIRMAN: We will have order, please.

MR. KENNEDY: I want to know, breaking that money down, Mr. Beck, did you use Union funds to purchase five dozen diapers for some of your friends at $9.68?

Mr. Beck again repeated his formula of refusal.

He had no answer for these questions that day any more than he had had answers for them when I first interviewed him at the Waldorf. And as the evidence continued to mount before the Committee, a different image of Dave Beck—the true image—began to emerge.

Next we called Nathan Shefferman. Senator McClellan asked Beck to remain in the room in the hope, as he remarked, that Shefferman's testimony might "refresh his recollection."

Shefferman had difficulty remembering some things but he answered questions.

When he had said at our first meeting that his relationship with Dave Beck had been an unusual one, he certainly had stated the facts. Take the matter of the $85,000 he had received from Beck to buy various items for the Beck family. These included such things as undershirts from Sulka's of New York, a radio, golf balls and clubs, sheets and pillowcases, football tickets, twenty-one pairs of nylons,

31

five dozen diapers, outboard motors, shirts, chairs, love seats, rugs, a gravy boat, a biscuit box, a twenty-foot deep freeze, two aluminum boats, a gun, a bow tie, six pairs of knee drawers—these are but a few of the purchases.

Wonder no longer who the "I" is in "I can get it for you wholesale." It's Nathan W. Shefferman.

Shefferman said he was unaware that he had been paid for the articles out of union funds.

Beck had sought to hide the payments. For instance, he had established a "Teamster Public Relations Account" in Los Angeles, which sounded innocent enough. But we learned that when he wanted to pay Shefferman, he transferred large sums of money from the Teamsters treasury in Seattle to the Los Angeles public relations account. Then immediately the money would be withdrawn from that account and transferred to Shefferman in Chicago.

The Committee also found that Shefferman and Beck had conspired to make a handsome profit in the land deal in which Beck bought the Washington site of the Teamsters headquarters.

Shefferman likewise testified that over a period of years he had given Beck $24,000 because he was "grateful" to him.

These were transactions between the man who headed the biggest and most powerful union in the country, and a representative of management groups.

Despite all this, at the end of the first hearing, Senator Mundt commended Shefferman and called his testimony refreshing. I was shocked; however, I recalled that he had also commended Alger Hiss when Hiss first appeared before the House Committee on Un-American Activities.

(Shefferman returned as a witness seven months later and, when asked questions regarding his extensive union-busting activities, refused to answer on the grounds of self-incrimination.)

The next day Beck was recalled and there were more specific questions—about his use of union funds for boats and bow ties and diapers and deep freezes and nylons and the rest. And still he declined to answer. He said he wanted his day in court with the right to cross-examine and he knew he would be vindicated.[3]

By the end of our hearing in March Dave Beck had been shown to be cruel, stingy, avaricious and arrogant. But had he not been so arrogant, his other faults would not have been so pronounced. He was outwardly as cocky and belligerent when he left the hearing room as when he arrived. I agreed with my brother when he remarked that my earlier sympathy for Beck had been badly misplaced.

Dave Beck was not finished in the Teamsters Union after these hearings. His position had been shaken and the decent elements of organized labor repudiated him. But in the Teamsters Union he was still in control. The rallying cry became, "Wait until he gets his day in court." There was the chant: "What's wrong with taking the Fifth Amendment? It's part of the Constitution." It began almost to sound as if somebody were performing a major patriotic act in taking the Fifth.

But when we proved a short time later that Beck was stealing money from the widow of his best friend, even the hierarchy of the Teamsters could not stomach it. We got hold of the end of this thread in April, when Carmine Bellino and I flew to Seattle. We learned on that visit that Beck with Simon Wampold, his attorney, and one Don Hedlund had set up a mortgage company through which Beck, as International president, channeled all Teamster funds to be used on mortgage loans. On all these funds they received a commission which they split three ways.

We saw Don Hedlund at his office at nine o'clock the night of April 8. He admitted the facts about the company, but said he could see nothing wrong; no conflict of interest; nothing improper. Hedlund talked to us as if we were small children who did not know the facts of life. He was an important figure in the social life of Seattle. He taught at the Jesuit College; naturally he wouldn't participate in anything improper. He could not understand why we did not seem to understand.

When he appeared as a witness in Washington, his attitude was still

[3] Within the year he got his wish. With considerable skill and courage, the District Attorney in Seattle, Charles Carroll, indicted and convicted Dave Beck and Dave Beck, Jr., of larceny. Beck was also indicted and convicted for income tax evasion. Beck's cases are on appeal.

the same. He couldn't understand how the actions and motives of Don Hedlund, "the pillar of his community," could be questioned. His college students were supporting him in this, his hour of trial, he told us, insisting again that nothing he had done was improper or wrong.

In reviewing Beck's books, we had come across a transaction involving a memorial fund of which Dave Beck was the trustee. It had been established for the benefit of Mrs. Ray Leheney, the widow of a former West Coast Teamster official and one of Beck's best friends. This was the transaction:

In May of 1956, some $71,000 was advanced to Beck and Hedlund by the International Brotherhood of Teamsters for what the bookkeeper for the Teamsters thought was the purchase of mortgages for the union. However, Hedlund and Beck used the money to purchase mortgages in their own names, interpreting the money as loans to themselves. These mortgages they held until December of 1956, by which time they had received payments that substantially reduced the value of the mortgages. Then Beck, this time in the capacity of trustee for Mrs. Leheney's memorial fund, used that money to buy the mortgages from himself and Hedlund. The purchase was made at the par value, $71,000. Beck and Hedlund then paid the union what the mortgages were actually worth, which was around $60,000, and pocketed the difference of $11,000. Hedlund and Beck split an $11,000 profit, which they had made first by defrauding the Teamsters, and then the widow of one of Beck's closest pals.

We questioned Hedlund about this at the hearing:

MR. KENNEDY: Let me ask you, do you think that what you did, and how you benefited from these transactions through the Investment Company and through the sale to Ray Leheney's widow, do you feel those activities on your part were completely proper?

MR. HEDLUND: That sale is one that was done from the heart rather than the head.

MR. KENNEDY: Doing it from the heart also gained you approximately $11,000 profit, you and Beck.

It was suggested that Mr. Hedlund's students were not in the best possible hands. Subsequently, I understand, this situation was rectified and Mr. Hedlund is no longer a professor.

Beck appeared for the last time on May 16, 1957. He had appeared briefly on April 24. He had made the statement that he could blow the top off the Capitol if he wanted to talk. We called him back to give him the opportunity. He took the Fifth Amendment.

Throughout the hearings he was nervous and fidgety, and during lulls in the hearings he would whistle to himself. He was a different man from the Dave Beck I had seen at the Waldorf on January 5, or before the Committee on March 26. Now he was dead, although still standing. All that was needed was someone to push him over and make him lie down as dead men should. The man to do that was available.

His name was James Riddle Hoffa.

Chapter 3 / INTRODUCTION TO JIMMY HOFFA

THE MAN who first introduced me to Jimmy Hoffa was Eddie Cheyfitz. From the outset, as I have said, he tried to steer our investigative attention away from Hoffa. And he sought diligently to implant the thought that after a wild and reckless youth during which he had perhaps committed some evil deeds, Hoffa had reformed. He could be a strong force for good in the Teamsters Union, Cheyfitz suggested. He urged me to sit down and talk with him; he wanted me to see what the man was really like, which I could do only by meeting him face to face.

Early in February, 1957, more out of curiosity than anything else, I finally agreed to have dinner with Mr. Hoffa and Mr. Cheyfitz at Cheyfitz's home. The date set was February 19.

On the afternoon of February 13, 1957, a soft-spoken, mild-mannered, prematurely graying man of about forty walked into the near state of bedlam that was our office in the first weeks of the Committee's life and handed his business card to my secretary. It read:

"John Cye Cheasty, Attorney, New York."

John Cye Cheasty had telephoned me from New York City the night before after having talked to one of our staff there. On the telephone he had told me: "I have information that will make your hair stand on end."

In those days there were few people I talked with who did not claim to have information that would make my hair stand on end, and I tried to see all of them. I invited Mr. Cheasty to Washington. About two o'clock the next afternoon he was ushered into my private office. I was having a late lunch and munched a sandwich as he sat down in the old black leather chair beside my desk and began to talk.

Within a few minutes I had forgotten my lunch.

This is what he told me—and what he testified to at Hoffa's trial: James R. Hoffa, he said, had given him $1,000 in cash as a down payment to get a job as an investigator with our Committee. Hoffa wanted him to be a spy and furnish secret information from our files. Cye Cheasty had taken the $1,000, and then had come to me.

As he talked, he took money from his pocket—seven hundred-dollar bills and some loose cash—and laid it out on my desk. He had ticket slips to account for the money, which he had spent on trips he had made from New York to Detroit and back, and from New York to Washington.

Though perhaps I shouldn't have been, considering what we already knew about Teamster officials, I was shocked by his story, and questioned him closely. We talked for more than an hour.

Cye Cheasty had been in the Navy and had worked for the Secret Service. He was now doing legal and investigative work in New York. His practice was not extensive, but he kept busy. He said Hoffa had approached him through a common friend named Hyman Fischbach, a lawyer for whom Cheasty had done some legal work. A few days ago, Cheasty told me, Fischbach had called him and invited him to join him in Washington on "business."

When they met, Mr. Fischbach explained that a client of his wanted a contact on the staff of the McClellan Committee. Did Cheasty know anyone on our staff? Could he get a job with us? Cheasty, as it happened, did have an acquaintance with Bob Dunne, one of our New York investigators. Shaken by Fischbach's suggestion, and immediately on guard, he asked who his client was. Fischbach showed him a name in a book: James Hoffa, Detroit. He offered to telephone Hoffa and confirm the offer. Over the phone, Hoffa told Cheasty to come to Detroit to discuss arrangements.

37

Cheasty and Fischbach flew out at once. They were met at the airport and taken directly to Hoffa's office. The Teamster leader gave Cheasty $1,000 in cash and agreed to pay him $2,000 a month if he got the job with us. The next morning the two men flew back to New York, where Cheasty immediately got in touch with Bob Dunne and outlined Hoffa's offer. His next step was to telephone to me.

As he talked I was continually conscious of the fact that here was a man to whom principle meant more than money. It would have been easy for him to have accepted the $1,000 and simply told Mr. Hoffa he couldn't get the job. Since we needed experienced men, it would have been easy, perhaps, to use his contacts with the Committee in New York to get taken on with us, then to feed information to Hoffa for $2,000 a month. Materially, he had nothing to gain by coming to me—and everything to lose. When it became necessary to bring into the open the fact that Jimmy Hoffa had tried to "fix" a Committee investigator, Cye Cheasty, regardless of how noble his motives, would suffer. Men who will bribe or fix can be dangerous. Furthermore, clients do not like an investigator or a lawyer who talks. Obviously, by talking to us, Cye Cheasty was jeopardizing his practice.

And yet he was willing to take the risk.

Matter-of-factly, and without dramatics, he told me his reasons. He was proud of his service in the Navy and the Secret Service, and he thought Hoffa's offer to him was on a par with attempts by the Russians to get U.S. Government employees to turn over secret information. He was hurt that something in his relationship with Hyman Fischbach had led him to think that Cye Cheasty would be even remotely interested. From the little he had seen and knew of Jimmy Hoffa, he considered him an ugly influence and a threat to the country. He was determined to fight him.

Cye Cheasty was not a strong man physically. I later learned that he suffered from a heart condition. And he was human. He had been genuinely fond of Fischbach and he was concerned because Fischbach's wife was pregnant. He did not want to hurt either of them, and asked if there were not some way to keep them out of the picture. Even before he had finished the question, I could tell he realized there was not. This, for him, was the most difficult part.

He carefully put his initials on the money he had received from Hoffa. I also initialed it. Then we walked together down the Senate Office Building corridor to the office of Senator McClellan, to whom he repeated his story. We asked him to return to the Committee offices and wait, while Senator McClellan telephoned J. Edgar Hoover. Mr. Hoover arrived within a few minutes and took complete control, arranging for a detailed interview of Cheasty that night by representatives of the Federal Bureau of Investigation.

Upon the recommendation of the Department of Justice, we decided that Cheasty should go along with the plan that Hoffa had proposed. Up to this point, what Hoffa and Fischbach had done was not a provable violation of the law. There was only Cheasty's word against theirs. More evidence was needed. The next step, then, was to see if Hoffa would, in fact, urge Cheasty to obtain documents and information from the files of the Committee.

Cheasty agreed to co-operate. In addition to the mental strain and the threat to his career this meant a personal financial sacrifice for him. For the present, at least, he would have to give up his practice, where he was making considerably more than the $5,000 a year the Committee could pay him. (We were legally limited to that amount because he was receiving a Navy disability pension at that time.)

From time to time I have heard people question his motives. Some have said: "Oh, he just wanted a job."

This is not a sensible conclusion. Aside from the fact that he came to work for our Committee at what certainly was hardly an attractive salary for any attorney, he also gladly gave up the $24,000 a year in cash that Hoffa was ready, able and more than willing to pay. If Cye Cheasty was "just looking for a job," Jimmy Hoffa was offering him a good one. To my mind he was a thoroughly unselfish man who was seeking only to do what was right and honorable.

On February 14—St. Valentine's Day—after being sworn in as an assistant counsel for the McClellan Committee, Cye Cheasty returned at once to New York to see if Jimmy Hoffa or Hyman Fischbach would make further advances. The calls came. Cheasty told them he had the job. From that point on, as was brought out at the trial, he was under the direction of the FBI, which guided his movements as he maintained constant contact with both Hoffa and Fischbach.

Hoffa wanted information. So I furnished Cheasty with material which he passed on directly to Hoffa. Hoffa gave him $2,000 more, which Cheasty turned over to his FBI agents. Always we were careful to furnish information that Cheasty would normally come by if he were a Committee investigator. Never, of course, was it information that would jeopardize the work of the Committee.

And that is how John Cye Cheasty came to work for the McClellan Committee—though I subsequently heard several other stories circulated.

Eddie Cheyfitz, Hoffa's attorney, later told me about some of the theories that the defense considered using in Hoffa's subsequent trial for bribery—a trial that was the direct result of Cheasty's work. One story they fancied was that the Committee was the briber and had paid Cheasty to frame Hoffa and Fischbach. Another was that the Committee had put wiretaps on Hoffa's telephones, overheard his conversations with Cheasty, and had then blackmailed Cheasty into coming to work for it. They ultimately abandoned these lines of defense because they couldn't be proved. The truth was and is that Cye Cheasty is an honest man—and Jimmy Hoffa had failed to recognize that there is such a person.

When Cye Cheasty came to me on February 13 and told me of Hoffa's proposal to him, I had been tempted to break the dinner engagement for February 19. But I felt that if I did it might seem peculiar and arouse suspicion of Cheasty. I decided to go to the dinner, knowing that Jimmy Hoffa thought he had a spy on our Committee.

The day of the dinner, Cheasty was in Washington, and in contact with Hoffa. Early in the day I supplied Cheasty with the names of four witnesses we planned to subpoena for our first hearing. Using the prearranged name of Eddie Smith, he telephoned the number Hoffa had given him. The number was listed to the office that Cheyfitz shared with his law associate, Edward Bennett Williams. Hoffa took the call, and arranged to meet Cheasty late that afternoon at the corner of Seventeenth and I Streets.

It was snowing when Cheasty set out for the rendezvous. The FBI testified during the trial that agents equipped with hidden cameras, kept both men under close surveillance. At their street-corner meeting, Cheasty handed to Hoffa the four names I had given him. Hoffa told Cheasty he was acquainted with three of the four. Then, as it was related to me later, Cheyfitz drew up in a car and picked up Hoffa and they drove off together to Cheyfitz's house to meet me for dinner. Cheasty made his contact immediately with the FBI, then called me at my office to say that he had delivered the information to Hoffa. Because I had been waiting for his telephone call I was a few minutes late arriving at Cheyfitz's house.

Both Cheyfitz and Hoffa met me at the door—Hoffa with a strong, firm handshake. Immediately I was struck by how short he is— only five feet five and a half. We walked into the living room of Cheyfitz's elaborately decorated house, but chatted only a few minutes before going in to dinner. The three of us were alone. Hoffa, I was to discover, can be personable, polite and friendly. But that evening, though friendly enough, he maintained one steady theme in his conversation throughout dinner and for the rest of the evening.

"I do to others what they do to me, only worse," he said.

"Maybe I should have worn my bulletproof vest," I suggested.

From that first meeting, it seemed to me he wanted to impress upon me that Jimmy Hoffa is a tough, rugged man.

We discussed employers whom he had encountered during his career. When they crossed him he destroyed them, he said. He told me of the fights he had been in. Always he had won. We discussed his difficulties with law enforcement agencies. He pointed out that mostly they had been unsuccessful in prosecuting him. We discussed the UAW-Kohler strike and he said if he had been in Walter Reuther's position he would have won that strike shortly after it started.

The conversation turned to Dave Beck, and Eddie Cheyfitz told us of his experiences while touring Europe with Beck and his son, Dave, Jr. The elder Beck "mothered" his son, he said; he never allowed Dave, Jr. to go out alone, insisted on ordering all the meals, selected all his friends, even though the younger Beck was a grown man. As a result, Dave, Jr. had become a jellyfish. In Cheyfitz's opinion, Beck had destroyed his son, and I agreed with him. I knew by this time something about the crimes Dave Beck, Sr. had committed as president of the Teamsters Union, but to me his attitude toward his son was his worst sin.

Somehow the dinner discussion moved on to lawyers' ethics. I questioned the propriety of using union funds to pay attorneys to represent union leaders who would not account for how union funds were spent. Both Cheyfitz and Hoffa maintained that such a practice was perfectly proper. I vehemently differed with them.

After dinner we returned to the living room. Hoffa sat on the couch. I stood with my back to the fire. Cheyfitz, the host, suggested: "Let's get into more controversial matters. Tell him about the paper locals, Jimmy."

Just before the 1956 Teamsters Joint Council election in New York, Teamster charters had been given to friends and associates of a racketeer named Johnny Dio, who was a friend of Hoffa. These charters gave Dio's friends a number of votes to use in the Joint Council election—though actually they had no union members and the locals existed only on paper. It was a bold election fraud aimed at making a Hoffa-Dio friend, John O'Rourke, president of the New York Joint Council. We were later to hold hearings on this paper local affair. I already knew from Cheasty that Hoffa wanted to learn how much information we had in our files on this case.

But that night Hoffa, admitting he was responsible for bringing the paper locals into the Teamsters Union, claimed he had rushed them in because he wanted to dodge the no-raiding pact that was to go into effect immediately after the AFL-CIO merger. This, as the Committee later found, was a complete fabrication. Hoffa had arranged for the paper charters for the sole purpose of influencing that New York election.

When the talk turned to the future work of the Committee, Cheyfitz and Hoffa let me know that they knew the name of a Portland, Oregon, Teamster official who would be subpoenaed before our Committee. It was one of the four names I had given to Cye Cheasty to pass on to Hoffa. With some grimness, I admit, I gave no indication that I knew where Hoffa had acquired his information.

Around 9:30 P.M., my wife telephoned. The snow that had been falling in the afternoon when Cheasty met Hoffa was still coming down and the roads were slick. A woman driver had skidded into a tree on our property. She was sitting in our living room, hysterical. I made my apologies and left.

As I was going out the door, Hoffa said: "Tell your wife I'm not as bad as everyone thinks I am." I laughed. Jimmy Hoffa had a sense of humor. He must have laughed himself as he said it. In view of all I already knew, I felt that he was worse than anybody said he was. In the next two and a half years, nothing happened to change my opinion.

On my way home I thought of how often Hoffa had said he was tough; that he destroyed employers, hated policemen and broke those who stood in his way. It had always been my feeling that if a person was truly tough; if he actually had strength and power; if he really had the ability to excel, he need not brag and boast of it to prove it. When a grown man sat for an evening and talked continuously about his toughness, I could only conclude that he was a bully hiding behind a façade.

I thought: Jimmy Hoffa has been reading his press clippings. And he is afraid I have missed them.

Later, during a hearing, I told him frankly that I did not think he was tough enough to rid his union of the gangsters and hoodlums he had put in power. The statement visibly upset him; his body tensed in the chair, his face contorted, and several days afterward, when he was again on the witness stand, he went out of his way to give a detailed answer. It is important to Jimmy Hoffa that he appear the tough guy to the world.

But the truth is that the tough ones are not the Jimmy Hoffas, with three hundred lawyers, and hired lieutenants riding in Cadillacs, armed with guns and clubs. The really tough ones are the men in Hoffa's union who have the guts to stand up to him and his hired hands. The really strong ones are the men who get knocked down again and again by Hoffa and who always get up to fight back. The really tough ones are the men Jimmy Hoffa cannot buy and cannot cajole and cannot threaten. The really tough ones are the Floyd Hooks, the Jim Lukens, the Barney Matuals, the Amos Renikers—men whose opposition to Hoffa we will discuss in detail later on.

As I drove from Cheyfitz's house that snowy night I knew that Hoffa must have spent the evening thinking he was playing a game in which he held all the cards—that with Cye Cheasty in his pocket he was looking down my throat. And I had spent the evening thinking he was thinking that. Considering later developments, I'm not sure who was right.

The next time I saw Jimmy Hoffa was at midnight three weeks later—in the United States Courthouse. He was under arrest. The FBI had just placed him in their custody after finding him with Committee documents in his possession—documents I had furnished to Cye Cheasty to give him.

Chapter 4 / THE TIME OF THE FIX

BETWEEN THE DINNER on February 19 and Hoffa's arrest on March 13, Cye Cheasty had had numerous conversations with him. During one of them, Hoffa expressed confidence that the McClellan Committee would fold up after a few months and that the Teamsters would have no more problems.

"We won't have any more trouble after this summer," he said. "We only have to sustain ourselves for four or five months. Bob Kennedy will want to spend the summer at Cape Cod with his family."

Hoffa had seen Congressional committees come and go before this. In 1953 and again in 1954 investigating committees from the House of Representatives had been on the threshold of uncovering major corruption in the Teamsters; corruption involving Mr. Hoffa and some of his chief lieutenants. Both times the investigations had been halted. The Congressmen went their way and Mr. Hoffa went his.

The 1953 Committee originally had been chaired by Representative Clare Hoffman, a Michigan Republican. Congressman Hoffman was highly critical of Mr. Hoffa. But his Committee, during the hearings, was hit by internal dissension. Clare Hoffman was voted out as chairman and was replaced by Representative Wint Smith, Republican, of Kansas.

Hoffa immediately employed as one of his attorneys former Governor Payne Ratner, also of Kansas. Shortly thereafter the hearings

45

stopped. There were reports that political pressure had been applied to kill the investigation.

Newspapermen were astounded. Could Jimmy Hoffa's pressure reach even into the halls of the legislative branch of the Government? They went to Chairman Smith and asked why his Committee had closed up shop.

"The pressure comes from way up there and I just can't talk about it any more specifically than that," was the answer.

Congressmen and Senators are historically reluctant to examine too closely the political pressures that influence another Congressman or Senator. Into this area where "wise men fear to tread," we went further than most; but in all honesty, not so far as we could have. Our Committee investigation gave no clear and definite answer to the question of what kind of pressure was used. However, quite apart from whatever really brought those 1953 hearings to an end, we did show that during them Hoffa had applied pressure on Congressman Wint Smith.

Hoffa, our Committee found, had given Payne Ratner three assignments—all stemming from Ratner's relationship with his fellow Kansan, Congressman Smith. He was to try to get Congressman Smith to postpone the hearings involving Hoffa; failing this, he was to persuade him to treat Mr. Hoffa more "courteously" than had former Committee Chairman Clare Hoffman. Finally, he was to make Congressman Smith see the wisdom of opposing any effort to have Mr. Hoffa cited for contempt.

On his first assignment Ratner failed. He told us he had suggested that the hearings be postponed on the grounds that Hoffa was at the time facing a grand jury investigation and the publicity from the hearings might influence the grand jury's work. The hearings proceeded.

But the record before the Committee showed that he felt he had met with success in his other two efforts to "influence" Congressman Smith.

Walt Sheridan, our investigator on the case, found Ratner at first accommodating, later mean, irritable and uncooperative. But in Ratner's files he came upon a number of interesting letters. Immediately after the 1953 hearings, Ratner had written to Hoffa:

Dear Jimmy: I listened carefully to all of the evidence last week and it is my considered opinion that you did nothing illegal or improper. I am proud to call you my friend. . . .

Wint told me today that he certainly got in bad with Hoffman and the staff by having gone along with me in his treatment of you Friday. I, of course, expressed appreciation to him and told him that I have always thought no one had to worry much about doing the right thing.

As he read this, Jimmy Hoffa must have felt that the money the Teamsters had paid Payne Ratner to "represent" him in this matter was well spent. He must have been even more elated when he read in a subsequent letter: "He [Congressman Smith] declared that it is his best judgment that there will be no further effort to cite you and if there should be it will not be successful."

Sheridan, in Ratner's subpoenaed records and correspondence files, had found evidence that tied Payne Ratner even closer to the Teamsters. Two letters, particularly, interested him. Addressed to Harold Gibbons, one of Hoffa's closest associates, they concerned the means by which a certain "package we have discussed over the telephone recently" was to be delivered to Ratner.

Sheridan set up an interview for Bellino and me with Ratner. I flew to Wichita to talk with him about his Teamster ties. Sheridan accompanied me to his office. It was a difficult interview. The former Governor was excitable and evasive. As we talked I noted that the device on his inter-office communications phone was "down" and I suspected that our conversation was being monitored. I asked him if this was true. He denied it. Then, adjusting the phone device, he said, "If it will make you feel better I'll put this up."

Immediately, his secretary came in and remained, taking notes throughout our interview. This was all right; in fact, Sheridan had told him at the beginning that he might have anyone with him that he wished, but he had declined the invitation.

After our interview, Ratner went to Texas to see Hoffa and his attorneys. They told him that he should have refused to turn his files over to us, claiming the lawyer-client relationship. There were a number of letters that he knew he would have difficulty explaining, and Hoffa laughed about the problems he was going to face before the

Committee. What explanation he could give for the "package" letters was a major topic of conversation. In a bathroom conference in the hotel Ratner and one of the Teamster attorneys threshed over his difficulties, finally deciding to use a certain major Democratic political figure to bring pressure on my brother not to call him.

The day I saw Ratner in Wichita I hadn't discussed the "package" letters, but when he appeared before the Committee I asked him about the package and what it was.

The "package" was a $1,000 check to buy tickets for the Teamsters to a Republican party dinner in Kansas.

Why, I asked, did he call it a "package" when he could have said more specifically "a check for $1,000"?

"You often do things in a jocular vein," he explained.

Questioned about $10,000 that he had received from the Steamfitters Union in St. Louis, headed by George Callanan, he told us that it had been given to him for using what he called his "alleged political prestige" to obtain certain changes in the Hobbs Anti-Racketeering Act. (Callanan had been indicted and later was convicted for violating the Hobbs Act.) Also, to our amazement, this former Governor admitted that it was ex-convict Barney Baker, one of Hoffa's strong-arm men who had done "organizing" work in Kansas, who had first approached him on Jimmy Hoffa's behalf.

Congressman Smith appeared before our Committee at his own request and denied that his hearings had been terminated because of any political pressure. He insisted that Ratner's letters to Hoffa reflected only a "lawyer tooting his own horn" rather than an objective appraisal of what had actually occurred.

Was Ratner the person responsible for the sudden ending of the 1953 Hoffa investigation? I think not.

From a close study of the files and records and from my personal contacts with Payne Ratner, it seems to me there was no doubt that he had been hired by the Teamsters for his "alleged political prestige." Virtually all his memoranda dealing with the hearings were categorized: "Wint Smith Matter"—not "Teamsters," or "Hoffa," or even "Congressional Inquiry." And after my interview with Mr. Ratner in his office and after seeing him before our Committee, I felt he was not of significant enough stature to have arranged such a coup. Rather, I had the impression that he was merely an additional avenue through which Jimmy Hoffa had applied what pressure he could on Wint Smith.

Furthermore, it was generally accepted at the time by newsmen and others who covered the 1953 hearings that the investigation had been called off in return for the promise that Hoffa and the Teamsters would support the Republicans in Michigan in 1954. In my judgment this, rather than the "alleged political prestige" of Payne Ratner, was the answer.

I might add here that Hoffa's shifting political preferences depend on who can help him at any particular moment. Like Frank Costello, Albert Anastasia or Al Capone, he is not interested in the party or the man but in "having a friend in court."

After our interview with ex-Governor Ratner, Carmine Bellino and I left Wichita by plane. Our problems with him were all but forgotten when, as our plane left the ground, we nearly collided with a plane that was landing. A few feet closer and the hearings of the McClellan Committee would have been postponed temporarily while they sought a new chief counsel and accountant.

Unfortunately, because it is a reflection on all of us, it was not only the 1953 Congressional investigation of Hoffa and the Teamsters that terminated unexpectedly.

While it was a former governor who came from the 1953 hearings with Teamster money in his pocket and a continuing connection with the Teamsters, when the 1954 hearings were abruptly cut off it was the chairman of the Committee who emerged wearing the Hoffa-Teamster mark of approval.

Representative George Bender, an Ohio Republican running for the Senate seat vacated by the death of Senator Robert Taft, took his Committee on a Midwestern tour to investigate the Teamsters. In September, 1954, he opened hearings in Cleveland, calling Hoffa's two chief lieutenants in Ohio, William Presser and Louis (Babe) Triscaro.

Appearing before the Bender Committee, Triscaro, the short, thin, dark-complexioned vice president of the Ohio Conference, whose bent nose is perhaps a relic of his prize-fighting days, took the Fifth on questions relating to his income. So did Presser, a big, hulking man who is president of the Conference and of Joint Council 41. They answered all other questions. After they testified, Congressman Bender postponed further hearings until November 9. Presser was to appear then, and Bender later announced plans to call Dave Beck to testify.

When the time came for the Bender Committee hearings to resume in Washington, Presser appeared and again took the Fifth Amendment. Bender did not question him. After only two days, the hearings "recessed at the call of the chairman."

Though the general public was under the impression that the hearings would again be resumed, and that there would be contempt citations, there was no doubt in Bill Presser's mind that it was all over. Four days after his appearance in Washington he addressed the quarterly meeting of the Ohio Conference of Teamsters, speaking of the hearings with an air of finality. "Of the people that were involved, not a single one was indicted for anything—no one was cited for any contempts—no perjuries. . . ." In short, Presser was telling his men the hearings would never be reopened—and he was right.

How did Presser know this? He did not say. But he did say: "We found, especially during the latter portion of the hearings, that we had a second friend on the Congressional committee, a friend that did a fair job for the people concerned . . . and his name is George Bender and it has taught me a lesson."

Why had those hearings—even as the investigations in 1953—been canceled so suddenly?

Walter Sheridan went into Ohio to try to get some answers. He talked to two officers of the Teamsters Union, both of whom recalled a meeting of the Ohio Conference of Teamsters in October, 1954. One of them, Walter Schulz, gave an affidavit to the Committee in which he stated:

". . . At the meeting William Presser made an announcement that the Teamsters Union was throwing its support to George H. Bender for Senator. Prior to this announcement the Teamsters had been actively supporting Bender's opponent, Thomas Burke, and had been very critical of Bender because of his activities as chairman of the Congressional Committee . . . When William Presser made this announcement . . . I asked him why we were switching our support from Thomas Burke to George Bender. Presser's reply was that Bender was the man to support and that he could not say anything about it. The members of the Executive Board were told to go back to their local unions and tell their membership that they should support George Bender rather than Thomas Burke."

Jim Luken, another Ohio Teamster leader who testified before our Committee, remembered a meeting of his Joint Council in November just after Bender's election. The man who was then president, George Starling (Luken has since succeeded him), told the Council that he had a letter requesting a contribution to pay the expenses of Triscaro and Presser in appearing before the Bender Committee. As Luken recalled it, about $40,000 was needed. Since the legal bills of the two had already been paid, someone in the meeting wanted to know why they were asking for additional funds.

Jim Luken told our Committee that he remembered the answer well. He had written it down so as not to forget. Starling said: "Other money was spent to pull certain strings to see that these charges were dropped."

Luken was shocked. "I wasn't shocked that a politician would take a bribe," he explained to the Senators. "I was shocked that somebody would be stupid enough to say so in front of seven people."

He went on to say: "I am sure Senator Bender's name was mentioned but I want to make it clear that I am not saying that this man said the money went to Senator Bender. It may have; it may not."

Bender's opponent, Thomas Burke, made a statement to members of our staff. The Teamsters had cooled on him toward the end of the race. Since he lost by a slim six thousand votes he had asked for a recount, but when he approached the Teamsters for their assistance in getting one, they had flatly refused him.

A year later, in 1955, George Bender, now a United States Senator, was the guest speaker before the Ohio Conference of Teamsters' quarterly meeting. Presser spoke of him in these glowing if ungrammatical terms:

". . . To you George Bender, the Republican whose name has been handled around as an anti-labor Senator, if it weren't for this one man, and his advice and the constant pounding we would have a lot of problems that do not exist . . . and Bill Presser is committed to George Bender anywhere down the line."

Bender lasted in the Senate for only the two years. In 1956, despite active Teamster support, financial and otherwise, he was defeated. But this did not end his connection with Hoffa.

By August of 1958, the McClellan Committee had uncovered a mass of crookedness and wrongdoing in the Teamsters. There were demands that Hoffa take steps to clean up his union. However, I was convinced by this time that he was completely incapable of doing the job—had he cared to. He was dependent on the racketeers and ex-convicts with whom he had surrounded himself. They were necessary to him—the Bill Pressers, the Babe Triscaros, the Barney Bakers. So when in August of 1958 Hoffa announced that he was appointing a special committee to investigate corruption in his union, I was suspicious. And when I heard that George Bender was to be the chairman of the committee I was flabbergasted. Although at that point we had not made it public, we had learned not only from Jim Luken but from a friendly source within the Teamsters that the Hoffa-Bender relationship was an intimate one dating back to the 1954 Bender investigation.

After Jim Luken testified, Bender had asked to appear before our Committee. He did so on July 8 and 9, 1959. By this time he had served for nearly a year as chairman of Hoffa's anti-racketeering committee.

Carmine Bellino had discovered initially Bender was paid $250 a day for his "work," besides being compensated for all expenses, even for the rental of his office, the secretarial help he had always had, his telephone bills, travel, etc. Shortly after he took the "job" we had made public the fact that he was getting $250 a day. He then was reduced in pay to $125 a day.

From August 18, 1958, through May 4, 1959, Bender charged the

Teamsters $58,636.07 in salary and expenses for "cleaning up" the union for Mr. Hoffa. Hoffa paid because George Bender had the highly respected though no longer applicable title of "Senator," before his name.

If there were any doubts that George Bender's appointment was more than a very expensive joke, his testimony before our Committee dispelled them.

We wanted to know what he had done to earn his $58,000. What racketeers or gangsters or ex-convicts had he recommended ousting from the Teamsters?

Here is an excerpt from his testimony:

MR. KENNEDY: Have you made any recommendations, for instance, on Sam Goldstein of Local 239 in New York?

MR. BENDER: No, sir, I have not.

MR. KENNEDY: He is in the penitentiary for extortion, and he is still a Teamster official.

MR. BENDER: Well, frankly—

MR. KENNEDY: He draws $375 a week and $25 expenses.

MR. BENDER: Well, he is a good man to be able to do that. But I have not—

But Bender wished to prove to the Committee that he had not been completely idle, although he was unwilling to say as much for Jimmy Hoffa. Examine this colloquy:

SENATOR GOLDWATER: George, let me ask you a question. Take the case of a man like Goldstein. Suppose you went to Mr. Hoffa and said, "Jimmy, you ought to kick this fellow out." Do you think he would do it?

MR. BENDER: Last week I went to him regarding a man, a matter came to my attention where a man was having relations with a 16-year-old prostitute and speaking very bluntly, he said, "Well, frankly, that son-of-a-bitch should be kicked out." He said, "He is no good. No man should be in this union who is doing that kind of thing."

SENATOR GOLDWATER: Was he kicked out?

MR. BENDER: That I can't tell you.

George Bender philosophizing on the state of Republican politics:

SENATOR GOLDWATER: Let's take a man like Glimco, in Chicago [the corrupt head of Local 777]. He is certainly no credit to the union movement. Have you made any recommendations relative to him?

MR. BENDER: Frankly, no. That matter hasn't come to my attention either. Incidentally, we have some characters in the Republican Party, Senator Goldwater—

SENATOR GOLDWATER: What?

MR. BENDER: We have some characters in the Republican Party who would look very bad if they were subjected to this sort of thing.

SENATOR GOLDWATER: The trouble is they don't get elected.

MR. BENDER: They do; many of them.

Bender then rambled on about politics, his in particular, telling how he had appointed the "best prostitute" in a particular district as Republican committeewoman.

"Frankly, unless you get the votes of the washed and the unwashed you can't win elections. . . . You don't have to be a prostitute yourself, but sometimes you have to get their votes."

Senator Goldwater left in disgust. Later in the day he said Bender's performance was a complete disgrace, almost enough to make him a Democrat.

Talking about the Teamsters headquarters, Bender had this to say:

". . . I have been so impressed with the manner in which that building is run, it reminds me of a church office. There is no gambling, and no liquor drinking or nothing of that kind going on there, and it is run very efficiently."

I asked Bender if he had recommended ousting anyone at all from the Teamsters Union since he had been appointed clean-up chief.

MR. BENDER: I am not going to go into that. My report is to Mr. Hoffa.

MR. KENNEDY: You came as a voluntary witness.

MR. BENDER: That is right, but on this matter, not to discuss my work or what I am doing.

He admitted that he had done nothing in the specific cases of Hoffa's Ohio henchmen, Presser and Triscaro, about whom our Committee had uncovered a mass of unsavory evidence. George Bender had personal knowledge of their activities dating back to 1954. Any honest man would have moved against those two the day he accepted his job. But Bender had grown closer to Presser and Triscaro since they had appeared before his Committee. Indeed, at the time Jimmy Hoffa hired him as a "clean-up man," Bender had been preparing to go to work for Presser and the Ohio Teamsters as a "public relations man." The payment he had already accepted he hurriedly returned when he discovered our Committee was investigating it.

While testifying, Bender denied vehemently that he received a payoff or bribe in connection with the 1954 investigation of the Teamsters.

The Committee had found that approximately $109,000—at least $30,000 in cash—went through George Bender's campaign committee bank accounts following that 1954 election. The money was never reported to state authorities—though there may be some question if it is necessary to report campaign funds received after an election is over and won.

I had known George Bender since 1955, shortly after he came to the Senate. He was assigned to the Permanent Subcommittee on Investigations, for which I was then counsel. I saw a great deal of him. He spent ten years as a state senator, fourteen years as a Congressman, and two years as a United States Senator. To me, it is incomprehensible that such a man should occupy the Senate seat once held by Robert Taft, a man who was a symbol of integrity and intelligence.

Jimmy Hoffa dealt with the Congressional committees in 1953 and 1954 as he deals with everything and everybody; he believes that money, or influence, or political pressure, or a combination of all three can fix any problem that faces him. As he once said to Washington newspaperman Clark Mollenhoff: "Every man has his price. What's yours?"

It must have been a setback to him the night he was arrested for attempting to bribe a Committee investigator to find that there was one man in America who was above and beyond a price.

J. Edgar Hoover had called my home late that evening to tell me that his men were ready to move in. I was out for a walk, but shortly after I returned to the house a second call came from the FBI. Hoffa had just been placed under arrest at the DuPont Plaza Hotel with the Committee documents that I had given to Cye Cheasty in his possession. I went at once to the Federal District Courthouse on Third Street and was waiting there in one of the courtrooms, in case I was

55

needed, when the Federal agents brought in Jimmy Hoffa. For a few minutes we were alone in the room.

"I don't know any of your agents," he said to me. I did not answer him, for the matter now was in the hands of the courts. There was an awkward silence and then, somehow, we began talking about physical exercise. He had read somewhere that I exercised a lot and that I did push-ups. We had about exhausted this topic when Hoffa's lawyer, Edward Bennett Williams, arrived.

"What's this all about?" he demanded. It was not my place to enlighten him, and I told him so.

I was convinced that the Federal Bureau of Investigation had given the Government an airtight case. Cye Cheasty was a good and honest man. He had served his country with distinction. The evidence supporting his testimony—there were fast moving pictures of Hoffa receiving the documents and paying off Cheasty—was solid. I felt that Jimmy Hoffa was finished.

A few days later, several newspaper reporters were in my office discussing the hearings, and getting briefed on developments. As they were leaving one of them asked: "What will you do if Jimmy Hoffa is acquitted?"

I now realize that I had never considered that possibility. Hoffa would be convicted. There could be no doubt of it. I knew the evidence; I knew the chief witness; I knew the case.

"I'll jump off the Capitol," I said, smiling. It didn't occur to me that any of them would quote me; it was an off-the-cuff remark. But several hours later a Washington reporter who had been present called to tell me that another newspaper reporter, from Hoffa's home town, Detroit, had built a story around the wisecrack, and used it. It was embarrassing then. It was even more embarrassing when Jimmy Hoffa was acquitted.

Ed Williams later, and quite justifiably, said he would send me a parachute.

Under our system of laws, if a jury of twelve good men and true finds a defendant not guilty, he is cleared of the alleged crime against him. He cannot be tried for it again. As a citizen or a lawyer I accept this, even when I have a personal knowledge of the case and feel strongly about the outcome. That's our system and I wouldn't change it.

So much has been written and said about this case that most people are aware that the jury consisted of eight Negroes and four whites, that the Teamsters paid the expenses of Joe Louis to come from Detroit to Washington and appear in the courtroom for two days, and that he publicly embraced Mr. Hoffa. It has been overlooked, however, that the judge, in a conference at the bench, took judicial notice of the make-up of the jury, pointing out that while the Government attorneys had selected jurors without discrimination as to race, Mr. Williams, Hoffa's attorney, had used his challenges against white jurors only. This circumstance, taken with the presence of Joe Louis and other events that transpired during the trial, shows a definite effort to influence the judge and jury in other ways than through accepted legal channels. Martha Jefferson, a Negro woman attorney, was brought from California to be at the trial, and another reputable Negro lawyer was employed for the same purpose. The law partner of the judge's brother was brought from Arkansas. Ed Williams, one of the nation's top criminal attorneys, hardly needed this legal assistance. And in the midst of the trial Williams posed with Mrs. Jefferson for a picture that appeared in a full-page ad in the *Afro-American*, a Negro newspaper. The ad praised Jimmy Hoffa as a friend of the Negro race. (Later our Committee heard testimony clearly indicating that Hoffa and his own Local 299 in Detroit discriminated against Negroes.)

When it was reported in the press that the ad had been delivered to the doorstep of every juror, that was enough for Judge Burnita Matthews. She locked up the jury to prevent further improper influences.

Then, while cross-examining Cheasty, Williams tried to establish that he had once investigated the National Association for the Advancement of Colored People. By the time the Government attorneys objected, the jury had heard Williams and it was too late. Cheasty testified that it was completely untrue.

Such methods seem extreme, and an insult to the court, to the judge, to the legal system, to the jury, and to the colored race. But it is Mr. Hoffa's philosophy that every man has his price whether it is money, pressure or prejudice, and he is willing to pay. Nevertheless, in my estimation, it was not these tactics that won Hoffa his acquittal. It was, rather, the work of Williams, his effective defense attorney, plus Hoffa's own strong testimony, together with the unpreparedness and ineffectiveness of the Government attorneys who prosecuted the case.

Naturally, this was a trial in which I was much interested. I appeared as a witness, giving the jury the complete story of Mr. Cheasty's connection with the Committee as I have given it here. Aside from that I was unable to be present, for we were conducting hearings at the time and the Committee's workload was increasing daily. But I received reports from Cheasty and from my wife, who attended the trial regularly. She admired, as I did, the quiet courage of Cye Cheasty. With the courtroom filled with Hoffa henchmen from all over the United States, Cheasty told me how much he appreciated having her there.

Some four or five days before Hoffa took the witness stand, Kenny O'Donnell, my administrative assistant, and I had attended a party at the home of Bob Ball, a reporter for the Detroit *News.* Eddie Cheyfitz was there and asked me if I thought Hoffa was going to testify. I said I did not know. He told me that Hoffa had been over his story with them again and again, but they had not yet decided themselves whether to put him on the stand. Then, after outlining the various defenses they had thought up and abandoned, and which I mentioned in the previous chapter, he went on to tell us a story that he must have thought was amusing. We didn't. He said Hoffa was sorry he had been stupid enough to be caught giving a bribe. He was concerned; "the boys" were laughing because he had handled it directly rather than through a third person.

I could not believe that under these circumstances Hoffa would take the stand. But take the stand he did. He swore that he had never known that Cye Cheasty was on our staff until the FBI arrested him. He swore that he had paid Cheasty $3,000 in cash out of a "revolving fund" in his office—but to represent him as a lawyer, not as a Committee spy.

58

The trial was in July, 1957. To round out the story, I might add that about a year and a half later Eddie Cheyfitz came to my office for a talk. He had always suggested that his friendship for Jimmy Hoffa and Dave Beck should not affect our relationship. Yet I had recently learned that he had tried to hire an investigator—whom I knew—to investigate me. The investigator was Tom LaVenia, whom I had asked to resign from the staff of the old McCarthy Committee in January, 1955, when Senator McClellan became chairman. When approached by Cheyfitz, he had refused to investigate me, he said, but he had accepted $10,000 to investigate the jurors for the defense in the Hoffa trial.

Cheyfitz said he had learned that I had been told this story and he had come to see me to deny it.

During our talk I raised the question of whether it was proper to know of Jimmy Hoffa's guilt and yet let him testify. That had not been his decision, said Cheyfitz. He added that he and Williams were ending their association with Hoffa as attorneys. Cheyfitz did terminate his relationship a short time later.[1] But Ed Williams was still Jimmy Hoffa's attorney well into 1959, when he appeared for the last time before our Committee.

I have said that the Government was unprepared in this case. We later investigated the background of the jurors, and it was apparent that the Government had been as careless in accepting the jury panel as the defense lawyers had been careful in selecting it. One juror, for example, had a police record of fourteen convictions, mostly for drunkenness. Another had nine convictions. Most of the charges against them involved common drunkenness and disorderly conduct. Some of the cases had been settled in forfeiture of bonds in lieu of pleas of guilt. Some of the offenses had actually occurred during the trial, before the jury was locked up by Judge Matthews. The son of another juror had been sentenced on a twenty-month to five-year jail sentence and was in jail on a narcotics charge at the time of the trial. Still another juror had been released from his Government job after refusing to take a lie detector test on the question of whether he was a homosexual.

[1] Eddie Cheyfitz died of a heart attack in May, 1959.

Such people are not prohibited from jury service. But they certainly are persons the Government might find antagonistic to the aims of law enforcement in a criminal court.

Furthermore, the Government attorneys had not expected Jimmy Hoffa to testify. When he took the stand, they were unprepared to conduct an adequate cross-examination. The day before he testified, representatives from the United States Attorney came to my office asking what background material we had on Hoffa. We began to compile it, but of course there was no time for the attorney handling the case to assimilate such a mountain of information in such a short time. As a result, while Hoffa testified with vigor and force, the cross-examination was unimpressive. It lasted only twenty minutes.

I was in the Senate caucus chamber questioning a witness from the Textile Workers Union when I became conscious of a stir and a buzz throughout the room. Then a note was handed up to me. Cye Cheasty had telephoned from the courthouse: Hoffa had been acquitted. I read the note with utter disbelief.

And yet it was not the first time he had been acquitted. It would not be the last.

I have often been asked why we did not subpoena Joe Louis to Washington to tell under oath why and how he came to attend the trial of Jimmy Hoffa.

To me, Joe Louis emerges as the most unfortunate figure in this whole case.

When we looked into his connection with the Hoffa trial, we learned that it was Paul Dorfman, a friend of Hoffa with contacts in the boxing world (as well as in the underworld), who had made the arrangements with Truman Gibson of the International Boxing Club for Louis's appearance. (Gibson is presently under indictment in connection with the boxing scandal in California.) We learned that Barney Baker, Mr. Hoffa's roving "organizer" and ambassador of violence, had arranged for Louis's hotel reservations in Washington.

Walter Sheridan went to Chicago after the trial to question Joe Louis. The former fighter was a lonely figure. Walt found him in a third-floor apartment, sitting in a chair and reading a newspaper, with both the radio and the television going. While he was there,

Louis's former manager Julian Black, whom Louis made and who owed Louis everything, appeared at the ground floor doorway and called up to him. Louis went dutifully down.

Joe Louis had been one of my heroes when I was a small boy. I had requested Walt to ask for the former champion's autograph for my son, whose name also is Joe. At the end of the interview, Walt made the request.

Louis said: "I'll give it to you for his son, but not for him. Tell him to go take a jump off the Empire State Building." I understood.

I do not believe that Joe Louis was aware of the seriousness of what was being asked of him when he came to Washington. He has made great contributions to this country. And he has been used again and again over the years by a long list of people he has encountered. Jimmy Hoffa simply joined that list.

All these feelings wrapped together is why Joe Louis wasn't called as a witness.

Some time after the bribery trial, I had a telephone call from a major television performer who told me that Joe Louis was on the payroll of Mercury Records. Later, during our investigation of juke boxes, we went into the files of Mercury Records and found that Joe Louis had worked for them in "public relations" for approximately seven months, starting immediately after the trial. We also found that the major owner of the company had received a two-million-dollar loan through the Teamsters Union pension and welfare fund. Mercury executives denied to me that Jimmy Hoffa or the Teamsters applied any influence to get Joe Louis his job.

For a while there appeared to be a happy ending to the story as far as the former champion was concerned. He married Martha Jefferson, the attorney who came from California to be at the Hoffa trial. They later separated.

In the late fall of 1957, Mr. Hoffa was tried in New York on charges of wiretapping. He allegedly had arranged with Johnny Dio, the New York racketeer, to have a wiretap artist, Bernard Spindel, put taps on the telephones of his subordinates in the Teamsters headquarters in Detroit. The trial ended when the jury could not agree on

61

a verdict. The jurors were eleven to one for conviction.

When the case was retried in the spring of 1958, Mr. Hoffa was acquitted. During this trial an attempt was made—unsuccessfully—to influence one of the jurors. The juror promptly reported the attempt to the presiding judge and was as promptly excused from the jury.

I have sometimes thought of this in connection with a curious encounter I had about that time.

It was in early June. The clicking of the typewriter keys was echoing through the corridor as I left our New York office in the U.S. Courthouse Building and walked to the elevator. Almost as soon as I pushed the button the elevator doors opened, and I was staring straight into the eyes of James R. Hoffa.

I said, "Hello, Jimmy" and got on.

He said, "Hello, Bobby." And we rode down to the street floor side by side.

I was headed for the La Guardia Airport and Utica, New York, to look into some matters concerning our investigation of the underworld meeting at Apalachin; he was just leaving the courtroom where his wiretap trial was still under way.

I asked him how it felt to be president of the Teamsters Union, a post to which he had been elected about two months after his bribery trial. He replied: "Greatest job in the world. But it's keeping me busy."

As we walked down the steps from the building into Foley Square, he asked how I was and whether I was commuting to New York. Then I inquired how his wiretap trial was going. He gave me rather an interesting answer to that.

"You never can tell with a jury," he said. "Like shooting fish in a barrel."

Outside on the courthouse steps we parted.

"Take care," he said.

Knowing, through an informant, of the attempt to reach one of the jurors, I put Jim Kelly of our New York staff on the case. Investigation revealed, and testimony confirmed, some interesting sidelights. After the trial was over we had a number of conversations with Bernard

Spindel, who had been Hoffa's co-defendant. At the time we talked, Spindel was angry at Hoffa. For a while he indicated that he would testify at our hearings, but when called before the Committee he took the Fifth Amendment.

However, before he appeared he did tell us a few things that we were able to verify. For instance, he said that his lawyer, Edward H. Levine, had received $10,000 in cash from Owen Bert Brennan, one of Hoffa's closest Teamster associates.

Levine corroborated this information. But apparently he had been uneasy. I asked him: "Isn't it a fact that you hid the money in one of your slippers, around which you tied a necktie, and held on to the tie all night so Spindel wouldn't take the money?"

Levine: "I put it in one of my slippers. I mean, I just wanted to make sure it stuck to me."

Hoffa, when first questioned, pleaded ignorance and referred us to Bert Brennan. And Brennan, of course, took the Fifth.

It was irritating, and nothing more than a way for Hoffa to avoid the stigma of claiming the Fifth directly, a trick he used repeatedly. But I think we finally managed to expose the device for what it was and make it clear to the blindest that Hoffa was simply hiding behind his men.

The opportunity came when I pressed him again about a $35,000 defense fund that had been raised during the course of the trial. Exactly how much money was involved? Where had it come from? To whom had it been paid? Hoffa didn't know. The only person who could answer these questions, he said, was Walter Schuler, a business agent for Bert Brennan's Local 337. It was his project.

I suggested that Mr. Schuler come forward then and there, and asked Hoffa to take a seat directly behind him.

Schuler gave his name and address and admitted he was a Teamsters business agent.

Then I addressed him: "Mr. Schuler, Mr. Hoffa spoke about the fact that there was a defense fund, or there was a fund, a sum of money raised in Detroit during this period of time and that you would be the one that could furnish the details. Would you tell us about that, please?"

63

Mr. Schuler: "I respectfully decline to answer because I honestly believe my answer might tend to incriminate me."

I turned to Senator McClellan:

MR. KENNEDY: Mr. Chairman, this is of course once again the pattern. Could I suggest that Mr. Hoffa obviously wants the Committee to have the information. Could I suggest Mr. Schuler, rather than testifying, that he tell Mr. Hoffa what the answer is—how much money was collected—and then Mr. Hoffa can tell us. Mr. Hoffa, of course, has all of those individuals around him who take the Fifth Amendment so that nobody will be able to testify regarding his activities.

THE CHAIRMAN: Won't you, Mr. Schuler, just come clean and tell us? Just for the sake of the flag? The country that gives you your protection of freedom?

MR. SCHULER: I respectfully decline to answer because I honestly believe the answer might tend to incriminate me.

THE CHAIRMAN: Will you whisper to Mr. Hoffa over there and tell him? Will you do that so he might give us the information of what you say?

Hoffa was on his feet, sputtering, but he seemed confused. His lawyers waved him down.

Schuler said: "I respectfully decline to answer. . . ."

I suggested: "Could we ask Mr. Hoffa to come forward and ask him if he won't ask Mr. Schuler the source?"

The lawyers around Hoffa were whispering instructions to him as he stood up.

Senator McClellan said: "Mr. Hoffa, will you help us clear it up? You don't want to help us?"

Hoffa, his answer now straight, if feeble, replied, "I do not want to infringe on a man's right to exercise the Constitutional privilege."

A quick look at some other cases we investigated that reveal something of Mr. Hoffa's relations with judges, juries, prosecuting attorneys and other public officials:

For instance, there was the Michigan judge to whom Hoffa indirectly made payments, through a public relations firm, at the time of the judge's campaign for re-election, and whose two sons, both attorneys, received money through Teamster lawyer George Fitzgerald.

Or, when Hoffa personally did not have the power to pay or push his way to what he wanted, he usually had someone who could apply the pressure for him. Like Robert Scott, a man who for a quarter of a century had been a top figure in the Michigan labor movement, with many friends in political life throughout the state.

The two men finally broke bitterly, but during the years that they were close, Scott testified, Hoffa made some unusual requests of him. For instance:

Hoffa asked Scott to intercede with a judge to get a new trial for Harry Fleisher, the head of the Purple Gang in Detroit who had just received twenty to forty years in prison.

He asked him to intercede with liquor commissioners and get a liquor license for Charles Harrison, known to police as "Black Charlie."

Once, Mr. Scott's assignment was to get inside information from a grand jury that was investigating Hoffa.

Another time, Scott testified, Hoffa asked him to intercede in obtaining a pardon from the Governor of Michigan for Frank Cammarata, a notorious gangster who has now been deported from the United States for the second time. Scott said Hoffa made other requests on behalf of other convicts from time to time. And once he asked Scott to "hide out" his ex-convict brother, Billy Hoffa, when Billy was wanted by the police for armed robbery.

Questioned about this on the witness stand, Hoffa was evasive. Finally he made this classic disavowal: "I am saying that to the best of my recollection I have no disremembrance of discussing with Scott any such question."

When about a year and a half ago one of Hoffa's criminal pals burned himself so badly setting fire to a cleaning establishment that he was unrecognizable, the police immediately assumed that Bob Scott had finally met with an accident. Before Scott came to Washington to testify, his life was threatened twice by anonymous phone calls. But he came. He wanted to be on record publicly against what he considered a menace to the labor movement he had served so long. And when it was necessary, he returned to testify a second time.

Was Mr. Scott's testimony accurate?

Before our Committee, Mr. Hoffa with one exception just couldn't remember. For some reason, he did admit that he had asked Scott to try to get a pardon from the Michigan Governor for Frank Cammarata.

How far would Jimmy Hoffa go to interfere with normal judicial processes? A long way, our record clearly demonstrated.

Scott told the Committee that the information he had obtained from inside the grand jury investigating Hoffa was that a bar owner, Turk Prujanski, had testified that Hoffa had tried to shake him down for five to ten thousand dollars to get his license restored; and that the money was to be split with Hoffa's friend on the liquor commission, Oren De Mass. Scott said that after Hoffa learned what Prujanski had told the grand jury he said he would have Prujanski run out of the state so he wouldn't be able to testify at the trial. Scott said Hoffa sent two men out to the racetrack to send Prujanski on his way. Prujanski ended up in California.

When he was brought back on a fugitive warrant, he no longer would talk about Hoffa's shakedown attempt. To the authorities he announced: "I refuse to answer any more questions. I am entitled to my rights, am I not? Throw me in jail."

So he was thrown in jail for sixty days for contempt of court.

Hoffa and De Mass were cleared of the extortion charges against them. The case had to be dropped when Prujanski refused to testify.

On another occasion, the record before the Committee showed, Hoffa intervened personally to make sure that criminal assault charges were dropped against a Tennessee Teamster business agent, William Arthur (Hard Hearing) Smith, a man with an affection for dynamite and violence.[2] In April, 1955, during an argument over the hiring of drivers, Smith brutally beat up Frank J. Allen, the manager of the Terminal Transport Company in Nashville.

In this case it was easy: Hoffa had only to suggest to Allen's employer that he would be better pleased if Allen didn't press charges. As he later remarked to reporter Clark Mollenhoff: "We need somebody like Smitty down there to kick those hillbillies around." (Hoffa

---

[2] Smith has a record of 19 arrests and 13 convictions. He is not related to Glenn Smith, mentioned later.

swore to the Committee that he could not remember whether he ever made such a statement to Mollenhoff or not.)

Another instance of Hoffa's arrogance was the tongue-lashing he gave Joseph Rashid, an assistant prosecuting attorney (now judge) in Detroit who was conducting a particularly vigorous examination of some Teamster officials charged with extortion. During a recess, Rashid was confronted by an angry Hoffa who warned him that "I have every politician in town in my office"; that he would spend every dime he could get his hands on to see that Rashid never went any place politically; and that he could frame him within ninety days.

So testified a courageous Detroit police officer, Sergeant Bernard Mullins, who had overheard Hoffa's futile tirade. As Mullins left the Committee witness stand Hoffa snarled: "I'll remember this sergeant."

Judge Rashid filed an affidavit with our Committee, corroborating Sergeant Mullins's testimony.

Hoffa had a frightening case of bad memory when we questioned him about this. But he did recall discussing Rashid's political future with him.

"I told him," Hoffa testified, "he would have political opposition every time he ran for office as far as I was concerned."

On Sunday afternoon, July 26, 1959, Mr. Hoffa and I were scheduled to appear on different television programs in Washington. He was to "Face the Nation." I was to "Meet the Press." Hoffa's appearance was thirty minutes before mine, and from the NBC studios in Washington I watched on a studio TV set as he was questioned by reporters.

For the most part I thought the program dull. The questions propounded to Mr. Hoffa dealt with his views on what legislation was needed in the field of labor reform. As I afterward told the reporters who questioned me, it would have been no different if the Attorney General had asked Al Capone what laws he thought should be enacted to stop crime.

But toward the end of Hoffa's program one of the reporters brought up our investigation of a Tennessee Teamster official named Glenn Smith. Mr. Hoffa seized on the opportunity of the moment. "It might be well for the public to know," he said, "that despite all the statements made by Mr. Kennedy and the Committee, the question of Glenn Smith was resolved in a court and he was found innocent." Millions of listeners must have concluded that Glenn Smith was a man who had been unjustly condemned by our Committee.

The fact is, Glenn Smith was an ex-convict who had twice served terms for burglary and robbery before joining the Teamsters Union. After he joined up with Mr. Hoffa his police record expanded as he moved from city to city on Teamster "organizing" assignments. Finally he wound up in Chattanooga, Tennessee, and, in 1952, he and twelve of his fellow Teamsters were charged with conspiracy to commit illegal violence.

The judge presiding at their trial was Raulston Schoolfield. By a series of maneuvers which the Committee found highly suspicious he freed Smith and the other Teamsters.

LaVern Duffy, an investigator I sent to look into the case, reported back to me that Smith had taken $20,000 of union funds to try to fix the judge. We presented the evidence he had uncovered at the Committee hearings. Glenn Smith took the Fifth Amendment. Judge Schoolfield was invited to testify and refused.

When state officials impeached and convicted Judge Schoolfield on charges growing out of our Committee hearings, I testified before the State Legislature. (I was cross-examined by Schoolfield and was impressed with the agility of his mind and his shrewdness.) Glenn Smith had testified the previous day, and admitted he took the $20,000 to get the cases before Judge Schoolfield fixed.

Despite this open admission, Smith continued as a union official. He claimed he hadn't violated the Teamster constitution. Moreover, Teamster lawyers represented him when he was tried for not reporting on his income tax the money he said he had received to bribe the judge. And with Hoffa's blessing his lawyers were paid from Teamster Union funds. They argued that Smith shouldn't have to pay taxes on the $20,000 because he had spent the money immediately to fix his case. Or that even if he had not, he shouldn't have to pay taxes on it anyway because he had embezzled it and embezzled funds are not taxable.

The jury brought in a verdict of guilty, which was reversed by the presiding judge. Although characterizing Smith as unfit to hold union office, and condemning his conduct as "sordid," he was highly critical of the Government's handling of the case and held that the charge had been improperly brought. He said his ruling might have been different if Smith were being charged with bribery of a public official, rather than with income tax evasion.

It was on this record that Hoffa claimed that Glenn Smith had been cleared of any wrongdoing.

There were times when it was depressingly easy to understand Mr. Hoffa's cynicism. I remember a rank-and-file Teamster named John Cunningham who came to see me in our New York office right after the Select Committee was established. He had a complaint about corruption within his union—the Milk Wagon Drivers. We talked, and I agreed to do what I could. Shortly afterward I heard that he had put out a press release that the Committee was going to conduct a full-scale investigation of his union's officials. This was untrue, and unfair to the incumbent officers of the union. Then I found that he had brought the same complaints to other Government agencies, who had investigated and found no factual basis to support them.

I heard nothing further from Cunningham until the so-called Teamster "insurgent 13" began battling the legality of Hoffa's election as International president in Miami, Florida, in the fall of 1957. They retained Godfrey Schmidt of New York as their counsel and were bitterly opposed to Hoffa. The head of the "13" was John Cunningham. At that time I did not connect the name with the man I had interviewed in New York at the beginning of the year. Later I met him again several times and was impressed with his purpose and apparent honesty.

The "13" brought court action to prevent Hoffa from taking office, a move that resulted in a settlement. Hoffa and the other officers elected were allowed to assume their duties as "provisional officers," and a Board of Monitors was appointed to oversee their activities until a new election is held. Rank-and-file members were allowed to select one monitor, the International Brotherhood of Teamsters another, both of these subject to approval of the court, which selected the third member, who was to serve as monitor chairman.

By mid-1958 I began hearing rumors that John Cunningham had switched, that he was now siding with Hoffa against Godfrey Schmidt, his own counsel and representative on the Board of Monitors. His actions were covert in the beginning, but then he came out in the open. I was shocked. I couldn't believe that right under our very noses Hoffa could take over the head of the "13" insurgents. We made an investigation. What we found was that John Cunningham had indeed become a Hoffa man. But there had been inducements. Since the middle of 1958 Jimmy Hoffa and his union had been paying some of John Cunningham's bills.

Every man has his price, says Jimmy Hoffa.

Chapter 5 / THE PALACE GUARD

ON JUNE 6, 1959, an extraordinary drama was enacted in a Senate hearing room. The president of a union local numbering 2,200 hard-working truck drivers was led in handcuffed by New York police, who had brought him down from the Rikers Island jail. This pleasant-faced, graying man—he looked more like a bank vice president than a union official—was a gangster. His name was Sam Goldstein; he was a twice-convicted extortionist, and a henchman of the notorious under-world figure Tony "Ducks" Corallo.

When he first appeared before our Committee in 1957 he took the Fifth Amendment on every question asked him. At the end of our hearings that year, James Hoffa promised to clear crooks like Gold-stein out of his union. In 1958, as token proof that he was keeping his promise, he gave us a written statement that Goldstein was no longer with the Teamsters in any capacity.

Yet now, in 1959, examining Goldstein again, we discovered that he was still president of his local and still receiving $375 a week in salary plus $25 a week for expenses—while in jail.

Sam Goldstein, in short, was an example of what Hoffa had not done and was not doing to clean up the Teamsters.

He was also typical of the thugs and racketeers thinly disguised as labor union officials that Hoffa has brought into the Teamsters. To cover all of them would require an encyclopedia, but we shall presently have a look at a representative half-dozen. A list of some of the others and their activities will be found in an appendix.[1]

In our August, 1957 hearings, when the Committee began to spread on the record Hoffa's close ties with racketeers, the nation got its first look at the man who in little more than a month would be elected to succeed Dave Beck as president of the most powerful union in the country—and at the convicted killers, robbers, extortionists, perjurers, blackmailers, safecrackers, dope peddlers, white slavers and sodomists who were his chosen associates.

In Hoffa, what the country saw was a man who was no stranger to a witness stand. He had previously appeared before another Congressional committee, and had come from his bribery trial only a month before our August hearings began. During the course of his career in Detroit he had been in and out of court on charges including malicious destruction of property, shooting, conspiracy and obtaining money under false pretenses; had been convicted and fined for violating the antitrust law, and given two years' probation for conspiracy.

The country saw in Hoffa also a man who, at the beginning of hearings, seemed confident that he would be able to charm his way through, and that the Committee would then forget about him and he would be free to go his way as before. So, during those first days on the witness stand, he was at times openly cordial in answering questions. Sometimes he called me "Bob," which later cooled to a formal "Mr. Kennedy"; but after the first year, to my amusement, he would not for the most part address me at all, answering my questions by turning to Senator McClellan and beginning, "Mr. Chairman" or "Senator."

But at times Jimmy Hoffa could be amusing, too. I still laugh remembering a day when I was sitting on a table at one side of the hearing room, my feet on a chair, and Hoffa walked by. He saw me and scolded: "Get your feet off. Don't you know you're dirtying government property?"

In the first of our series of hearings he relied principally on a bad memory to get him through; for the AFL-CIO had taken a stand against letting their union officers take the Fifth on matters that in-

[1] See Appendix.

volved their administration of union affairs. So we heard repeatedly from Hoffa answers such as this:

"To the best of my recollection I must recall on my memory I cannot remember." And even: "I can say here to the Chair that I cannot recall in answer to your question other than to say I just don't recall my recollection."

Not even playing back for him transcriptions of his own telephone conversations helped; in fact, nothing we could do seemed to stimulate his memory. Senator McClellan finally commented in exasperation: "If these things do not refresh your memory it would take the power of God to do it. The instrumentalities of man obviously are not adequate."

Before Hoffa returned as a witness in 1958, he seriously considered taking the Fifth Amendment and in fact at one point had pretty well decided to do so. Afterward he told the Committee that he wished he had, that it would have saved him a lot of trouble. However, he feared that if he did claim the Fifth, the court-appointed Teamster monitors might attempt to remove him from office—so he came to try to talk his way through the hearings.

He was now Teamster president, with all the power that union office could offer. And as we uncovered more and more evidence of corruption attributable to his administration, he dropped his mask of amiability and became aggressive and contemptuous. But he was smoother in telling us that he had lost his memory, and he found new ways to avoid answering. For one, he had hit upon the device of taking the Fifth Amendment by proxy—"Ask Bert Brennan."

He had also discovered that long, rambling answers could delay the hearing and sidetrack an embarrassing line of questioning; it sometimes took him nine or ten hundred words to say "yes" or "no."

Another delaying practice he developed to perfection was, after listening to a summary of some other witness's testimony about Hoffa's corrupt activities, to say blandly, "That isn't in the record—I have read the record. Nothing like that is in the record."

If the Chairman decided to take the time to call this bluff, twenty minutes would be lost digging into the record to locate the testimony that had just been summarized. Once the record had been read to him, Hoffa would go off on a lengthy, uninformative tangent.

Sometimes his façade of bluster and bluff would crack and for an hour during a hearing he would appear morose, discouraged and beaten. But the man has great stamina, and he would bounce back again as forceful as ever.

The hearings were always tedious and a physical and mental strain. I recall one day, particularly, when Hoffa was scheduled to appear but adjournment time came before we got to him. Senator McClellan indicated that he might hold a night session. I was bushed. I looked at him and smiled wearily.

Hoffa, standing just across the counsel table from me, saw my look of fatigue and snickered. "Look at him, look at him! He's too tired. He just doesn't want to go on."

I think he saw the whole investigation simply as a fight between the two of us—Bobby Kennedy and Jimmy Hoffa don't like each other. To him, it was a personality clash, not the United States versus corruption. I don't think this was a publicity gimmick, though certainly his publicity people pushed it. But I saw his look that day and it was the expression of a man scoring a tremendous victory. I was tired and he wasn't. It was as if he regarded the hearings as a sort of endurance contest—a game of Indian wrestling on a national scale.

In the most remarkable of all my exchanges with Jimmy Hoffa not a word was said. I called it "the look." It was to occur fairly often, but the first time I observed it was on the last day of the 1957 hearings. During the afternoon I noticed that he was glaring at me across the counsel table with a deep, strange, penetrating expression of intense hatred. I suppose it must have dawned on him about that time that he was going to be the subject of a continuing probe—that we were not playing games. It was the look of a man obsessed by his enmity, and it came particularly from his eyes. There were times when his face seemed completely transfixed with this stare of absolute evilness. It might last for five minutes—as if he thought that by staring long enough and hard enough he could destroy me. Sometimes he seemed to be concentrating so hard that I had to smile, and occasionally I would speak of it to an assistant counsel sitting behind me. It must have been obvious to him that we were discussing it, but his expression would not change by a flicker.

During the 1958 hearings, from time to time, he directed the same shriveling look at my brother. And now and then, after a protracted, particularly evil glower, he did a most peculiar thing: he would wink at me. I can't explain it. Maybe a psychiatrist would recognize the symptoms.

Almost as soon as the Committee began to develop the evidence on Hoffa and his friends during the August, 1957 hearings, it became apparent that the inner sanctum of the Teamsters Union hierarchy has no counterpart in the United States today. We listened to testimony from the dregs of society. We saw and questioned some of the nation's most notorious gangsters and racketeers. But there was no group that better fits the prototype of the old Al Capone syndicate than Jimmy Hoffa and some of his chief lieutenants in and out of the union.

They have the look of Capone's men. They are sleek, often bilious and fat, or lean and cold and hard. They have the smooth faces and cruel eyes of gangsters; they wear the same rich clothes, the diamond ring, the jeweled watch, the strong, sickly-sweet-smelling perfume.

And they have criminal records to compare with those of the old Capone mob.

Consider John Ignazio Dioguardi, alias Johnny Dio. Dio is a long-time garment industry racketeer, an extortionist and a Sing Sing ex-convict who was charged in the acid-blinding conspiracy of labor columnist Victor Riesel. In the 1930's Thomas E. Dewey, then New York District Attorney, called Johnny Dio "a young gorilla" who "by the time he was twenty had become a major gangster."

Throughout his career Dio worked both sides of the labor-management street. He was a director of the United Auto Workers Union, A. F. of L.,[2] in New York, while at the same time owning an interest in a string of cheap dress manufacturing firms. He was convicted of violating the New York State income tax law for failing to report an extra $11,200 he received in the sale of one of these dress firms, in

---

[2] Not to be confused with the UAW-CIO headed by Walter Reuther. The UAW-AFL broke away from the CIO group in 1939.

return for the assurance that the new owner would keep the shop nonunion—as it had been under Dio.

Yet this is the man to whom Jimmy Hoffa turned as far back as 1953—the man he made his chief instrument—in his efforts to grab control of the New York Teamsters from International Vice President Tom Hickey, known—and rightfully so—as "The Honest Teamster."

Suave, dark and well dressed, Dio came before the Committee August 8, 1957, some two weeks before Hoffa first appeared. The day he came into the office he was tense and nervous. His hand trembled as he lighted a cigarette. The charges facing him—conspiracy in the Riesel blinding, another case of extortion—had given him a haunted, hunted look.

I told him he could remain in the office until it was time for him to testify. After leaving a message that I would call a few minutes before he was to appear, I went up to the crowded hearing room and made my way through the swarm of spectators, photographers, TV and movie cameramen, reporters, lawyers, witnesses, friends, attendants, stenographers, senators and investigators to the counsel table.

Apparently there had been some misunderstanding, for shortly afterward Dio and his lawyer entered. He was immediately recognized.

Photographers rushed across the room to snap his picture. There was a murmur among the spectators as they pointed to him. As Senator McClellan rapped the gavel for order, I sent a staff man to tell Dio he could leave the room until we were ready. Photographers followed him into the corridor and down the hall, still flashing their bulbs at him. He retreated, lost his temper and suddenly, like a cornered animal, turned and screamed, "Don't you know I have a family?" and lashed out with his fist at one of the photographers.

Another cameraman caught the now famous picture of him swinging, his lips curled in an angry snarl, a cigarette dangling from the corner of his mouth.

When he did testify, Dio took the Fifth on all questions—including whether he knew Hoffa.

Dio was not a major underworld figure like Frank Costello or Albert Anastasia. If it were not for the blinding of Victor Riesel and the importance of his uncle, James Plumeri, in gangster officialdom, plus his friendship with Hoffa, he would be considered not much more than a punk. However, he seemed to impress Hoffa. He talked like a hoodlum, he had certain contacts and connections that Hoffa felt could be helpful to him in his drive for power in New York. And Hoffa's wife and Dio's wife were very close.

Early in our investigation, I had called on New York District Attorney Frank Hogan and asked for his assistance. Both he and his chief assistant, Alfred J. Scotti, pledged their full support; their assistance was a major help in a number of important investigations. From their office the Committee received a number of legal wiretaps made of phone calls by Dio to Jimmy Hoffa. They concerned a series of meetings in 1953 in which Hoffa had tried to pressure Dave Beck into letting Dio take over organizing the taxicab drivers in New York—which would have been a slap in the face of "Honest Tom" Hickey.

In May, 1953, Dio called Hoffa to discuss ways to impress Beck in advance of a meeting of Teamster executives to be held at the Hampshire House in New York. They decided Dio was to call strikes of "his" UAW-AFL local and put on a major show of power.

There was this recorded conversation:

DIO: I'll tell you what I'm going to do though. We're lining up—I think we're going to have about twenty strikes before that meeting.
HOFFA: Well, that's good.
DIO: Well, the reason—before I pulled it I thought I'd consult with you on it.
HOFFA: I think that's [inaudible] show him who the ———got the people.

About this conversation, Hoffa said: "I cannot hardly remember the meeting. . . ."

Did he and Dio agree on whether Dio should come into the Teamsters?

"I don't remember. I am trying to refresh my memory out of these conversations, but they are such with other people that I don't know how I can do it."

On May 12, 1953, the eve of the meeting in New York, Dio and Hoffa talked again. Hoffa was planning to fly that night from Detroit. Dio told him that, as they had planned, the cab strikes were starting.

According to Tom Hickey, who was present at the Hampshire House meeting, the next day Hoffa insisted to Beck and his aides that these strikes were evidence of Dio's qualifications for a Teamsters charter.

A Hoffa-Dio conversation recorded just after the May 13 meeting indicated that Hoffa had attempted to recruit the support of Martin Lacey, another important New York Teamster.

"I just came from that fellow's office. . . . Ah—getting a charter," said Hoffa. Dio asked: "Who's that, Marty?"

Hoffa: "Yeah . . . he went on—definitely on record against it."

To the credit of Dave Beck, he refused to permit Dio to come into the Teamsters.

Jimmy Hoffa was able to remember one telephone conversation he had had with Dio. This one took place only one month before Hoffa's first appearance on the witness stand.

"He called me up to tell me that he had been convicted of extortion and he wanted to know if his wife would need any assistance would I help her," Hoffa said.

A few weeks after the Hampshire House meeting, a grand jury in Detroit began looking into the activities of Hoffa and the Teamsters. The newspapers reported that Hoffa had made all his union subordinates wear a tiny device called a Minifon into the grand jury room, so that he would have recorded evidence of their testimony.

The Committee asked Hoffa about this, and to help him remember played for him the tapes of a conversation he had had with Dio two weeks before the grand jury proceedings started:

DIO: I got a couple of those things.
HOFFA: Good.
DIO: So, ah, maybe—maybe I'll have four of them tomorrow.
HOFFA: Fine.
DIO: All right?
HOFFA: Yeah, John.

I asked Hoffa: "You just cannot tell us anything about what the 'four of them' was?"

He answered: "It could be four of almost anything."

Two weeks later, on June 16, 1953, Hoffa telephoned Dio and there was this conversation:

DIO: Did my man get there all right?

HOFFA: Yes; he was here last week.

DIO: Yeah.

HOFFA: He—he was to see you over the weekend that's why I thought he would tell you the whole story.

DIO: Yes. Well, I didn't see him because I was busy.

HOFFA: I see. He was back here again this week, two of them.

DIO: Well, he'll be back.

HOFFA: He's here now.

DIO: Is he there now?

HOFFA: And they are doing that work.

DIO: Uh-huh.

HOFFA: Uhhh—he had to have 13 last week for supplies.

DIO: Huh?

HOFFA: He wanted—

DIO: Well, I gave him a few hundred when he left.

HOFFA: He wanted $500 for [inaudible] supplies.

DIO: Uh-huh. I'll a—

HOFFA: Now, ah—insofar as work is concerned you better have him call you before he starts.

DIO: Yeah, but look, Jim; you remember you do all your discussing there with him because if you don't like anything tell me. You know what I mean?

HOFFA: Well, he's doing all right.

DIO: Well, I'm going to tell you this. Those are the best—

HOFFA: Yeah, you're doing a wonderful job.

DIO: They are the best; they work for the UN and everything else, now—and whenever you want to need 'em any part of the country if you want to find out they're your people you let me know. You know what I mean?

HOFFA: Yup.

I asked Hoffa what Dio meant by "They are the best; they work for the UN and everywhere else."

Hoffa's answer was "I just don't recall."

After we had jogged his memory a little more, Hoffa admitted that he had ordered and received some Minifons at this time. He did not recall whether they had been the subject of his conversation with Dio or what use he had made of them.

HOFFA: What did I do with them? Well, what did I do with them?

KENNEDY: What did you do with them?

HOFFA: I am trying to recall.

KENNEDY: You could remember that.

HOFFA: When were they delivered, do you know? That must have been quite a while.

KENNEDY: You know what you did with the Minifons and don't ask me.

HOFFA: What did I do with them?

KENNEDY: What did you do with them?

HOFFA: Mr. Kennedy, I bought some Minifons and there is no question about it, but I cannot recall what became of them. . . .

This continued for a while and at one point I asked him if he had ever worn a Minifon himself.

HOFFA: You say "wear." What do you mean by "wear"?

Finally, in exasperation, Senator McClellan said: "I have done as much to refresh your memory as I know how to do. If you cannot recall it from that, and you want to leave the record that way, if you want to think that this committee is so stupid and that the public is so stupid that they will believe that you could not remember having done a thing like that, you leave the record that way."

I suggested to Mr. Hoffa that from all of the conversations we had played for him, he ought to be able to remember.

He answered: "Well, I will have to stand on the answers that I have made in regards to my recollection and I cannot answer unless you can give me some recollection, other than I have answered."

He made 111 similar answers to our questions that day.

When, in 1953, Dave Beck cut short Hoffa's plans to take over Hickey's taxicab organizing efforts, it did not cool Hoffa's desire to seize power in New York or diminish his hope of getting Dio to help him do the job.

So it was that three years later Hoffa and Dio became involved in the now notorious paper local case. Briefly, it was a plot to steal the presidency of New York's powerful Joint Council 16 from the incumbent, Martin Lacey, who had Tom Hickey's backing.

Hoffa and Dio had as their accomplice in this Antonio (Tony Ducks) Corallo, alias Antonio Freno, alias Mr. Selzo, an underworld figure of great influence whose unusual nickname stems from his reputation for "ducking" convictions in court cases in which he is arrested. Tony Ducks, whose police arrest list includes drug and robbery charges and who is on the Treasury Department's narcotics list, lost only one bout with the law. In 1941 he was sentenced to six months for unlawful possession of narcotics. He had managed to muscle into the Teamsters movement in New York and had absolute control of five different locals.

Carmine Bellino, who has seen his share, said Corallo was the meanest, toughest gangster he had ever seen. Evidently others agreed. One New York employer told me he hired Corallo simply to walk into his plant and "glare at the employees" to keep them in line. This seemed to me rather funny at the time—almost comic strip material. But when Tony Ducks appeared on the witness stand and turned his glare on us, I changed my mind. The only thing worse for sheer evilness that I have ever seen was that look of Hoffa's.

As their man to unseat Martin Lacey, the Hoffa-Dio-Corallo forces picked silver-haired, distinguished-looking John O'Rourke, a New York Teamster leader who was opposed to Tom Hickey. In what the Committee showed was a blatantly rigged election they won by a handful of votes. The following year, 1957, John O'Rourke, by the grace of Jimmy Hoffa and with the help of the underworld, took over in New York for the Teamsters. And when Hoffa became International president in October, he backed O'Rourke against Tom Hickey, for the International vice presidency in New York.

O'Rourke is the Teamster voice in New York today, and he is the man on whom the responsibility falls for ridding the Teamsters Union of "The mob." He isn't capable of doing the job. In May, 1959, he himself was indicted on charges of conspiracy, coercion and extortion in connection with the juke-box business in New York.

I felt sorry for him after he appeared before our Committee. When he took the Fifth Amendment he seemed deeply hurt. He walked from the hearing room and there, away from the eyes of the spectators and the television cameras, he wept. I stopped as I passed by in the hall and told him I was sorry.

"I understand you are just doing your job," he said.

Later a former mutual friend came to visit me and suggested that we might meet privately to discuss O'Rourke's problems in running

81

the union. I went to my friend's house the next time I was in New York, for I was anxious to see if anything could be done to improve the situation. O'Rourke met me there and told me that he had been in the hospital when Dio's racketeers infiltrated the Teamsters Union in New York; that he had had nothing to do with it.[3]

Before I left he promised that he would take specific steps to get rid of one particularly corrupt Teamster in the New York area. He didn't keep his word.

Hoffa's successful takeover in New York was only one step—though a big one—in his rise to the top of the Teamster heap. His drive for control began in Detroit. The men he surrounded himself with there were typical of those he was to recruit as his power spread, first throughout Michigan, then into Chicago and the Midwest, through the South, to New York and the East, until it became all-embracing with his election to the International presidency.

And certainly one of the first men he recruited on his way was Owen Bert Brennan. Brennan, who has been arrested several times and was convicted with Hoffa of conspiracy and violation of the anti-trust law, is probably Hoffa's oldest and closest crony. In September, 1957, I interviewed him in our Committee offices on the seventh floor of the Post Office Building in Detroit.

At one point his lawyer, George Fitzgerald, stepped out of the room and for a few moments we were alone. During a lull in the conversation, I walked over to the open window and looked out on the street below.

"If I fell out of here now, they'd say you pushed me."

He didn't change expression.

"I'd like to," was his unsmiling direct reply.

Bert Brennan is a wiry, muscular, little man with cold eyes and close-cropped hair. He always looks healthy and tanned—and mean. He talks tough; he acts tough. An incessant smoker, he has a habit of biting a cigarette between his front teeth (just like the movie bad-man), curling his lips back and talking while keeping his cigarette

[3] Dio had brought into the union movement about forty hoodlums with 178 arrests and 77 convictions between them.

perfectly in place. Like Hoffa, Brennan worked hard at portraying the tough guy.

Hoffa's and Brennan's lives have been intimately entwined in deals in and out of the labor movement. He knows more about (and on) the International president of the Teamsters than any of the other men around Hoffa. According to the testimony of Bartley Crum[4] before the Committee, reporting a conversation with Hoffa, Brennan once warned Hoffa that if "he [Brennan] were called or indicted or tried, he would spill his guts on Hoffa. . . ." In a deep sense, Brennan symbolizes why Hoffa doesn't clean up his union: to get rid of Brennan would be self-destruction.

Hoffa and Brennan fought their way up together in the Teamsters Union, using gall, collusive deals and a group of police characters. Brennan is president of Local 337 in Detroit, which has headquarters in the same building as Hoffa's home Local 299. When Hoffa became president of the International in 1957, Owen Bert Brennan was elected vice president.

The men Hoffa and Brennan have around them in Michigan, their stronghold of corruption, tells a story in itself. One of these was Herman Kierdorf, until August, 1958, a business agent for Joint Council 43 in Detroit. Kierdorf spent from 1933 to 1935 in Leavenworth for impersonating a Federal officer, from 1942 to 1948 in Ohio State Prison for armed robbery. He was released from prison and subsequently from his parole at Hoffa's intercession. Before the Committee, Kierdorf took the Fifth Amendment, and shortly thereafter retired from the union. He took with him into retirement a $4,800 Cadillac for which he gave the union a note for $1,400. Not long afterward he was convicted of possessing a gun silencer and given a one-to-five-year prison term.

His nephew, Frank Kierdorf, served a term in Michigan Penitentiary for armed robbery. Almost immediately upon his release Hoffa put him in charge of Teamster Local 332 in Flint. A reign of terror for small businessmen followed: arson, dynamitings, beatings were all

---

[4] Bartley Crum died December 9, 1959, as this book was being prepared for publication.

part of his organizing technique. When the Committee asked Hoffa in 1945 whether he had investigated the charges against Frank Kierdorf, he replied that he had: "I asked him about it and he said he didn't do it," Hoffa told us blandly.

On August 3, 1958, Frank Kierdorf set fire to a Flint cleaning establishment and turned himself into a human torch. He was delivered to a hospital, his body burned and charred beyond recognition. He died a few days later. Shortly before his death, the prosecuting attorney, a religious man, told him: "You only have a few hours to live, you are about to face your Maker, your God. Make a clean breast of things. Tell me what happened."

Through burned lips, Frank Kierdorf gave his dying declaration: "Go —— yourself," he said.

At the end of our 1958 hearings, Hoffa presented us with a list of Teamster officials whom he had expelled or fired.

The late Frank Kierdorf, "Human Torch," was one of them.

By 1949, with the help of Brennan and others, Jimmy Hoffa had consolidated his position in the Michigan Teamsters; but outside his home state he was still largely unknown. For him, the key to the entire Midwest was Chicago. He needed a powerful ally there—and he found his man in Paul Dorfman. Dorfman, our testimony showed, was a big operator—a major figure in the Chicago underworld who also knew his way around in certain labor and political circles.

A slight man with thinning red hair and an almost benign manner, Dorfman took over as head of the Chicago Waste Handlers Union in 1939 after its founder and secretary-treasurer was murdered. In 1957 the AFL-CIO kicked him out for corruption.

He has tied some strange knots in the strings he pulls. According to our testimony, he was closely linked with such underworld figures as Tony Accardo, who became head of the Chicago syndicate after the death of Al Capone, and with Abner (Longie) Zwillman—a top gangland leader in the United States. (Longie Zwillman committed suicide shortly after being subpoenaed by our Committee.) Red Dorfman is also considered a power in some political circles, both Democratic and Republican. He is prominent in professional boxing and a close friend of Truman Gibson, the head of the former International Boxing Club.

Hoffa made a trade with Dorfman. In return for an introduction to the Chicago underworld, the Committee found, Hoffa turned over to him and his family the gigantic Central Conference of Teamsters Welfare Fund insurance.

Martin Uhlmann, a graying veteran accountant from the General Services Administration, and Jim Findlay, an intense, tireless worker loaned to us by the Army Department, took on the job of investigating the deal.

After months of tedious digging they found, and the hearings later showed, that there was nothing whatever to recommend Red Dorfman, his wife, Rose, his son, Allen, or their company, Union Casualty, to any responsible union leader—or anyone else for that matter. When bidding for the welfare fund insurance began, Allen Dorfman, who became the broker, did not have an office, did not even have an insurance brokerage license. He was hurriedly established in the insurance brokerage business so that he might be in operation by 1950, when the insurance award was to be made. He got it, of course, though low bidder for the teamster business was Pacific Mutual Life Insurance Company, a reputable firm with assets about five hundred times greater than Dorfman's company ($376,000,000 to $768,000).

Our investigation revealed that in eight years Allen Dorfman and his mother, Rose, received more than $3,000,000 in commissions and fees on the Teamsters insurance. Expert testimony further established that $1,250,000 of that amount was in excessive commissions, another $400,000 was in excessive service fees. A total of more than $1,600,000 was the pay-off to the Dorfmans.

And this money was coming out of Teamsters members' pockets.

During the period 1952 to 1954, Hoffa allowed the company to increase their commissions and the premium rates of his members —and at the same time permitted the insurance benefits of the members to be cut. The Teamsters were paying more and getting less. And in 1956 the benefits of the membership were cut again.

Our Committee showed that Allen Dorfman took $51,000 worth of premiums and deposited the money in his own bank account.

This whole operation was so outrageous that the New York State

85

Insurance Department, one of the best in the country, withdrew the right of the Dorfmans to do business in that state.

Many other states in addition to New York have taken action against them, but in some they are still allowed to continue. The political influence which Paul Dorfman wields still is effective.

In January, 1958, after our Dorfman investigation had been going on for many months, I was in Las Vegas with Carmine Bellino, checking Allen Dorfman's hotel records. While we were working in the office of the hotel manager, the door suddenly swung open and in walked Allen Dorfman himself. A shocked look crossed his face— and I am sure that same look crossed my own. There were a few moments of idle chatter. And then he wanted to know why we wouldn't leave Hoffa and him alone.

The next time I saw him was when he appeared before the Committee and, like his father, took the Fifth Amendment.

Paul Dorfman and Jimmy Hoffa are now as one. Everywhere Hoffa goes, Dorfman is close by. Most important decisions by Hoffa are made only after consultation with Paul Dorfman.

Allen Dorfman is also close to Hoffa, but the relationship is different. A neat, good-looking man, he had an excellent war record with the Marines and was decorated for bravery. Four years after his discharge his income was $5,000 a year. When his father and Jimmy Hoffa took him up on "top of the mountain" and offered him a chance to make some $300,000 a year, the temptation was too great. Paul Dorfman doesn't mind, but, with his previous record, I don't think Allen Dorfman enjoys taking the Fifth Amendment.

A few months after the Dorfman hearings, I was at home one evening when my administrative assistant, Kenny O'Donnell, telephoned to say that in Chicago the Dorfmans' lawyer had attacked me because of our investigation.

"Among other things, he called you a sadistic little monster," said Kenny. "I think you ought to sue him—you're not so little."

From time to time, we ran into some of Jimmy Hoffa's hoodlum Teamster lieutenants, who made a big show of pretending that they took their Teamster duties seriously.

Of these, Joey Glimco was a prize example of a union leader who had no interest in union members in Chicago or elsewhere. The head of Teamsters Local 777 in Chicago, and an ornament of the city's underworld, Glimco has been arrested thirty-six times, twice in connection with killings.

When Glimco came before the Committee in 1958, he was under a subpoena to furnish us with his local's books and financial records. He brought them with him—but on the witness stand he pretended that his sworn duty as a union official was not to permit the records out of his sight. To his surprise, we readily agreed. I felt that by keeping him in Washington we were doing a favor for Chicago law enforcement. I took him down to our office, arranged for a chair to be placed in the hallway just outside the door where the records were to be examined.

"As you realize, we will want to keep these records overnight," I told him. "I have arranged for a bed for you to sleep on and the men's room is halfway down the corridor."

There was a cafeteria in the building so he would be able to eat breakfast, too, I added, and left him in his chair to keep vigil.

An hour later I went back. He had vanished. He never again mentioned his books and records or his phony obligation to maintain custody of them.

Several years ago merchants in Chicago's Fulton Street Market testified before a Federal grand jury that in order to operate they were required to make kickbacks to Glimco. Some said they paid under fear of death. Trial was delayed for three years, and by this time, the witnesses had changed their stories. Yes, they admitted, they had paid Glimco—but it was because they wanted to give him a Christmas present. Christmas presents in June? Well they just liked him, they said.

Glimco, without consulting the membership, took $124,000 from the treasury of his taxicab Teamsters local in order to defend himself in this action—although the Teamsters were not involved in the case.

Glimco, like Hoffa, keeps no bank accounts, never writes checks and deals only in cash. He pays his own bills and expenses, as well as those of his girl friend, out of union funds.

Joey Glimco appeared before the Committee for the last time in mid-1959. I was riding up in the elevator on my way to the hearing room when I was almost overcome by a heavy, sickly-sweet smell. I tried to remember what madam was testifying that day, until I got out and, walking down the hall with Glimco to the caucus room, realized that he was the source of the oppressive odor.

Hoffa is well aware of the kind of people that he deals with in Chicago, as an incident related by Robert Scott indicates. (Scott, you may recall, is the union leader Hoffa once asked to hide his brother Billy from the police.) Scott told Walter Sheridan, our investigator, about a trip he and Hoffa made together to Chicago. Hoffa retired to his hotel room early. Scott took a walk. On returning, he stopped by Hoffa's room to see if his boss was asleep. He tried the doorknob and it was unlocked. He stepped into the room.

"I didn't get inside the door before Jimmy had rolled out of bed over to a table and came up standing on the other side of the room with a gun in his hand," said Scott.

To consolidate his power in his growing empire, Hoffa employed roving emissaries of violence. Robert Barney Baker was one of these.

In our 1958 hearings, Hoffa testified: "Now Barney Baker works for the Central Conference of Teamsters *under my direct orders.*"

An ex-convict (jailed three times in the 1930's), the 325-pound Baker was a former professional boxer, longshoreman, confidant of top hoodlums and a bouncer before joining the Teamsters. His rise was rapid. Starting in Washington, D.C., he soon became the general organizer for the Teamsters in Missouri and finally was promoted by Hoffa to his present job. Assault and mayhem in crushing opposition to Hoffa were often a part of his day's work.

In 1936 Baker was shot down in what police describe as a gang war near a Thirty-fourth Street restaurant in Manhattan. With him that night was John O'Rourke, later to become Jimmy Hoffa's hand-picked Teamster vice president in New York. Another man with him that night was killed. Testifying before our Committee some twenty-two years later, Barney recalled the ambush: "Myself, a fellow named Joe Butler, Farmer Sullivan, a trainer-manager of mine, and Mr. John

O'Rourke we walked from this restaurant. . . . I believe just before getting to the New Yorker Hotel around fifty or seventy-five feet there is a parking lot. And all I heard was a lot of noise and I hit the pavement. They shot myself, Mr. O'Rourke and Mr. Butler. . . . Mr. Joe Butler passed away."

Barney claimed he didn't know why he was shot.

He tried to make a joke of the whole thing, telling about his criminal associates with such good humor that the press and members of the Committee were highly amused at his testimony.

For instance, we asked him about the men who had been involved in the killing of Anthony Hintz, a famous New York murder case during the 1940's.

MR. KENNEDY: Do you know Cockeyed Dunn?

MR. BAKER: I don't know him as Cockeyed Dunn. I know him as John Dunn.

MR. KENNEDY: Where is he now?

MR. BAKER: He has met his maker.

MR. KENNEDY: How did he do that?

MR. BAKER: I believe through electrocution in the City of New York of the State of New York.

A few minutes later we asked him about "Squint" Sheridan.

He said: "Mr. Sheridan, sir? . . . He also has met his maker." I asked: "How did he die?" Baker said: "With Mr. John Dunn."

MR. KENNEDY: He was electrocuted?

MR. BAKER: Yes, sir.

MR. KENNEDY: He also was a friend of yours?

MR. BAKER: Yes, he was a friend of mine.

We asked about Danny Gentile, the third man involved in the Hintz killing.

MR. KENNEDY: Where is he now?

MR. BAKER: I don't know where he could be now—excuse me. I believe he was implicated in a certain case in New York. He must be in jail.

MR. KENNEDY: That was the Hintz killing. You see we have testimony that you were closely associated with these people, Mr. Baker.

MR. BAKER: Yes, I knew them real well.

He boasted that he also knew such sinister underworld figures as Joe Adonis, Meyer Lansky, the late Benjamin "Bugsy" Siegel, "Trigger Mike" Coppola, "Scarface" Joe Bommarito, Jimmy "Blue Eyes" Alo, Vincent "Piggy Mac" Marchesi, and others.

During much of Barney Baker's testimony, Jimmy Hoffa sat in the hearing room and chuckled as he heard the man who "works under my direct orders" admit association with killers, gangsters, gamblers, racketeers, traffickers in narcotics and human flesh. And when we asked Hoffa if this didn't bother him at all, he said: "I am sure, hearing him testify here that he knew every one of them . . . it doesn't disturb me one iota."

We heard testimony from union men around the country who told of Barney Baker's unique abilities when it came to "organizing." Sometimes the mere threat of his presence in a room was enough to silence the men who would otherwise have opposed Hoffa's reign.

In testimony before the Committee Mollie Baker, Barney's divorced wife, mentioned the missing ransom money paid for the release of the kidnaped Bobby Greenlease six years ago. Her information was apparently limited, but she swore that Barney, through a St. Louis underworld contact, knew something about it. Law enforcement officials rank several Teamsters as chief suspects in the disappearance of the Greenlease ransom money.

In Florida, Walt Sheridan talked to a woman named Ruth Brougher, for whom Barney had left his wife. The tall, five-times-married blonde, who was then serving a fifteen-year prison term for an underworld killing, told Walt that Barney had supported her in high style, a style that included houses with swimming pools, hotel penthouses, and a hundred dollars a day "walking around money." Once, she said, he had told her about the time he "killed Joe Penner's duck" by "throwing a stink bomb" onto the stage; another time he bragged that the day he was released from prison he went straightaway and beat up the man whose testimony had convicted him. Later, Ruth Brougher appeared as a witness before the Committee and verified the information she had given Walt.

On the witness stand, Barney Baker claimed he was simply the innocent victim of two vengeful women who were trying to get even with him because he had withdrawn his romantic charm.

It was a romantic charm for which the Teamsters rank and file paid dearly.

Because the name of Harold Gibbons belongs high on any list of Hoffa's playmates I want to mention him here, but only in passing since he will be dealt with fully in another chapter. After Brennan, he is probably the most important figure in Hoffa's chain of command —some say he is even closer to Hoffa than any of his other advisers. Before our Committee hearings destroyed the pretty myth, Gibbons was pictured as the Teamsters egghead, an intellectual and philosopher way above the everyday hurly-burly of union infighting and gouging.

I interviewed him first in my office in the spring of 1957, shortly before the phantom local case was to begin in New York. He had no lawyer with him but he answered most of my questions readily. The next time I talked to him was when he came before the Committee.

In conversation and even when testifying he refers to himself in the third person: it is not "I" did this or "I" did that, but "Gibbons" did this and "Gibbons" did that. I noticed that by the time of the 1959 hearings, Hoffa had acquired the habit.

Gibbons was born in Pennsylvania in 1910, and as the youngest of twenty-three children had a difficult early life. He told me once that he had not met all his brothers and sisters and was not sure how many he had of each. When he was nineteen he moved to Chicago; eventually he went to work in a warehouse with the WPA, and by 1934 had become active in American Federation of Truckers. He was involved in the Chicago taxicab strike in 1937, and from then on, throughout the war and until 1947, held various union jobs. In 1947, Beck brought him into the Teamsters and, the Committee found, also arranged for him to purchase a local union in St. Louis and, with Hoffa's support, take over Joint Council 13.

In running his little command, the Committee found, Gibbons is as ruthless as Hoffa.[5] He talks about democracy but completely disregards it—even in his private life. His house outside St. Louis is plainly furnished and his family lives modestly. Gibbons himself, a tall and thin man with a cold superior look, has an apartment or a hotel room

[5] See Chapter 7: The Captive Unions.

in the city and lives expensively and well. He wants to enjoy the finer things, and Teamster money is used to help him.

This bright, self-centered, arrogant man is not popular within the Teamsters Union; he could not exist a day without Hoffa. Several top Teamster officials near to Hoffa urged us, unnecessarily, to investigate him. Gibbons, who is active politically, tried to use his contacts to have his appearance called off. As the hearings showed—and not for the only time—Senator McClellan was unmoved. Mr. Gibbons appeared as a witness.

These are by no means all the men around Hoffa or the stories of all those who have made his rise to power possible.[6] We had derogatory information on over 150 Teamster officials, more than one hundred of whom appeared before the Committee and took the Fifth Amendment. With the exception of Dave Beck and a handful of people around him, the Teamster officials who betrayed the trust to the union membership were lieutenants of Hoffa. Where Hoffa has the least influence—in the Western Conference of Teamsters—we found very little corruption and there again, except for Dave Beck and Brewster, it involved people having close connections and ties with Hoffa.

[6] See Appendix.

Chapter 6 / THE MONEY

WHEN OUR PLANE touched down at the Willow Run airport near Detroit, Pierre Salinger, brief case in hand, the inevitable cigar in his mouth, and an almost visible halo of excitement encircling his head, was waiting for us in the sweltering summer sun. It was July 28, 1958 —just a week before Jimmy Hoffa was due to appear before our Committee for his second series of hearings.

Salinger was a dark, extremely alert and intelligent young man who could grasp the importance of a document better than almost anyone on the staff. So his urgent telephone call about a document he had got hold of in a particularly sticky investigation had brought Carmine Bellino and me rushing from Washington.

What he had was a signed, sworn affidavit that in 1949 Hoffa had demanded and received cash pay-offs from Detroit laundry owners in return for a sweetheart contract. The payments, it said, had been arranged through the labor consultant firm of Jack (Babe) Bushkin and Joe Holtzman, two of Hoffa's most helpful pals in Detroit.

Our Committee had already shown that Hoffa made "business" deals with employers; we had shown that he kept huge sums of cash on hand. But he consistently had denied to us that the cash was pay-offs from employers.

This affidavit was important evidence to the contrary. Salinger had received it from William Miller, a former Detroit laundry owner,

93

only a few hours before our arrival. For three consecutive years, Miller said, he and all the other laundry owners in the city had contributed to a purse raised for Mr. Hoffa by the Detroit Institute of Laundering. The cash was collected by two officials of the Institute, John Charles Meissner and Howard Balkwill, who saw to it that Mr. Hoffa got the money.

Meissner had been executive secretary-treasurer of the management group. He was now retired. Balkwill was still the chief executive officer. Meissner and Balkwill, then, were the first men in Detroit we wanted to see to get corroboration of Miller's statement.

As Pierre Salinger drove through the traffic toward Meissner's suburban home, he filled us in on the background of the 1949 dispute between the laundering management group and the Teamsters Union —the dispute that had led to the sweetheart contract and the pay-off.

Laundry drivers of Teamsters Local 285 had still been working a six-day week that year—and, as testimony showed, they were tired of it. In February, their local union head, Isaac Litwak, sat down with Laundry Institute officials headed by Meissner and Balkwill, determined to get a five-day work week for his union members. Across the table from Litwak, the laundry representatives put their heads together, counted costs, and decided they could not possibly afford a five-day week. Negotiations ran on for weeks, then months. In May, Litwak, impatient, threatened a strike.

Management negotiators again put their heads together. While they could not afford a five-day week, neither could they afford a strike. And as strike talk continued, they became alarmed. Obviously, they concluded, they couldn't deal with Litwak. He had even thrown one of their lists of proposals in the wastebasket. They decided they had to go to some higher Teamster authority. According to his own affidavit, William Miller suggested getting in touch with Jimmy Hoffa to see if something could be "worked out."

Balkwill and Meissner agreed to try. After several days, Miller's affidavit continued, they reported that they had been successful. They could obtain a contract for a continued six-day week—in return for a cash fund to pay off Jimmy Hoffa. Were the owners all agreeable? According to Miller, they were.

When we arrived at the home of John Charles Meissner, in a quiet

Detroit residential section, it was humid and hot and clouds were blotting out the sun. A thunderstorm was brewing. Meissner was puttering in his garden. He was a tanned, healthy-looking man of medium build. As we walked across his lawn to where he was kneeling, he had a friendly though inquisitive look on his face.

We introduced ourselves. We showed him our credentials and sat down—Salinger and Bellino on a wooden bench, I on an overturned pail. We told him outright, without softening the blow, why we had come: about the pay-off in 1949 to Jimmy Hoffa. I told him we wanted his co-operation; that we needed his help. He was shocked. "Never heard of such a thing," he said, and vehemently continued to deny that the laundry owners had paid a "shakedown" to anyone during the 1949 negotiations. We evidently didn't understand, he said, that we were talking about reputable businessmen, people with a standing in the community.

Mr. Meissner has an honest way about him. Without blinking, he looked me straight in the eye. And he lied. Mr. Meissner lied then and continued to lie for several days thereafter.

Carmine Bellino now set out to try to track down Howard Balkwill while Pierre Salinger and I continued our discussion with Mr. Meissner. We went with him into his house and I asked if we might use his telephone to call William Miller. When Miller answered, I asked him to refresh Mr. Meissner's memory. He agreed. I handed the phone to the former secretary of the Institute.

Salinger and I stood nearby while they talked. Mr. Miller, apparently, was making his position clear, telling Mr. Meissner what he had sworn to in the affidavit.

We heard Meissner say: "Bill, I just don't know what you are talking about." He put down the receiver.

We then served a subpoena on him, ordering him to come to Washington. He became angry. And so did his wife, who had heard the telephone conversation and our discussions with her husband. She ordered Salinger and me from her house. We left, and went off to see how Carmine was making out in his interview with William Balkwill.

Mr. Balkwill is still president of the Institute and has taken over Mr. Meissner's old job of executive secretary as well. His office is a dilapidated frame building on Detroit's Grand Avenue.

We found Carmine there, waiting for us on the front porch. Balkwill's secretary was in, but he was out. The screen door was locked. We showed the secretary our credentials and asked if we might come inside and wait.

"I don't believe you are who you say you are," she told us through the screen. "You can't come in until Mr. Balkwill comes." She remained seated at her desk and the screen door remained latched.

So the three of us sat down on the porch steps of the old building to wait for Mr. Balkwill.

Thunder had been rumbling for some time; now rain started to fall, and soon a heavy, windswept downpour drenched the porch—and us. Still the secretary remained seated and her door remained locked. Finally, Howard Balkwill arrived; his secretary unlatched the door, and dripping from every seam Carmine, Pierre and I trailed in after him.

Balkwill is a large, robust man and looks a little like an auctioneer at a country fair or, perhaps, the man who forty years before was the big tackle on his high school football team. And, like his retired colleague, he righteously denied that there had been any pay-off—to Hoffa or anyone else. We had been badly misinformed, he said. The conversation was unpleasant. I was impatient and irritated. Balkwill and Meissner—these two "upright" businessmen in one day were hard to take.

We served Balkwill with a subpoena to produce his records. He turned them over to us there in his office. For thirty minutes Carmine Bellino examined the books of the Laundering Institute while Salinger and I went through the correspondence. Bellino came up with a number of thousand-dollar checks made out to cash. There was nothing to show where this money went, or to whom it had been paid. We immediately assumed that this was the money that had been paid to Hoffa—but as it developed (and as Balkwill and Meissner later testified), it was actually bribe money to John Paris, a close friend of Hoffa and head of the Laundry Workers local in Detroit, who has since died.

After leaving Balkwill's office, I assigned every staff member in the Detroit area to track down the other members of the Detroit Laundering Institute, interview them, and see if they would admit paying into the fund William Miller said had been collected. Bellino and I left Detroit convinced that Miller had told the truth in his affidavit. While he had not actually seen Balkwill and Meissner pay over the money, they had told him where it went. Within forty-eight hours, the reports from Detroit were in. I read them with a certain grim satisfaction: Our men had found several other laundry owners who admitted that they had contributed to the Balkwill-Meissner fund.

When Meissner and Balkwill arrived in Washington to appear before our Committee some five days later, there was a marked change in their attitude—and in their stories. They had learned by this time that we had made a survey of other members of the Institute. There had been a fund and it was a cash fund, they both admitted. The story they now told the Committee was this:

When Isaac Litwak started talking strike, they got in touch with a Detroit laundry owner, Moe Dalitz, who also is a Las Vegas and Havana gambling figure. Moe Dalitz was supposed to have "connections," and indeed he did have. He arranged a few days later for Mr. Meissner and Mr. Balkwill to sit down to lunch with Jimmy Hoffa's labor consultant friends, Joseph Holtzman and Jack Bushkin. At Carl's Chop House, just a stone's throw from Hoffa's Detroit Teamster headquarters, they discussed how they might get around Isaac Litwak. After a bit, Holtzman left the restaurant to see if it was possible to go over Litwak's head. When he returned, he told them he could get them the contract they wanted—for a price.

What price?

Twenty-five thousand dollars, all in cash, said Mr. Holtzman.

Balkwill told the Committee: "We nearly fainted. It is a lot of money, we couldn't pay it."

And while they couldn't pay it, neither could they afford to go back to the bargaining table with Isaac Litwak—described as a man "who wouldn't take a cigar."

So Meissner and Balkwill began "negotiating" with Holtzman and found him far more "reasonable" than Isaac Litwak. They "negotiated" the fix price down to $17,500, agreeing to pay the money for Mr. Holtzman's "expenses" in three installments: $7,500 in 1949;

$5,000 in 1950; and $5,000 in 1951. To raise the money, they assessed each laundry owner so much per truck: $45 in 1949 and $22.50 in 1950-51.

What did they get for their money?

Back went the officials of the Institute to the bargaining sessions with Isaac Litwak. Litwak, apparently confident that the laundry owners would soon capitulate, stood by his guns on the five-day week. Balkwill, Meissner and company stalled and watched the door and waited.

Late in that last session the door opened and in came Jimmy Hoffa.

Mr. Hoffa told the group there would be no strike. He wanted the contract signed on the owners' terms and signed immediately or he would step in himself. Mr. Litwak was stunned and angry—Meissner described him as "furious"—but he had no choice. He surrendered. The contract was signed without a five-day-week provision.

What happened to the cash payment?

Mr. Balkwill "assumed," so he testified, that Mr. Hoffa received part or all of it. Mr. Meissner said "assumed" was the wrong word. He said he "conjectured" that Mr. Hoffa got some of the money. Both denied having told Mr. Miller that they knew for a fact that Hoffa received the money, but Balkwill admitted that Holtzman said that he had to take care of "some people."

THE CHAIRMAN: In other words, there was never any doubt in your mind at all except that this was a payoff?
MR. BALKWILL: No.

William Miller, however, backed away from certain portions of his original affidavit. He was anxious to point out that he had never actually *known* to whom the Laundering Institute officials had given the money. What he had told us was only hearsay, he said.

We learned that coming into Washington Meissner and Balkwill had traveled on the same plane as Hoffa. He warned them to remember that it was Holtzman to whom they had given the money. They remembered.

This is of added significance because when we first asked Hoffa about this matter, before any of the laundry owners had testified, he stated that he knew nothing at all about these negotiations or payments. He denied that he took any pay-off money from the laundrymen or from Joe Holtzman or Jack Bushkin. We knew, and he admitted, that he had borrowed $5,000 from Holtzman and $5,000 from Bushkin—without note, interest or security. But that $10,000 in cash was a "loan," not a pay-off, he said.

Holtzman was dead at the time of our hearings. Bushkin took the Fifth Amendment.

Two other laundry owners confirmed Miller's story. One of them, Vincent Watkins, had been on the negotiating committee. He remembered the decision to approach someone "higher up" in the Teamsters and later hearing that "it was going to cost some money."

The other man, Conrad Lantz, recalled having heard that the fund was to go to Joe Holtzman, who, he testified, had direct communication with Mr. Hoffa.

Though Hoffa denied that he ever took bribes from employers, we found that he frequently had on hand enormous amounts of cash—far more than his income as a Teamster official could account for. His own simple explanation was that he "accumulated it." Carmine Bellino found the attempt to trace where it all came from and where it went a frustrating experience, since Hoffa deals only in cash: he maintains no bank account; he has written only one personal check in his life that we are aware of (that was to Edward Bennett Williams); his records are apparently nonexistent; and his memory, when it comes to where he gets his money or where it goes, is terrible.

One explanation of how he "accumulated" it, which put a severe strain on my imagination, was his account of the way he regularly comes by some $5,000 or $10,000 each year. It is not bribe money from employers, he swears, but race track winnings.

Mr. Hoffa admitted to the Committee that he knew absolutely nothing about betting on horses. But he claimed his business partner and fellow Teamster official, Bert Brennan, knew a great deal. So each year Mr. Hoffa gives Mr. Brennan half of whatever money Mr. Brennan wagers. In return, Mr. Brennan gives Mr. Hoffa half of whatever he wins. This has been going on for ten years.

"There is race tracks in Detroit," Hoffa told the Committee, "and my . . . business associate in Detroit has some horses and he places some bets and we are fortunate to win some money."

They had phenomenal good fortune.

From 1948 through 1957 they divided a total of more than $150,000 in race track winnings.

Hoffa claimed his share of this money was put down each year on his income tax as "collections" received, and later as "wagerings."

Another time he said: "Mr. Owen B. Brennan keeps the records and I don't do the betting and I don't keep the records."

Whereupon the Committee called Owen B. Brennan and questioned him. Mr. Brennan, as was his way, "respectfully declined to answer. . . ."

Herbert L. Grosberg, the accountant for the Teamsters and for Mr. Hoffa, figures up his income tax each year, Hoffa said. He doesn't bother with keeping any records of where the money comes from. He throws away the pieces of paper on which he figures the return, keeping only the copy of the income tax report itself. Grosberg was questioned, but he shed little light.

Mr. Grosberg admitted that he disposed of Mr. Hoffa's net worth statement in the face of an Internal Revenue probe. He destroyed it because George Fitzgerald, the Teamsters' and Hoffa's attorney, told him to do so, he said.

How could Mr. Hoffa remember, over a period of a year without the benefit of any records, how much money he had won gambling—and remember it down to the exact dollar and cent? Mr. Grosberg's testimony indicated that Mr. Hoffa had a fantastic memory.

On every question involving his race track winnings, Bert Brennan took the Fifth Amendment. Since Mr. Brennan would not say where or when or how he actually acquired the money, we put this question squarely to Jimmy Hoffa:

MR. KENNEDY: Let me ask you this: Did any of that money come directly or indirectly from any employer?
MR. HOFFA: It came from Brennan to myself. It came from racing gambling—from racing earnings.
MR. KENNEDY: Did it come directly or indirectly?
MR HOFFA: It came from Brennan to myself.

MR. KENNEDY: Well, that could have been indirectly from an employer. I am asking you the question whether it came directly or indirectly from an employer?

MR. HOFFA: Well, I am in return saying that Mr. Brennan handled that end on wagering and at the end of the year Mr. Brennan told me this was the net results of our wagering. This is what I declared on my income tax.

After the day in August, 1957, when Hoffa first embroidered into the record his colorful story, "Success at the Races," Bert Brennan must surely have become the most sought-after man in the history of the American track. But what his infallible "system" was Mr. Brennan, alas, would not tell.

Some two years after Hoffa first came up with his race track yarn, my brother told him: "I have never been completely convinced, Mr. Hoffa, to be frank with you, that Mr. Brennan did win this money at the race track."

Mr. Hoffa said, "Why don't you ask him?"

Senator Kennedy: "I did and he took the Fifth Amendment."

Mr. Hoffa: "Maybe he had a reason."

When my brother cast serious doubts on his "wagering" story, Mr. Hoffa snapped: "Disprove what I said."

In 1954, trying to account for all the cash he had available, Hoffa had told the Hoffman Committee that he borrowed considerable sums from the union's business agents who worked under him. Like his "wagering" story, this tale seemed to me more of an alibi than an explanation. Consequently, a few weeks before he was to come to Washington to testify for the first time, I sent Carmine Bellino and Pierre Salinger to Detroit to look into his union records and to ask him about these loans.

They made an appointment and found him seated at his desk on a raised platform, surrounded by his Detroit lieutenants. First off there was a discussion of the circumstances under which Carmine and Pierre would be allowed to examine the books. Hoffa told them they would have to look at them in a room in union headquarters and that his accountant and one of his lawyers must be present at all times.

Bellino was willing to examine the books in the building, but he wanted nobody looking over his shoulder.

"We don't work that way," he told Hoffa plainly.

Furious at being crossed in front of his men, Hoffa flew into a tantrum. He jumped up and started shouting: "Go to hell! Take the records to Washington! The hell with you!"

His angry blast lasted for several minutes. When things calmed down, Bellino asked Hoffa's lawyer, George Fitzgerald, to telephone me and work out a method of procedure. Fitzgerald called and we settled on what we thought was a fair arrangement. Bellino, later in the day, told Hoffa of our agreement. Hoffa again took off like a rocket but this time at his own lawyer, Fitzgerald. Bellino said he could hear him screaming at Fitzgerald in the hall outside the office, cursing him in the foulest possible language and finally threatening to fire him. It was so bad that Bellino, becoming embarrassed for Fitzgerald, broke in and told Hoffa that he would give way on certain points.

Eventually Carmine and Pierre were allowed to get on with their job. They reported back that Hoffa said he had repaid all the loans but did not know when he had paid them. And on that point the records were unilluminating.

Hoffa never would grant any of us another interview, but whenever an investigator was studying records in the Teamster headquarters he was always around. And one day, much later, in 1959, Carmine Bellino had an even worse run-in with him. He and Walt Sheridan had been examining some records in the Teamsters building in Washington, and at Hoffa's request stopped in at his office on their way out. By this time Bellino's work had turned up major corruption in Hoffa's administration of union affairs, and Hoffa had made it clear that Bellino bothered him.

During their talk they had an argument about a telephone call that Bellino had made to Hoffa's hotel; Hoffa accused Bellino of doing spy work for the AFL-CIO, and called him a liar when he denied it. Bellino retorted, "No—that's what you are."

Hoffa jumped up from behind his desk, his fist clenched and ready to lash out when Sheridan stepped between them. At that moment Harold Gibbons entered the room and with a jerk of his thumb motioned them toward the door. Bellino and Sheridan are certain he must have been listening outside or on a monitoring device.

So from the beginning until the end, our experiences with Hoffa were unpleasant. Whether we were talking to him about his business interests or the sources of his mysterious cash, his attitude was sullen and belligerent and his answers contradictory.

When he first appeared on the witness stand in August, 1957 he ticked off the list of nine business agents—men whose jobs depended on his good will—from whom he had borrowed anywhere from $1,000 to $3,000 each. Every one of these "loans" had been made under terms unlike any ever heard of by the Committee: no notes signed; no security offered; no interest charged, and no promise of payment. Each loan had been in cash—which the lender said he happened to have at his home. Not one of them had had to write a check or withdraw money from his savings account, and for five years no one of them had asked for repayment.

Nevertheless, we were startled when Mr. Hoffa denied under oath that he had paid any of this money back. Bellino and Salinger both had written memoranda on their interview with Hoffa in Detroit and both remembered distinctly his telling them that he had paid it all back. On the witness stand, however, he not only denied having made any repayment, but he denied ever telling Bellino and Salinger that he had.

I strongly suspected that Mr. Hoffa invented the story of the loans in the first place to account for cash he had on hand, the real source of which he did not want to reveal. I also am convinced that after telling Bellino and Salinger he had repaid all the money, he realized he had not reported sufficient income to the Internal Revenue to allow for the payments. So he had to change his story when he was put under oath.

Other than Hoffa's word and the word of men who worked for him, there was not a shred of tangible evidence that any money had, in fact, ever changed hands.

Carmine Bellino later developed three interesting points.

1. Herman Kierdorf, one of the business agents Hoffa named (and an ex-convict for whom he had interceded), had made monthly re-

ports to his parole officer of his savings since leaving prison. According to these reports, he could not possibly have had the $2,000 on the date he said he made Hoffa the loan.

2. Mr. Hoffa received four salary checks totaling $1,115.80 in the month of January, 1953. In addition, he kept other salary and expense checks totaling $4,826.81 received from December 30, 1952 through September 3, 1953—a period in which he was supposedly in desperate need of funds. He did not cash any of these until October 14, 1953.

As Bellino said: ". . . if he [Hoffa] was in such dire need of cash, he had checks in his pocket which he could have cashed and used."

3. Hoffa applied in May, 1957, at the City Bank of Detroit for two loans. Both applications called for a report of accounts and notes payable, but he failed in either case to mention the debts he supposedly had outstanding to his friends in the Teamsters Union.

With these facts plus his statement to Salinger and Bellino as a basis, I made it clear when Mr. Hoffa next appeared before the Committee that his story of the loans was highly suspect.

We found that a close relationship existed between Jimmy Hoffa and employers. We found that he was more than willing to do favors for them. Big favors, such as settling strikes against the wishes of his men. And we found that employers were anxious to do favors for him. Big favors, such as setting him up in business so that he could reap big profits. He helped them. They helped him. And they always insisted that the exchange of favors was coincidence.

The classic example of Jimmy Hoffa's attitude on this score came clearly in focus in the money-making deal called "Test Fleet." Back in 1948 one of the big Michigan trucking companies, Commercial Carriers, decided that its truck drivers would no longer be allowed to own their own equipment and drive it for the company as owner-operators. In protest, the drivers went on strike. The walkout was considered successful—up until the time Jimmy Hoffa came onto the scene.

The company's attitude was that they had made a management policy decision and that the drivers were staging a wildcat walkout. Mr. Hoffa sided with the company and against the strikers. He told the truck drivers to go back to work on the company's terms. Under this pressure from Hoffa, the strike was broken.

Shortly afterward, a new trucking company was formed in Tennessee—Test Fleet, later known as Hobren Corporation, an interstate company that was to own its own equipment but work for Commercial Carriers. One of the officers of record in the original company was James Wrape, the lawyer for Commercial Carriers; the company thereafter was run by the Commercial Carriers accountant, E. R. Biedler. Several weeks later, the ownership of the company was put in the names of two women: Josephine Poszywak and Alice Johnson—the maiden names of Mrs. James R. Hoffa and Mrs. Owen Bert Brennan. The company continued to be run by Wrape and Biedler. All that the women or their husbands had to do was to cash the dividend checks each year. And these were considerable. I questioned Hoffa about them when he was testifying in August, 1957.

MR. KENNEDY: Has this been a profitable operation?

MR. HOFFA: You have the record. I think you could say that it was.

MR. KENNEDY: Well, I am asking you the question.

MR. HOFFA: Since it is not my company, I can only say that I think that it was.

MR. KENNEDY: It was. You do not know. Your wife has not let you know how much money she made?

MR. HOFFA: I think I know how much she made.

MR. KENNEDY: Approximately, how much do you think she made in that company since it was set up?

MR. HOFFA: I can't tell you, offhand, but a guess. I can give it to you this afternoon, if I can get it.

MR. KENNEDY: We have some figures here.

MR. HOFFA: Read them off, brother.

I read them off. They showed that on a $4,000 original investment the two wives did, in ten years, a gross business of $1,008,000, with a net profit after taxes of $155,000.

Hoffa told our Committee there was no connection between his position on the strike and the fact that the company set up Test Fleet for him. He insisted that there was nothing whatever wrong about his ownership in a trucking company, and he admitted being in a number of other trucking businesses. He thought it was advisable, in fact, for more Teamster officials to own trucking companies. It would give them a better feeling for the problems of the employer. It was interesting, however, that Hoffa's ownership in trucking companies was always hidden behind his wife's maiden name.

The Teamsters who never got their jobs back after the 1948 strike thought that Hoffa did not have to own a company to have ample feeling for the problems of employers. Though Commercial Carriers, with Hoffa's approval, did not let them own their equipment, it not only allowed Hoffa to own his equipment, but set him up in the business. The strikers were bitter then. They are still bitter. They came to see me when I was in Detroit in 1957. They had been fighting Hoffa for nine years. They knew what their rights were and they wanted justice.

As Bert Beveridge, the president of Commercial Carriers, recalled the circumstances of the strike, Hoffa had tried hard to represent the union properly and to get the jobs back for nine strike leaders who were let out. But in Beveridge's files we found an interesting letter addressed to Carney Matheson, an attorney for the trucking industry, also a friend and business associate of Hoffa:

. . . We have been informed by George Dixon's New York attorney friend that he is starting suit for the drivers that we failed to hire back for different reasons, basing his suit on prejudice. Jim Hoffa has told me to forget about it. . . .
Actually it appears we do not have a contract and it is Messrs. Hoffa and Brennan's instructions to treat all employees as new employees hired in after the strike, which would mean payment on a 2 per cent basis. . . . some of them are expecting 4 per cent.

This letter very importantly establishes in words of the trucking executive whose firm put Jimmy Hoffa and Brennan in business that Teamster officials Hoffa and Brennan were advising the company how to act *against* the union member-workers.

It often seemed to me that Jimmy Hoffa was more of a business-man than a labor leader. He had a wide variety of personal business interests. In fact, he had even more than his predecessor, Dave Beck. However, there was an important difference. Beck used to boast: "I have made very successful investments." Yet, though Jimmy Hoffa put money in more business ventures than Beck, aside from Test Fleet almost all were financial flops. By comparison, he was much less successful, but his interests were far more complicated and difficult to trace.

But we did trace many of them and they consisted of a near fantastic variety of investments, which included stock in all kinds of different firms, including four trucking companies, an investment company, a wholesale grocery company, a boat unloading company, an oil company and mining ventures, a girls' camp, a men's camp, a brewery, a race track, a taxicab company, a professional prize fighter and a Florida land scheme.

He had other and more questionable ways of making money. For instance, on the payroll of a juke-box local headed up by one Jimmy James, we came upon the names of Josephine Poszywak and Alice Johnson. Each of them received $100 a week over a considerable period in a malodorous but profitable little arrangement designed to restore peace among the warring factions of the industry—the juke-box owners association and its "enforcing arm," the union local, on the one hand, and the Detroit underworld headed by Angelo Meli and Scarface Joe Bommarito on the other. Hoffa was close to Bommarito and Meli, and for a time after the women's names appeared on the payroll of Jimmy James's local, there was calm and accord in the industry.

Why did Mrs. Hoffa and Mrs. Brennan get a total of about $6,000 from Jimmy James's local—when neither of the women had the remotest connection with it?

James would not answer our questions and took the Fifth Amendment. So did Brennan. But Mr. Hoffa had an explanation. He told the Committee that he and Brennan had loaned Jimmy James some money—about $2,500—to get the juke-box local started. The $6,000 he "thought" was generous Jimmy James's way of returning the loan. The employers who established James's union said this was not true, that the complete financing came from them.

Once I asked Hoffa about $20,000 in cash that he invested in another venture. Where did this cash come from, I asked him.

"From individuals," Mr. Hoffa said.

107

And what individuals? His answer to the Committee on that was impossible.

"Offhand," he said, "that particular amount of money I borrowed I don't know at this particular moment, but the record of my loans, which I requested, I have, and out of all the moneys I loaned over this period of time I went into these ventures."

This answer summarized the confusing, contradictory, suspicious situation regarding Hoffa's money and its source.

An angry man who would identify himself only as "Oscar" telephoned our Detroit office one day in September, 1957. His call led us into an investigation of one of the most complex of all Mr. Hoffa's financial manipulations—the Florida land scheme called "Sun Valley." Hoffa's front in this fraud was Henry Lower, a self-styled "colonel" and a fugitive from a California road gang when he went to work as a Teamster official.[1]

Following the end of our August hearings I had gone out to Detroit to work on new Hoffa leads, but was out of the office when Oscar first telephoned. When I returned, the secretary gave me his message: "He wants to talk only to you," she said. "He wouldn't give any other name or leave a telephone number. But he is upset about something."

When the man called back, it was immediately apparent that he was agitated about something Jimmy Hoffa and "Colonel" Henry Lower had done. "I want to tell you about those two," he said. "I've got to see you." He would not discuss his complaint on the telephone.

I suggested that he come by the office.

"I wouldn't come near there," he said. "I don't want to be seen around your office. Just call me Oscar," he said.

Finally I prevailed upon "Oscar" to come to my room at the Sheraton Cadillac Hotel that night. As I waited for him, I reviewed the little we knew about Henry Lower.

Hoffa, in his testimony on the witness stand the month before, had told us that a man named Henry Lower had once loaned him $25,000 in cash, "because I asked him." Henry Lower, he said, had at one

[1] Lower was convicted of a narcotics charge and sentenced to prison during our Committee investigation.

108

time been a representative of the Teamsters Union, but was now in real estate.

MR. KENNEDY: Where in real estate?

MR. HOFFA: In Detroit and Florida and I don't know where else.

MR. KENNEDY: Does Mr. Lower . . . have any relationship, business relationship, with the Teamsters Union?

MR. HOFFA: Only so far as the fact that the Teamsters members can buy lots in Florida if they care to from Mr. Lower.

MR. KENNEDY: Anybody can buy lots in Florida.

MR. HOFFA: You asked me a question and I answered it.

"Oscar" walked with the bearing of an athlete. He was a pleasant-looking man with a high forehead and an open face. But he was mad at Henry Lower and Jimmy Hoffa. I could tell that from the moment he came into my room.

Within a short time I learned that his name was Joseph Kritch and that he was a former professional baseball player. "Colonel" Henry Lower had approached him some time before and had offered him a job selling lots "in a wonderful project we have going in Florida." Lower had explained that the project was sponsored by the Teamsters Union and led Joe to understand that Hoffa was the man behind it. There would be a fertile field for sales among Teamsters Union rank-and-file members, said Colonel Lower. So Joe Kritch had set out to sell lots.

Recently, Kritch said, Henry Lower had started talking about assessing everybody he had sold lots to for more money for improvements, such as streets. Since previously he had said the streets were all in, Kritch had become suspicious and had gone to see Jimmy Hoffa about it, suggesting an investigation.

Hoffa said, "See Henry Lower and tell him about it."

"I believe Hoffa is behind the whole project," Kritch told me.

Then some of the home owners went to Florida. They told the Committee that they found no roads, no improvements; they could not even find their own lots.

"I have sold some of these lots to people who have put their life savings into it," said Kritch. "I can't look them in the face."

But he was anxious to face Henry Lower. "I've been thinking

109

about that man," he said nervously. "I've bought a gun and I'm going to shoot Henry Lower."

We had a long talk and I pointed out to him that he would not help himself or his friends by taking matters into his own hands. Assuring him that we would make a full investigation, I told him that he could best make it up to the people who had lost their money by helping us. Before he left, he promised that he would do anything he could, and that he would not use the gun.

The next morning I tried to get hold of Henry Lower, but he was not at the office in Sun Valley or at his home in Detroit. He would not answer the telephone at either place. Becoming aware that he was ducking us, we set out to discover all we could about Sun Valley.

In 1955 and 1956 Teamster members throughout the Midwest had suddenly found themselves victims of a high-pressure selling campaign boosting a new land development in Florida. Advertisements began appearing: "Stake your claim in the Teamsters' model city of tomorrow"; "Entire Sun Valley program has been endorsed by the Florida Chamber of Commerce and your [Teamster] Joint Council." Movies of what purported to be Sun Valley were shown at Teamster meetings. Rank-and-file members were told they would be able to buy lots at "cut-rate prices," and selected Teamster business agents, given free trips to Florida, returned with glowing reports to the membership of the wonderful new city.

The Committee learned that Hoffa had made Lower a Teamster official and that he held that position while he was promoting the Sun Valley project, collecting some $90,000 in fees and expenses. Records also showed that Hoffa had arranged for Lower to get a Teamster loan and later had signed notes that enabled "the Colonel" to get $75,000 in loans from a Detroit bank.

The Committee subpoenaed the bank's initial memoranda dealing with this loan. It indicated that the loan was being urged upon them by Hoffa; that they had lost an $800,000 Teamsters account earlier because they had not made a Teamster-approved loan, and they did not want to lose another. As it developed, Mr. Hoffa's signature on Lower's note was enough to assure the loan. This loan started Sun Valley.

Our search for Henry Lower continued for several days. Nobody knew where he was or when he could be reached. Finally, one of the girls in our Detroit office telephoned the Sun Valley office and pretended to be an old friend of Henry Lower from out of town. In a short time Henry Lower answered the call.

Carmine took the phone and identified himself. Mr. Lower stopped running for a night. He said that he had not been well and that we would have to arrange any meeting with him through his attorney. We called the lawyer and an interview was set up that same night at Lower's home in a recently developed suburb of Detroit. The lawyer told us that Mr. Lower was under a doctor's care and that he (the attorney) wanted to be present during our discussion.

A doctor was with Henry Lower when we arrived at the modern, neatly furnished home. Mr. Lower was seated in a living room chair clad in pajamas, bathrobe and slippers. We sat and waited while the physician gave him an injection of Demerol. I was to remember that shot later when Henry Lower was sentenced to jail for narcotics violation. And I was to remember his nervous discomfort throughout our meeting. He seemed under a strain. We had no desire to subject him to severe questioning and our meeting was as informal as possible. He was reasonably co-operative and at times he was unknowingly helpful.

Lower told us that Sun Valley had been his own idea and that Hoffa had told him to "put it on paper" and let him see it. At one time, he said, he took the Teamster chief to inspect the site where Sun Valley was to be located. Throughout our conversation, he tried hard to keep from offering us any information that might hurt Hoffa. But he confirmed Joe Kritch's darkest suspicions—that this was Hoffa's project.

We asked Lower about the $25,000 that Hoffa told the Committee he had borrowed from him. Lower said he had loaned Hoffa the money because he was grateful to him. The loan was in cash and delivered in a brown paper bag because, Lower said, that was the way Hoffa wanted it. Furthermore, he said he had given Jimmy Hoffa a 45 per cent option on Sun Valley—an option to purchase anytime at the original price! This put Hoffa right in the middle of the venture.

We were not to get the full story on Sun Valley from Henry Lower.

111

That was to come only from weeks of investigation—analyzing records, interviewing Teamster members and bank officials, taking affidavits from them and others who had any information on the Florida property scheme.

I was anxious to get hold of the option that granted Mr. Hoffa 45 per cent interest in Sun Valley, anticipating that on the witness stand Lower, like so many of Hoffa's associates, would claim the Fifth Amendment rather than answer questions. However, we were unable to run it down, and when Hoffa next appeared before the Committee he said he would try to find it. He never did. His lawyer, George Fitzgerald, confirmed that the option had existed, but he too was unable to locate it. In the end, in order to have some documentary evidence that Hoffa actually had an interest in Sun Valley, I had George Fitzgerald put into writing the fact that the option did exist.[2]

When we had garnered all the facts, Hoffa was involved even more deeply in the sordid story: Lower had gone to Florida banks looking for "a half a million" in loans to develop Sun Valley. He told Mr. Ford, then the president of the Florida National Bank, that if he got the $500,000 to improve the land he would make sure that a like amount —$500,000—in Teamster funds would be placed in an account in the bank, interest free. The money would remain in the bank until the half-million-dollar loans were repaid.

Mr. Hewitt, vice president of the bank, gave an affidavit to our Committee that described Henry Lower's proposition.

"At the outset of the negotiations for the loans," he said, "the two principal owners of Sun Valley, Inc. were identified to our bank as Mr. Henry Lower and Mr. James R. Hoffa, an official of the Teamsters Union in Detroit. . . . Our bank was told by Mr. Lower at the outset of the loan negotiations that Mr. Hoffa had a principal interest in Sun Valley, Inc. At first, Mr. Lower said that this interest of Mr. Hoffa could not be revealed publicly. He did not say why. On November 16, 1956, Mr. Lower told me personally in the presence of Mr. McCarthy [a bank official] and our current president, Mr.

---

[2] On December 11, 1959, as this book was being prepared for the press, the Committee received a copy of a letter purporting to be the agreement between Lower and Hoffa.

Willard, that as of that time he was free to reveal Mr. Hoffa's interest, when he had not been previously."

On June 20, 1956, the bank made a $300,000 loan to Sun Valley, payable to Henry Lower, who gave as his address the Teamster headquarters in Detroit. At the same time, $300,000 in Teamster funds was deposited, interest free, in the Florida bank—as Lower had promised. In November, the bank loaned him $200,000 more—and the Teamsters deposited another $200,000, interest free, in the bank.

Had this half a million dollars been placed in an account where it would have gained 2 per cent interest, it would have earned the Teamsters Union $10,000 a year. When we later asked Hoffa why he had made this transfer of funds to a bank in Florida and permitted the interest income to fly out the window, he answered bluntly, "Because I wanted to."

The plan to make a profit on this deal was simple. Lots cost Henry Lower only $18.75 each. They were sold for prices ranging from $150 to $550. Altogether about two thousand were sold, mostly to rank-and-file Teamsters, although John Dioguardi got hooked on one of them. So did some other more innocent outsiders—such as relatives of Joe Kritch.

Like many another deal Jimmy Hoffa became involved with, this one was headed for financial disaster. The reason, primarily, was that Henry Lower was diverting to his own personal use the loan money with which he was supposed to be making improvements. The roads were not built, sewers and electricity not installed—and some of the lots, we found, were still under water! Carmine Bellino, after a close examination of the records, said that at least $144,000 from the Florida bank went into Henry Lower's pocket and into another Lower project in Detroit—not into improvements on the property.

As word spread of what was happening to Sun Valley, bankruptcy proceedings became inevitable. The Teamster members who had bought lots stood to lose their investments.

Meanwhile, Lower had again disappeared. Our investigators in the Detroit area made concerted efforts to trace him, and ultimately we were able to subpoena him, but he claimed he was too ill to testify. It was not until July of 1959 that he finally appeared before the Committee.

His physical condition had not improved. He walked with a cane and a heavy limp. He had lost weight, his clothing was loose-fitting and shabby. His face was drawn and worn. He was awaiting sentence on the narcotics charge against him. With the Teamster pin in his lapel he took the Fifth Amendment on all questions.

Had Sun Valley become a financial bonanza, Jimmy Hoffa would have cleaned up. When it failed, he lost nothing. He had risked only Teamsters Union funds—and the savings of those rank-and-file members who, unfortunately, lost their cash in the process.

Lower's interest in Sun Valley was taken over by another friend of Hoffa's, Benjamin Dranow, under highly questionable circumstances. Dranow too visited a Florida bank (a different one than Lower had gone to) and told them, as Lower had, that if they would lend money on Sun Valley, whose name he had changed to Union Home and Land, he would be able to have one million dollars of Teamster funds deposited in the bank, interest free. The bank turned him down—the bank president having a "hunch" everything wasn't proper.

Hoffa and Dranow were involved in several other deals together, one of which was the purchase of 26,000 Teamsters Union jackets, to be given "free of charge" to rank-and-file Teamsters of Hoffa's and Brennan's locals. It cost the union in 1958 and 1959 $350,000. Furthermore, by assigning the contract for the manufacture of the jackets without asking for bids, Dranow cost the Teamsters' treasury an extra $50,000, as we learned from a subcontractor to whom the order was farmed out. This man, Phil Petill, told our Committee he could have saved the union at least two dollars on each of the 26,000 jackets.

Furthermore, we found that most of the jackets did not have union labels and were made under contracts with non-union shops.

Phil Petill also said he understood that originally it was contemplated that each of the million and a half Teamsters in America would have one of these jackets. That, of course, would have meant a cost of $15,000,000 to the Teamsters Union—and a profit of $750,000 for Hoffa's pal Benjamin Dranow.

Paul Schutzer, courtesy Life, © *1958 Time Inc.*

Arthur Morgan, of Minneapolis, a Teamster symbolic of those who opposed the reign of Hoffa, fights back tears as he relates threats his family received because he had given earlier testimony.

Paul Dorfman (left).
His family received Hoffa's
Teamsters insurance plus
$1,600,000 excess profits.

(Below) Nathan Shefferman, labor-
management middleman; Joe Curcio,
Teamster paper local leader; and Tony
Accardo, heir to Al Capone's empire—
all took the Fifth Amendment.

Johnny Dio, racketeer, punched a photographer covering the hearings.

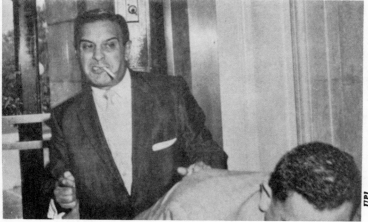

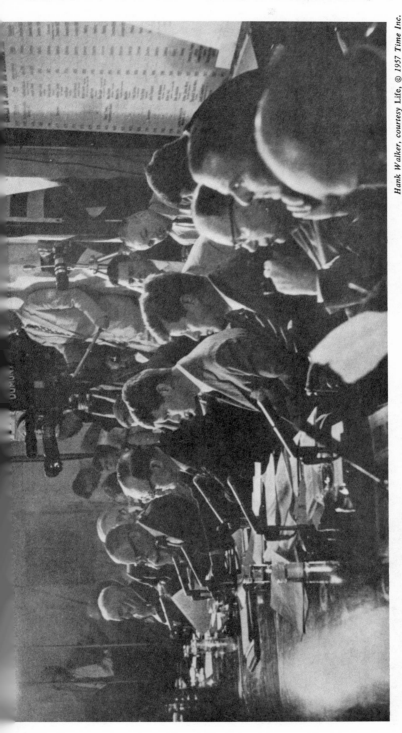

Hank Walker, courtesy Life, © 1957 Time Inc.

The author and the Committee at work in the Senate caucus room. Seated from left are Senators Erwin of North Carolina, McNamara of Michigan, Goldwater of Arizona, Chairman McClellan of Arkansas, Chief Counsel Kennedy, Senators Kennedy of Massachusetts, Mundt of South Dakota, visiting Senator Butler of Maryland and Chief Accountant Bellino.

"Chee, Boss, I can't wait to get dem cops in de union" was Bill Mauldin's cartoon caption in the St. Louis *Post-Dispatch* when Hoffa announced plans to organize the police.

The expressive eyes and hands of Jimmy Hoffa . . . He was often a bright witness, with what Senator Ives described as an amazing "forgettery."

This is one of a series of photographs taken by the FBI as John Cye Cheasty gave Committee documents to Hoffa in exchange for cash.

Frank Kierdorf, Teamster agent and friend of Hoffa, was burned to a crisp when he set himself on fire in committing arson. He died from the burns.

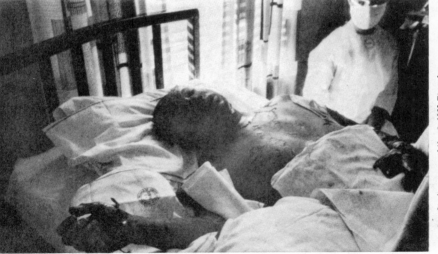

Joe Clark, courtesy Life, © 1958 Time Inc.

The author and Jimmy Hoffa clash. "It is important to Jimmy Hoffa that he appear the tough guy to the world."

Dave Beck philosophizes for reporters during a recess. ". . . when Dave Beck first took the witness stand . . . I felt sorry for him."

Ed Clark, courtesy Life, © 1957 Time Inc.

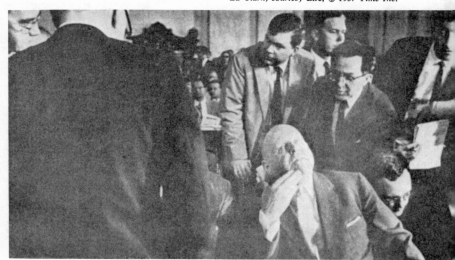

Block brothers,
Louis (left) and Max,
milked management
and the
Butchers Union.

Wide World

Wide World

The Gallo brothers
were two of the
most extraordinary
witnesses to appear
before the Committee.

UPI

John O'Rourke,
Hoffa's head man
in New York,
wept after
his appearance.

Ed Clark, courtesy Life, © 1957 Time Inc.

Wide World

Paul (The Waiter) Ricca
sold the Teamsters
a house they never used.

James Cross,
Bakers Union president,
got fat off the union,
was expelled
by the AFL-CIO
for corruption.

Owen Bert Brennan,
Hoffa's sidekick (right),
and George Fitzgerald,
Teamster lawyer,
used union loans
to make money.

Carmine Lombardozzi, Brooklyn underworld figure, was a delegate to the Apalachin gangland convention. Jim Elkins, Portland racketeer, was one of the best witnesses to appear before the committee. Judge Raulston Schoolfield, of Chattanooga, declined an invitation to testify. He was later impeached in Tennessee.

As it was, Dranow got a commission of some $17,000. When I questioned Hoffa about this, he said heatedly that I was wrong on my facts.

"No, sir," he stormed at me. "You can't show me in the record."

I said, "Mr. Hoffa—"

He cut me off. "Show me in the record if you please. I read the record and checked the record and there is nothing in the record that indicates Benjamin Dranow got any commission at all, except $2,000."

When I tried again to insist that this was in the record he cut me off a second time and said to Senator McClellan: "No, sir. I would appreciate the Chair, if you will, to let me see the paragraph . . . it just isn't there."

So we took a recess to dig into the record and, to save time, I walked around and showed it to Hoffa, hoping he might simply admit when the session started again that he had been wrong. I pointed out the page where the pertinent testimony appeared. "Read it," I suggested.

Hoffa started to read, but stopped and looked at me with an angry expression.

"Oh, no," he said. "Fool me once, blame you; fool me twice, blame me." Reporters were gathering around and I asked him to read it all. He jumped up and growled: "You're sick. That's what's the matter with you—you are sick."

The recess over, the Chairman read him the record. Hoffa quickly changed the subject.

All sorts of people, it seems, who cannot get bank financing because they are considered unreliable or bad risks, find Mr. Hoffa has a ready ear. Consider, for example, the $12,000 loaned to Ahmed Abass, a numbers racketeer whose unlikely name had appeared seventeen times on a police blotter; and the $40,000 loaned to John Bitonti, a numbers racketeer with a record of twenty-three arrests. Then there was Paul De Lucia, elder statesman of Chicago's underworld, known also as Paul (The Waiter) Ricca. A former bodyguard of Al Capone, and considered by some his heir-apparent, Paul Ricca, sometime in 1955, suddenly needed a lot of "honest" money in a hurry to square his accounts with the Bureau of Internal Revenue. The Teamsters obligingly bought his showplace home outside Chicago for his asking price of $150,000—considerably more than the appraiser's estimate. So hurried was the deal that—as Jerry Adlerman, our Chief Assistant Counsel, was to show—the union failed to get a clear title on the entire estate; for more than a year the Teamsters legally owned only half the property, though they had more than paid for all of it. Included in their share was half the tennis court and part of the swimming pool; Paul the Waiter owned the other part. It was a nice picture for all concerned.

When we pointed this out, Mr. Hoffa, in a rare display of beneficence, announced: "We want to thank Mr. Adlerman for giving us the information so that we could properly clear the title."

The Committee, of course, was anxious to hear Mr. Hoffa's explanation of why two Teamsters Union locals in Detroit paid such an exorbitant price for a home so distant from their headquarters. Hoffa had a ready answer: he had grand plans for this estate, he testified. He was going to make it a school for business agents and union stewards.

The only thing wrong with that, however, was that the local zoning restrictions made it impossible to turn the house into a school. And the Teamsters have never used it as a school.

On September 11, 1953, a check for $5,000 was written on the account of the Central Conference of Teamsters in St. Louis, made payable to James R. Hoffa. It was cosigned by Harold Gibbons and James R. Hoffa. On September 29, Mr. Hoffa opened a new account in the Detroit City Bank for a dummy unincorporated society he named the "Central States Organization." Mr. Hoffa listed himself as "chairman" of this "society." Into this new account he deposited the $5,000 he had taken from the Central Conference of Teamsters, and he alone was authorized to make withdrawals.

On December 30, 1953, the last day of the year, $4,900 was withdrawn from this Central States Organization account on a check written to "cash" and signed by Mr. Hoffa. He declared it as personal income on his Federal tax return.

Hoffa told the Committee that this money "was placed in the Detroit bank to use as I saw fit for organizational expenses."

Questioned about this society he finally admitted it existed only as the name of a bank account. In short, Jimmy Hoffa took money from a legitimate union account, set up a dummy account, then withdrew the cash. He spent it, he paid income taxes on it, he is not required by anyone to account for it.

This story is worth telling principally because it could have been, as easily, $49,000 or $490,000. When Mr. Hoffa paid the taxes on the money, he was in the clear.

If we are to draw any important conclusion from the relationship of James R. Hoffa to such men as Benjamin Dranow and Henry Lower, and the rest, it is this:

The vast millions of dollars assigned to the various treasuries and funds of the International Brotherhood of Teamsters, as vested property of the rank-and-file dues-paying members, are under the complete and absolute control of Mr. Hoffa, and are available to himself and his friends and cronies. He has to account to no one else. And he accounts to no one else.

Chapter 7 / THE CAPTIVE UNIONS

THE TRAVESTY that Hoffa makes of democratic procedure within the Teamsters Union is perfectly exemplified by his own election as International president at the Miami convention in October, 1957.

This convention was rigged from start to finish.

From an examination of the Teamsters' own records, our investigators were able to prove that under the terms of the union's constitution, more than half the delegates—56.2 per cent—had been selected illegally; about the legality of an additional 39 per cent there was serious doubt. In short, we could establish that only 4.8 per cent of the delegates who elected Jimmy Hoffa had any clearly legal right to be at the convention and to vote.

The selection of unqualified delegates had been brazenly open. For instance, we found one local in New York whose delegates had not been elected until thirteen days *after* the convention ended. Even those from Hoffa's own local were not named in accordance with the provisions of the constitution.

Delegate James Clift of Local 337 in Detroit (Bert Brennan's union) testified before the Committee on September 14. This was ten days before the convention was to open, but already twenty days after the deadline date set by the constitution for the election of delegates.

118

MR. KENNEDY: Were you elected as a delegate?

MR. CLIFT: I will be.

MR. KENNEDY: You will be elected?

MR. CLIFT: Yes, sir.

MR. KENNEDY: Do you have a meeting scheduled to elect you?

MR. CLIFT: Yes, sir.

MR. KENNEDY: When is that scheduled?

MR. CLIFT: Tonight.

Mr. Clift did not seem at all concerned that he was to go to the convention as a delegate who had been elected in violation of Teamster law. He felt sure, he told us, that the lawyers who work for the Teamsters Union would straighten out the whole problem. He was right. They simply told Dave Beck that he could waive the constitution.

Before the convention, I had had hopes that John English, secretary-treasurer of the International and a man who had given his life to the labor movement, would use his prestige to help defeat Hoffa as International president. I had seen him frequently, and he had praised our work in the Beck case; so with a discredited Beck on the way out and the convention coming up, I was anxious to know where he stood. But when I went to see him for the last time at his office in the marble palace in the spring of 1957, he told me that Jimmy Hoffa was a great organizer, that he would work where Beck had done little. He said nothing about Hoffa's corruption.

Disappointment must have been evident in my face, for he said: "And what do you want me to do? I've been with this union all my life. I've been a Teamster for fifty years. What do you want me to do? . . . Do you want me to lose my pension, everything?"

However, there were courageous men at that convention.

Jeff Cohalen, now a Congressman from California, made a stirring speech and stood on his feet and battled against the corrupt Teamster forces who dominated the convention. Frank Brewster put his future with the Teamsters on the line and went down fighting.

But the die was cast.

Newsmen covering the convention, observing the election and the men responsible for it, coined such editorial comments as: "It's

119

all over but the looting" and "Hoffa punishes his enemies and rewards his accomplices."

Throughout 1957 and 1958, as our Committee spread on the record the sordid story of Hoffa's corruption, I began to hear more and more frequently: "If Hoffa really is as bad as the evidence indicates, why don't the rank and file rise up and toss him out?"

I knew the reason. They couldn't. For months the staff had been hearing stories of men who had tried, but because of the money, goons and those lawyers that Hoffa owns, had been unsuccessful. We felt that this was a point that the Committee should establish unmistakably. I also hoped that public exposure of what the Hoffa type of democracy means might help the men who were fighting it. So in 1958 we sent investigators to Pontiac, Michigan, to Peru, Illinois, to Joplin, Missouri, and elsewhere, to get the fullest possible stories.

I might add here that the courage of the men who fought Hoffa filled me with an overwhelming feeling of admiration and yet sadness. Admiration that they had such courage, and sadness that as I sat in the giant caucus room of the United States Senate and listened to their stories, there was nothing that we could do to help them in the immediate future. They would give their testimony and then return to the battle not really any better off than when they came.

What help we could be to them would be a long-range proposition. I knew that and they knew it, too. And yet they came ahead— and yet they fought. These are tough men.

One of the courageous Midwestern Teamsters who came to Washington to testify has waged a long, hard battle to free his local union of the viselike grip of Jimmy Hoffa, and Hoffa's henchmen. He has not won, but he has not stopped trying. Because of his fight, he and his wife and his friends have been through a hellish nightmare.

The day before his departure for Washington to tell the Committee how Hoffa had ruthlessly suppressed rank-and-file democracy in his local, this Teamster received a letter:

DEAR EMIL:[1]

After a sleepless night I've decided to write you a sister-in-law letter. . . .

[1] The names in this letter have been changed.

Phil has no idea that I am doing it, so I would appreciate it if you would not tell him. I hope you understand this note in the light in which it is written. . . .

Here's the pitch . . . you and your family or any of the Clan are welcome in our home, but under the circumstances this particular trip which you are coming to Washington, I don't think it advisable to even know our address, name or phone number. . . . I have been following this teamster deal very closely and I don't want my family even remotely connected with anyone connected to the investigation. We've lived around the big city too long, I guess—Candy and I spent too much time alone in our isolated community to take any chances . . . and knowing the extent to which they spread their retaliation I don't think I'm being overly cautious. . . .

I hope that you understand. . . . I think you have been very brave in this whole venture over the past few years. . . . I'm sorry that you even have a job that has tossed you into this tempest. I know that you will tell a good story and perhaps it will contribute to some successful legislation for the elimination of dictatorship in the business world. Most of the Senators have gone home, so you will probably appear before Bob Kennedy's fact finding board . . . they say they are very nice and I know they are doing a wonderful job. . . . I wish you all the luck in the world.

Please forgive me for being selfish in this matter . . . and please try to understand that I'm not being prudish or anything. We will be on our way to New Hampshire either tomorrow or early Thursday morning, so don't waste your money on a telegram. . . . Phil's leave was cut short so we couldn't make the California trip as planned . . . so we are heading for the mountains and the sea shore to make up to Candy for Disneyland.

Thank you for being understanding. . . .

/s/ JUNE

Today Emil is more dedicated than ever in his opposition to a dictatorship that breeds a fear so terrible that it severs family bonds. Editorial cartoonists portray "the Teamsters" as a grasping octopus, a tidal wave of corruption about to engulf the nation's capital, a brass-knuckled fist, a shadowy underworld figure. Such images are accurate symbols of Hoffa's rule, but they attach an unfair stigma to the real Teamsters, the men who load the freight and drive the trucks and deliver the milk. As a group the rank and file are decent, honest, hard-working men who, like Emil, hate what Hoffa is and

121

what he stands for. Given half a chance they would indeed "rise up and throw him out."

Let's take a look at democracy in the Teamsters Union as Jimmy Hoffa permits it to be practiced. Let's see, in a half-dozen typical cases, what has happened when men have revolted against his rule.

For Barney Matual of Peru, Illinois, a lean, wiry little fellow with the weather-beaten look of a farmer, the trouble started on a December afternoon in 1954 when Hoffa rode into town and called a meeting of the officers of the four little locals in Peru, La Salle, Oglesby and Utica. With Hoffa were Paul Dorfman, Richard Kavner, a St. Louis Teamster agent under Harold Gibbons, and the three Floyd brothers, who controlled Local 179 of Joliet, Illinois.

Hoffa announced that the four local unions were to be merged into one and incorporated with Virgil Floyd's Joliet local. He gave them until April 1, 1955. If the merger wasn't accomplished by then he would "shove" them into Floyd's local.

Barney Matual, who had served the Teamsters honestly and proudly for twenty-three years, told our Committee the story of what followed. He saw union democracy going out the window. He measured the men around Hoffa and realized they meant business. He knew who Paul Dorfman was. He saw the pistol under Kavner's belt. He had read only days before that Virgil Floyd had been convicted in Federal Court of taking $2,000 in "shakedown" from a contractor. He was aware that Jimmy Hoffa was anxious to dominate all the locals in the Central Conference.

He also knew that joining the Joliet local would mean traveling sixty miles to meetings; paying higher union dues; being under a president who had just been convicted of selling out the union membership.

He told Hoffa that he would handle the matter in a democratic way and would put it to a vote of the rank and file. That was the way things were done in the Teamsters Union around Peru.

At the next membership meeting of the four locals the men voted 694 to 7 against Hoffa's "proposal" to merge with Floyd's local. But realizing Hoffa's power, they decided to merge their own four small unions into one. They put the numbers of their four locals into a hat, drew one out—46—and became Teamsters Local 46, with Matual as its president and business agent.

Shortly afterward, while attending a union meeting in a hotel in Springfield, Illinois, he received word that he was wanted in another room. There he found Virgil Floyd waiting—and with him Barney Baker, Hoffa's 325-pound wandering ex-convict "organizer." Baker warned Matual he had better co-operate with Virgil Floyd. And he spoke in such a way that Mr. Matual began to wonder if he would get safely from the room.

He told the Committee: "I was partly frightened, a little bit." He said that looking up at Baker, who outweighed him by more than 150 pounds, "I didn't wholly agree [to co-operating with Floyd] but I partly agreed."

A short time later Virgil Floyd began to invade his territory. A Teamster auditor came in to check his books, though they had only recently been audited. Then one day in came a personal representative of Teamster vice president John T. O'Brien of Chicago, with a letter from Dave Beck announcing that Matual's local was under trusteeship. Matual and his fellow officers were angry. Trusteeships are meant for locals in trouble; theirs was sound and solvent. They informed O'Brien's representative that they would not accept trusteeship.

A few days later Vice President O'Brien himself came to Peru. "I want your charter and seal," he told Matual.

"You are making a mistake, John," Matual replied. "These people here are dead against a trusteeship. If you take that charter and seal out of here they are going to go independent. You're going to lose them."

O'Brien must have recognized the truth in Matual's words, for he sat down and placed a long-distance call to Dave Beck in Seattle. He said, "Dave, do you know why I was sent here? Their books are clean and their contracts are good. They got money in the bank. . . ."

On the other end of the line Dave Beck undoubtedly was remembering that he had ordered the local into trusteeship at the urging of Jimmy Hoffa. Why had Hoffa wanted it?

To O'Brien he said: "I don't know why. I'll call Washington, D.C., and find out." Then Matual spoke to Beck and asked for a chance to talk with him. He too realized that Hoffa was behind the move, and wanted to explain the background of the feud with Hoffa. Beck arranged for a meeting a month later in Dallas.

At 3 P.M. on July 12, 1956, Barney Matual sat outside the door of Beck's hotel suite in the Statler Hilton, his brief case bulging with documents proving that his local was a solid, prospering organization. Inside, Beck was closeted with Jimmy Hoffa, Harold Gibbons, John O'Brien and several others.

The night before the meeting, when Matual had arrived at the hotel, he had passed Jimmy Hoffa in the lobby.

"Hello, Barney. How are you?"

"Hello, Jim. Fine."

And Hoffa said, "Barney, I get what I want."

Matual slept on that statement. The next day as he waited outside Beck's suite Jimmy Hoffa was inside with Beck "getting what he wanted."

Mr. Matual, in his testimony before the Committee, gave an account of that meeting.

"We had an appointment with Mr. Beck for three o'clock," he said. "We had to wait until four o'clock, after he held his meeting with Hoffa. Then he [Beck] opened the door and we went into the meeting. There was Mr. Hoffa, Mr. O'Brien, Dave Beck, Harold Gibbons, Dick Kavner, Einar Mohn and a few others. We came in with a brief case with contracts, financial standings—showing that the local was all right.

"Dave Beck didn't even give me a chance to open up the brief case. Hoffa popped up and said, 'I got a letter . . . in my pocket . . . [that says] you have a sweetheart contract. . . .' So I said, 'Jimmy, you are all wet. I haven't signed a contract so far. I have only been in office in Local 46 six months.'

"He said, 'Are you calling me a liar?'

"He jumped to his feet, and I jumped to mine. And I said, 'All right, let's have it.'

"Dave Beck jumped between us. Dave Beck said, 'I am going

to give you a trusteeship if I have to spend $50,000, $100,000. . . . My boy Jimmy knows what he is doing.' "

Matual, incensed, retorted that he would never take a trusteeship. "My father came to this country from Lithuania looking for this freedom and I have it and I am going to keep it," he said. And he walked out of the meeting.

Legal warfare started. International representatives changed the locks on the union headquarters and took $533 from the office safe. Barney Matual put the local's bank account into a trust fund so the International could not get at it and changed the building's locks again. The International then formed its own local in his area. It originally had no membership but it was a form of harassment. However, the International continued to accept per capita tax money from Matual's local and he continued to send it in as proof that the International still recognized his local.

In 1957 when Matual went to negotiate a new contract with Union Star Brewery, the major employer in the area, John Clinch, the lawyer for the company and also an officer of the firm, refused to deal with him unless he brought in someone from the International. (Our Committee later showed that, while representing the brewery, Clinch accepted $4,000 from the Teamsters International as "legal services" for "representing" a dissident group within Matual's local.) When Clinch refused to bargain with him, Matual called a twenty-four-hour strike and the company then signed the contract. This was August 1, 1957, and Matual was still fighting against trusteeship. (A few weeks later, Hoffa told our Committee that he had no knowledge of the situation in Peru—in spite of all our evidence to the contrary.)

In December, 1957, the Teamsters were ousted from the AFL-CIO because of corruption; eleven months later Matual and his union went independent and later joined with District 50 of the United Mine Workers. This led the Star Brewery, operated by Mr. Clinch and his family, to refuse to recognize their contract. Again, a strike broke out. Clinch and O'Brien of the Teamsters were in telephone contact. The Teamsters marched through Local 46's picket line and attempted to break the strike. When this tactic failed, Clinch signed a contract with O'Brien covering the brewery workers who were in Matual's Local 46,

125

though at this time O'Brien represented none of the employees. O'Brien, when the Committee questioned him, took the Fifth Amendment.

Clinch came to see me prior to the hearing and brought his wife with him. "You have evidently made a mistake, Mr. Kennedy. I am a lawyer, a member of the bar. We have a financial interest in a major business concern. We are respectable people in our community. We are certainly in favor of everything you are doing. It's terrible how these racketeers control the labor movement. I'm sure, however, you don't want me."

Clinch is not fit to tie the lacings in Barney Matual's shoes.

Barney Matual is still outside the Teamsters, still fighting for his survival—a victim of Hoffa's kind of democracy.

Another story our Committee heard begins with Clyde Buxton, of Joplin, Missouri. He was a member of Teamsters Local 823. In 1953 he and a number of his fellow Teamsters sent a petition to Jimmy Hoffa, protesting against the way their president, Floyd Webb, was administering the union. Webb, however, was a friend of Hoffa and Hoffa immediately sent him the petition. Within a few days Clyde Buxton was beaten and slugged into unconsciousness by an assailant with a ball-peen hammer. To an investigating committee of rank-and-file members, one of whom testified before the Senate Committee, Webb arrogantly admitted that he had ordered the attack. But he had been disappointed in the outcome.

"What I wanted was some funerals," he said, "and there are going to be some if you guys don't keep your nose out of it."

Webb showed he meant business. Three of the men who had signed the petition were told by their union steward to cross off their names or lose their jobs. Several weeks later a man who refused had his union book lifted.

Next Webb warned an official of the Roadway Express Company that the firm would catch "hell" unless it fired two particular employees—both of whom were signers of the anti-Webb petition. Twelve days later, after a twenty-four-hour strike, the two men were fired.

Now the rebel rank-and-filers went to court. Buxton filed an action in tort to recover damages for his slugging. In a settlement Webb paid him $4,000—which he took from the union treasury.

The two men fired by Roadway Express took their case to the NLRB. They were awarded their back salaries—$4,825 from the company and a like amount from Webb. Webb's share again came out of the union treasury, as did all attorneys' fees in both cases.

Then Amos Reniker, a leading figure in the opposition group, filed suit asking that Webb be removed as union president. That night a bomb blast rocked Reniker's house. Damage was not serious but in the night Reniker's telephone rang and a voice warned: "The next time we will blow you to hell."

As Reniker's move to oust Webb gained momentum, the International used its old weapon, and placed the local in trusteeship, with Jimmy Hoffa as the trustee. Hoffa immediately put his old friend Floyd Webb back in charge to run the local union for him. Webb and Hoffa now had absolute control.

In the meantime, union members had filed suit, asking that an election be ordered. The court agreed and Reniker's group named a slate of officers to oppose the men Webb selected. A few days before the election word came from Hoffa: all Reniker's candidates were ineligible because of the provision requiring that they pay their dues by the first of the month. Reniker's group had paid their dues, but under the union-established check-off system. (As this arrangement is set up the company, which checks the dues off on the first day of the month, can't possibly get them to union headquarters before the second, third or fourth of the month. The Teamsters officers realize this and often use the gimmick to rule everyone ineligible but the incumbent officers, who work for the union and pay their own dues.)

Taking no chances, Hoffa and Harold Gibbons made special trips to Joplin to praise Webb and criticize Reniker before the membership. They made it clear that they expected this local to stay under their control.

The court then stepped in and blocked the election because of the undemocratic manner in which it was being handled. After prolonged litigation another election was set up for 1956. Again, in came Mr. Hoffa to inform the members that the officers under Webb's administration had done no wrong, and that Reniker and his group had cost the union $70,000 in litigation fees. He suggested that they throw Amos Reniker out of the union. Again the court delayed the election.

When Paul Tierney, an investigator for our Committee, went to Joplin to look into the situation, he of course talked with Amos Reniker. Immediately after Tierney left town, four men accosted Reniker and one grabbed him by the front of the shirt. They warned him: "Now if you don't quit talking about Mr. Hoffa and quit talking to those Senate investigators and quit talking about Mr. Webb we are going to make you awfully sorry, boy."

Amos Reniker was not intimidated. In September, 1958, he appeared before our Committee and told exactly how democracy in Joplin had suffered from the actions of Jimmy Hoffa and Floyd Webb. At the time of these hearings Webb and his men were still in power. Webb took the Fifth Amendment when he appeared before us.

Reniker told the Committee: "It looks to me like the situation has gotten so big that when the rank and file can't take care of their own problems and don't have any say in their own problems then there should be laws made to protect the rank and file."

In Pontiac, Michigan, one night back in 1953, a fleet of twenty-five black Cadillacs roared into town. Each carried four or five men, all armed with clubs. The cars drew up outside the union hall, where a man named Floyd Hook and his fellow rank-and-filers of Local 614 were having a meeting to discuss what to do about a couple of dishonest officers. Jimmy Hoffa had arrived. He had come to instill in these people some understanding of the proper place of union members in his Teamsters. Floyd Hook was going to be straightened out. Tough Jimmy Hoffa would have eighty armed men do it for him. But Hook and his men locked the doors, called the police and went on with their meeting.

This happened after the union had twice applied to Hoffa for help, presenting evidence that the two officers in question, Dan Keating and Louis Linteau, were taking pay-offs from employers in return for not enforcing the contract.

The first time Hoffa had said he would look into it. Nothing happened. The second time the delegation called on him he said he had investigated. He had found that Keating and Linteau were not crooked. (The Committee learned that Hoffa's idea of conducting an investigation is to ask the Teamster official if he committed the crime he was charged with. If the official says no, that ends it—especially when, like Keating and Linteau, he happens to be a good friend.)

Nevertheless the delegation had pressed for an election of new officers. According to Floyd Hook, Hoffa told them: "There will be no election and if you fight me you will never get an election."

I asked Hook, "So what did you tell him?"

"I told him we was going to fight him, and we have ever since."

A tough, good-looking truck driver who has been a Teamster all his life, Floyd Hook does not take kindly to threats. And neither, when Hoffa descended on their meeting with his hired goons, were he and his fellow members intimidated. They turned their information on Keating and Linteau over to the prosecuting attorney and the two officers were indicted. Dave Beck placed the local under trusteeship, and named Hoffa as trustee. Immediately Hoffa put Keating and Linteau back in to run the local for him!

Still Floyd Hook did not quit. He now sought to have the trusteeship lifted. As he explained it to the Committee: "We had approximately eleven to twelve hundred men that signed petitions. We sent them to Mr. Beck, the President of the Teamsters, asking for the trusteeship to be lifted and that we could hold an election. He acknowledged receipt of the petitions and that is the last we heard from him."

About this time the Hook family began to be subjected to vicious persecution. A car followed Floyd Hook wherever he went. On nights when he was out on the road, a Cadillac remained parked across the street from his house. Threatening telephone calls were made at all hours to his family.

Think for a moment of what it would be like to be awakened every hour of every night from midnight to 6 A.M. by malicious telephone calls. The first night, or the first three or four nights, perhaps, would not be intolerable. But think then of the second week and the third, the second month, the third and the fourth—and still the telephone rings and still the voices threaten: "Your husband just had an accident, they are going to bring him home on a white slab." "Tell your children to be careful on the way to school today, it would be unfortunate if a truck ran them down." These were the calls that tormented Floyd Hook's family.

Mrs. Hook had a nervous breakdown and her husband sent her to live with relatives in Indiana. He stayed to fight. In January, 1954, on a trumped-up charge, Hook was fired from his company. The union, of course, would not help him. Hook finally followed his wife to Indiana to get a job. The telephone calls found him even there.

Although handsomely defended at union expense, Keating and Linteau, and two other union officials convicted at the same time, served short prison sentences which grew out of the indictments for taking money from employers. While in prison, and for a year after their release, they continued to receive their union salaries. Thereafter they went on pension. Altogether, they received more than $140,000 after they were convicted of betraying the union membership.

Why was Jimmy Hoffa so solicitous of Keating and Linteau? Why did he refuse to listen to Floyd Hook when he first complained that Keating and Linteau were dishonest? Why did he refuse to take action against them when they were indicted? Why did he put them back in charge of the local after Dave Beck placed the local in trusteeship? Why allow them to receive defense money and salaries while in jail?

Robert Scott, the Michigan labor official who was once a close friend of Hoffa, testified that Keating had told him (Scott) that he was making kickbacks to Hoffa, giving him a percentage of whatever he got from employers. Scott also told us that Keating had said Hoffa would get Frank Fitzsimmons[2] off if the others would plead guilty. In return, he promised to pay them while they were in jail. And this, we found, is exactly what happened.

Hoffa denied to the Committee that he received kickback money from Keating, as Scott had testified. Here was his testimony:

MR. HOFFA: I was not charged with any crime connected with them, nor was I on trial. I was not afraid they were going to expose me, because

[2] Fitzsimmons, vice president of Hoffa's own Local 299, was indicted on the same charge as Keating and Linteau. Charges were not pressed and he was released.

130

they have nothing to expose. But, insofar as they were concerned, we felt—I felt they had been with the union sufficient time, worked the hours they had worked, knew their families, and decided to recommend that they be taken care of, and we did.

MR. KENNEDY: Mr. Hoffa, if you are looking around for charitable organizations to contribute union funds to, I am sure you can get a better group than four individuals who violated their union trust. They received money from employers. These were not people out on the picket line who got into a fight or something. These were people who received money from employers. How can you possibly explain your being so solicitous for them, unless you received some of the money yourself. Can you explain that?

MR. HOFFA: I think I have made my statement.

MR. KENNEDY: You don't have anything else to add to it?

MR. HOFFA: Nothing.

MR. KENNEDY: Then, when they got out of jail, they continued to receive their money, all from union funds? Do you have anything to say to that?

MR. HOFFA: I have made the statement that I care to make for that answer, unless there is some other question.

When Keating and Linteau went to jail, Hoffa turned the union over to a man named Floyd Harmon. In May, 1958, Harmon was to stand for election. Two Teamsters were nominated to oppose him. Both were declared ineligible.

To insure that the election of the other officers on the slate would also be to his liking, Hoffa sent a committee of Teamster officials to Pontiac. The man in charge of this committee was Barney Baker.

Hoffa's friends won all the seats in this election.

Among the stories of how Jimmy Hoffa and his lieutenants coldly rolled democracy under in the Teamsters Union, the events that occurred in St. Louis, Missouri, when it came time for Harold Gibbons to take control, first of Local 688 and later of the Joint Council 13, must be included.

Here a labor union became nothing more than a commodity to be bought and paid for on the open market.

Gibbons's entry into the Teamster movement occurred in 1949. At that time he headed a CIO local in St. Louis that had the same warehouse jurisdiction as the Teamsters Local 688. Local 688 was headed by Lawrence Camie. A "merger" was decided upon; Camie and the rest of his executive board resigned, the Teamsters paying Camie $36,000 to give his job to Gibbons. This was called "severance pay." In all, the executive board of Local 688 got a total of $78,000 for turning over the local to Gibbons. Harry Karsh, a business agent, who didn't long remain severed, received $18,000.

The rank and file of Local 688—the men who footed the bill for Gibbons to come in and rule them—had nothing whatever to say about it. There is no proof that they were even told. Neither the constitution of the International nor the by-laws of the local contains any provision permitting such payments.

Though Gibbons denied it to our Committee this amounted to nothing more or less than a cold cash purchase of the union—using the funds of the union he was to take over to buy out the officeholders.

Senator McClellan remarked: "This is quite typical and that is the very thing that this Committee is concerned about. The membership are just handled like they were chattels, and not human beings, and not given a chance to express their views or their will or to determine what will be done with their money. But a few labor leaders got together and made a deal out of which they expect to profit."

From 1953 until 1958, Gibbons ran the St. Louis Joint Council as its trustee, appointed to that position on Hoffa's recommendation. A number of the locals under the command of this "egghead Teamster" were ruled like little dictatorships by his hand-picked officers—some, men with criminal records. Opposition to Gibbons was literally, not figuratively, beaten down, as James Ford testified. Ford was a man who spoke out against Gibbons in union meetings once too often. He was thrown over a stair railing, and wound up with a broken nose, a split cheek, no lower teeth, three broken ribs and a punctured lung. According to one of his assailants, a man with a long police record, Gibbons sent a sizable group to take care of Ford—three or four carloads.

After Hoffa became International president, it was decided in December, 1957, to take the St. Louis Joint Council out of trusteeship. There was little doubt that Gibbons, with his close relationship to Hoffa, would be successful in holding on to the presidency. But when the St. Louis Teamsters realized that there was actually going to be an election, after so long a time, opposition to Gibbons burgeoned and spread.

As it became apparent that a very close race was in the making, onto the stage to save Gibbons came Harry Karsh and his Carnival Workers Local 447. Karsh, of course, is the same man who had been "severed" for $18,000 when Gibbons bought Local 688.

The Joint Council's research bulletin, which contains the names of all locals belonging to Joint Council 13, states specifically there are twenty locals in the council with seven votes each, and it does not list Local 447 among them. The official list of locals put out by the International Brotherhood of Teamsters showed that Local 447 was affiliated with no joint council; its jurisdiction was the entire United States of America. But as trustee of the St. Louis Council, Gibbons claimed he had the right to bring in Harry Karsh's local if he pleased. And with his election in the balance, he pleased.

Robert L. Lewis, the tough, honest, outspoken secretary-treasurer of the Brewers and Malters Union, St. Louis, ran for recording secretary on the anti-Gibbons slate. He told us of the shock and dismay that greeted Gibbons's announcement that Karsh's local was part of the Council.

Lewis said that Gibbons originally claimed as trustee the right to cast the votes for Local 447 in the election.

MR. KENNEDY: Could you tell us what your reaction was?
MR. LEWIS: Well, it was quite an explosion. We made it clear that we were not going to hold still for it. Then he asked if Mr. Karsh could not vote the votes.

Lewis said there was great opposition to the proposal.

"Well, I thought it was only fair, Mr. Kennedy, that Mr. Karsh bring his delegates in like everybody else was expected to do. All the other locals must have their delegates present. No one would be allowed to vote any votes for the delegates."

No one knew who the delegates from Local 447 were. Lewis said, "I asked Mr. Karsh for the names of his delegates and he gave me a lot of mumbo-jumbo about their being in Puerto Rico, South America and God knows where."

MR. KENNEDY: Did you ask him to get the names and addresses of these delegates?

MR. LEWIS: Yes, sir. I asked three times. I asked for just the names. He wouldn't give me the names. Mr. Gibbons stuck his head out the door and told him, "Keep your mouth shut; don't give him any information." Mr. Gibbons claimed he had the names, but they were downstairs, locked in a file somewhere. I don't know why they were locked.

It is of significance that these conversations took place in December, 1957, for we proved in our hearing that Local 447 had no delegates at that time. It had no delegates until January, 1958, when Karsh appointed six.

This was not the only stumbling block that Gibbons placed in the way of his opposition. He circularized by mail all the delegates who were to take part in the election, but refused to furnish Lewis's group with a list until it was too late for them to get out a letter. "This is a fight to the finish," he told Lewis, "and no holds are barred."

THE CHAIRMAN: Is that the democracy that he bragged about in the union?

MR. LEWIS: I have heard democracy talked about, but I have seen damn little of it practiced.

Lewis discovered that the members of Karsh's local had paid no per capita taxes to the Joint Council as required by the constitution—further evidence that they were not really considered members. However, Harold Gibbons attempted to rectify this defect. Our investigator, Thomas Eickmeyer, found that on December 16, 1957 and on January 13, 1958, a total of some $2,660 was paid to Joint Council 13 to cover up the per capita payments that had been missed since June, 1955. The checks were signed by Harold Gibbons as trustee of Local 447. Karsh finally got together six delegates in the flesh. Two of them later testified before the Committee.

One, a man named Vernon Korhn, from Tampa, said that he received a telephone call from Karsh telling him he was now president of the local, and suggesting that he get "at least five good men that know show business to be on the advisory board to serve as officers of the union." Korhn said he got together five men, all management foremen in various fairs and carnivals. Joint Council 13 paid their travel expenses to St. Louis and their lost time, although subsequently it was reimbursed by Local 447. When the six carnival delegates arrived in St. Louis they all went in and voted for Gibbons. Their votes were placed in a separate envelope "to be counted only if the election was contested or close."

Without the seven votes of the Carnival Workers, the full anti-Gibbons slate would have been elected. Three members of the anti-Gibbons slate won anyway. A fourth anti-Gibbons candidate was tied with a Gibbons candidate.

The most outrageous thing about this whole situation, however, was that Harold Gibbons allowed these men to be delegates and officers of the local, and to participate in the election even though they were not eligible under the dues provision of the Teamsters constitution. None of them had had their dues paid by the first day of the month for a period of two years. Here there wasn't even the mitigating factor of the check-off system, as in Joplin and elsewhere, where this gimmick was used to rule ineligible all opponents of Hoffa. Here the constitution was flagrantly ignored, because, of course, it helped Hoffa and Gibbons to ignore it.

The records brought before the Committee show that only Harry Karsh of the seven officers was eligible to hold a position. It also developed that none of these men was bonded as required under the constitution. Furthermore, it was determined that despite efforts of the International union to cover the matter up by issuing a false report, the carnival local union had not even made proper per capita payments to the International union and, therefore, the union itself was no longer in "good standing" and their charter was in "automatically revoked" status.

What did Harold Gibbons, the self-styled fighter for democracy, say to this flouting of the constitution?

MR. GIBBONS: . . . You can go through there through this international constitution and find two dozen places where it does not apply to this organization. This is an organization in an utterly new field and the problems of administering this in line with the constitution are many and different.

THE CHAIRMAN: Where is the provision, Mr. Gibbons, in your constitution that gives you or an international president a right to waive any part of the constitution or make an exception for a local such as this in any particular field?

MR. GIBBONS: There is this section in which the president has the right to interpret the constitution.

The Chairman pointed out: "The right to interpret does not mean a right to waive."

Mr. Gibbons went on to admit that "literally" they had violated the constitution. Then referring to me he stated, "I think he has made a pretty good case here to the effect that we have violated."

But when I asked him whether he would be willing for the election to be decided on the basis of the legal votes cast at the time, he said he would not: it did not appear to him to be a serious violation of the constitution.

Gibbons came before the Committee as the intellectual Teamster, the man who disapproved of crude, violent tactics.

But, as the Committee proved, he was not averse to using the tactics of the racketeers who had tried to steal the Joint Council election in New York. He has depended on the Barney Bakers and Harry Karshes, as Hoffa depends on them.

He claimed he had kicked out gangsters and hoodlums. I am sure he had. However, I asked him: "Who will clean out the ones you have brought in?" He poses as an advocate of union democracy. Yet, as we have seen, the rank and file in many locals he controls have no voice in the operation of the union.

The Committee in its first year of operation went into the case of the paper locals in New York. I have already mentioned briefly this attempt of Hoffa's, with the help of Johnny Dio and Tony "Ducks" Corallo, to take over control of Joint Council 16 and its 140,000 New York Teamsters.

This power grab, as the testimony showed, was based on a plan to create a number of phony Teamster local unions in the New York area and thus invent enough votes to swing the Joint Council election Hoffa's way—that is, to John O'Rourke. At Hoffa's request, according to Einar Mohn, charters were issued to seven phantom locals, five of which actually had no members at all. But they did have officers. Dio made sure of that. When the charters arrived in New York, he and Corallo turned them over to their associates—including a number of extortionists, gangsters, gamblers and punks, like Nathan Carmel, Jack Berger, Aaron Kleinman, Milton Levine, Jack Priore, Max Chester, Sam Goldstein, Al Reger, Harry Davidoff, Joseph Curcio, Arthur Santa Maria. And when the Joint Council election rolled around open fraud was practiced. Men who were not Teamsters and had never been Teamsters turned up and voted. The Committee heard evidence of this. For instance:

Anthony Barbera was in Joe Saud's bar when someone came in and said, "Let's all go down to the Amphitheater and vote." So he went along with the crowd. We asked him whether he had voted, as the records showed. He told the Committee: "I don't know whether I voted. . . . I was drunk."

Then there was Armando Simontacci, a machinist. He lived near Joseph Curcio—one of Dio's "boys." One day Joe Curcio told Mr. Simontacci he was an officer of a Teamsters Union. Mr. Simontacci had never belonged to the Teamsters Union—but he was not one to turn down such an honor. He wanted to be good neighbors with his friend, Joe Curcio. He didn't refuse. Then after the election, Mr. Curcio came to his neighbor and told him that he was no longer an officer.

Sam Getlan, former slot machine operator who once worked for Frank Costello, was secretary-treasurer of the Jewelry Workers Union. He didn't know anything about being an officer of the Teamsters Union—until he started getting mail addressed to him at his office.

Mr. Getlan never did vote in a Joint Council election, he told the Committee—yet someone voted in the election under his name.

Another man who was listed as an officer told us he couldn't possibly have voted, as the records indicated. He had been in a floating crap game at the time.

Because of the intervention of District Attorney Frank Hogan and action brought in New York courts, Hoffa's seizure of the New York area was blocked at the time of the paper local case. Actually it was only delayed.

A major figure who aided Hoffa and Dio in setting up these paper locals was John McNamara, who held office as secretary-treasurer of Local 808 and, for a time, as president of paper Local 295. McNamara was the man who went to Washington to pick up the paper-local charters from the Teamsters International headquarters and take them to New York; he was the man who distributed them; with Dio, he worked out the detailed plans for setting them up.

But McNamara (convicted with Dio for extortion in a case later reversed by the Appellate Court) ran into rank-and-file opposition because of his activities.

People who ask why the rank and file put up with gangsters and corruption have only to look at what happened in Local 808 to realize the terrible truth of the matter is that the rank and file are powerless.

Michael Clements and Edward McCormack are veteran rank-and-file Teamsters. They are tough-minded, stubborn men, like Floyd Hook or Barney Matual. They don't like to be pushed around. Pushed too far, they fight back.

Clements, McCormack and others in Local 808 got fed up with McNamara and his dictatorial command and his gangster friends. To get rid of him and of them, they proposed a slate of opposition candidates to run against him in the next election, which was to be held December 14, 1958. Prior to the election, both sides agreed to bring in the Honest Ballot Association to supervise the voting.

McNamara was opposed by McCormack for the job of secretary-treasurer. The first count showed a tie; 439 votes for McNamara and 439 for McCormack. There were some challenged votes. Two paper ballots were opened. Each candidate got one of these and the count was then 440 to 440. Two more paper ballots put McNamara ahead 442 to 440. But he had also challenged six voting machine ballots that the Association found were illegally cast. There was no way to tell for whom these six votes had been meant, and they obviously might have affected the outcome. So the Association recommended another election for the office of secretary-treasurer.

McNamara, however, refused to abide by the Association's decision.

George Abrams, executive secretary of the committee on labor elections of the Ballot Association, told our Committee that his group had supervised thousands of elections and that "this is the only case to our knowledge where a recommendation has not been followed."

The anti-McNamara slate won three trustee positions, while the pro-McNamara men won the presidency and the recording secretaryship. McNamara, of course, would not budge from the office of secretary-treasurer.

Another conflict blew up over the office of business agent, for which rank-and-file rebel Michael Clements ran against Henry Fitzpatrick, but the Honest Ballot Association found Clements had a clear margin of victory, and certified him as the newly elected business agent.

The over-all result then was that the anti-McNamara slate won four offices and the pro-McNamara two offices. Thus, even with McNamara refusing to vacate his position, the anti-McNamara group controlled the seven-man executive board with four votes. However, the situation was not quite that simple.

When Clements reported for work as business agent, he testified, McNamara at first refused to allow him in the office, then he refused to pay him, on the grounds that he did not have enough money in the union treasury. At the same time, though, he hired Fitzpatrick, the man Clements defeated, as a "clerk" and continued to pay him a salary.

It also turned out that McNamara, Fitzpatrick and others of the McNamara slate were receiving so-called "back pay," a wage increase that McNamara maintained had been authorized in 1949 but never put into effect owing to insufficient funds.

Skeptical, the new trustees went to the union hall to examine the books. When McNamara objected, the trustees refused to sign the papers certifying the union records.

Mr. Clements told us: "Brother McNamara stated he would bring charges against them and it was their duty to sign the books, and it was not their concern to question the expenditures made but only to see that they tallied with the canceled checks."

MR. KENNEDY: Were charges brought against them?
MR. CLEMENTS: Charges were brought against them.
MR. KENNEDY: So what happened?

139

MR. CLEMENTS: The trustees were suspended for one year from their jobs. . . .

The trustees appealed this action to the Joint Council, which was now controlled by Hoffa's friend John O'Rourke. O'Rourke upheld McNamara and ruled that the trustees were guilty as charged. He held that it was their "unfamiliarity" with union procedures, however, that made them guilty, and therefore they should be reinstated.

During this whole time, of course, McNamara had been collecting his "back pay" and was again entrenched in control. The trustees had learned their lesson. If they stepped out of line, McNamara could bring "charges" against them. They now knew they could not win.

After describing how they had been stymied in their efforts to run the union decently and democratically, Clements made this appeal before the Committee:

"Might I add at this point that people like myself . . . the little labor man, can do nothing unless our legislators and lawmakers will help us. Where can we go now? If we go to court and try to force a run-off election the court will tell us, 'Have you exhausted the machinery and the remedies of your union? Did you go to your Joint Council? Did you go to your International? Or after that the convention?'

"We are not going to get any place making those kind of appeals."

The Committee questioned McNamara and O'Rourke about their conduct. Both took the Fifth Amendment.

Teamster officials who fight Hoffa are rare. To oppose him means that they must risk personal safety and the security of their jobs. Most leaders dare not cross Hoffa.

Jim Luken, of Cincinnati, is one who dares.

When Jimmy Hoffa was called to Washington during the Committee's hearings in 1958, the presidents of Joint Councils around the country were called on to extend to him a vote of confidence. A number of them did not vote. But only one in the entire country had the courage to vote "no."

That man was Luken. He is president of Cincinnati Joint Council 26 and also president of Teamsters Local 98, a milk drivers' union. He has been a milk truck driver and a Teamster since 1941, and an official of the union since 1949. For almost that long he has opposed the rule of Jimmy Hoffa and Hoffa's number one Ohio chieftain, William Presser.

His opposition to Hoffa and Presser has meant trouble for him. He described to the Committee some of the threats and harassments to which he and his family were subjected. Once, for example, a Cincinnati undertaker called his home to say he had just been informed that Mr. Luken was dead. He wanted to know where he was to pick up the body. On another occasion funeral flowers were delivered to Luken's house. The card was signed with the name of a Teamster official.

When intimidation failed, he told us, his enemies tried bribes. Presser offered him the presidency of the Joint Council in Cincinnati—if he would co-operate with Mr. Hoffa and Mr. Presser. The Joint Council then had a president—but Presser said "resignations can be arranged."

Luken ultimately became president of the Joint Council, but he was elected over Presser's opposition, having made it clear that he would not "co-operate."

Presser has worked hard to put every possible obstacle in Jim Luken's path. In 1951, he brought his brother-in-law, Harry Friedman, into Cincinnati to take over juke-box Local 122. Friedman, who has a long criminal record, and had just been released from prison, made all the trouble for Luken that he could. But Friedman wasn't around long. He added to the list of arrest charges against him—which included forgery, blackmail, illegal transportation of whisky and auto theft—a conviction for filing false affidavits. He went back to prison, this time to the Ohio State Penitentiary.

Then Presser brought in another man, Ralph Vanni, who, Luken said, tried to steal contracts from him by offering employers softer deals. He left town when it was discovered that he was trying to extort money from employers.

In the Teamster elections of 1958 the Hoffa-Presser forces resorted to a variety of unscrupulous methods to get control of Local 100, the largest of Cincinnati's Teamsters Unions, and later of Joint

Council 26. For instance, one of Luken's lieutenants was accused of rape.

I interviewed the woman who made the charge. She admitted to me that it was false, as Luken had told our Committee, and said that she had been paid $195 and promised another $1,000 if the man was indicted.

Her admission, plus her physical appearance, was so repulsive that I could not stomach the thought of calling her to Washington to testify.

Robert Morris was the Presser-Hoffa spokesman in Cincinnati during this era. In the midst of his dispute with Luken's people, Morris's car was bombed. Promptly Luken and his lieutenants asked for a lie detector test from the Cincinnati police department and challenged Morris to be tested about whether he had bombed his own car. Luken and his men all passed the lie detector test. Morris refused to take it. It developed that Morris had telephoned his insurance agency just before the bombing and had asked if he would be able to collect insurance money if his car was blown up.

Threats, abuse, bribes, trumped-up charges—Jim Luken and his followers have faced them all and have not yet been beaten in their fight against Jimmy Hoffa and William Presser. Luken stands alone as a Teamsters leader who stood up to be counted against Hoffa, and survived. It has not been easy. He expects more trouble. But he believes that labor union democracy is worth fighting for. And he intends to continue the fight.

This, then, is the story of democracy in the Teamsters Union—or rather, the story of the complete absence of democracy in the Teamsters Union where Hoffa exercises control. Can anyone familiar with it still ask why the decent, honest, hard-working rank-and-file teamsters don't rise up and throw out Jimmy Hoffa and his gang? The answer is simple:

They have tried in dozens of towns and cities across the country—and they can't.

Chapter 8 / **"BUT HE GETS GOOD CONTRACTS"**

JAMES HOFFA'S APOLOGISTS excuse all else—his venality, his shady business deals, his gangster connections, his roughshod abuse of democratic procedures within the union—on one ground:

"All right, maybe he's a crook and a roughneck," they say, "but he looks out for the rank and file; he gets good contracts for his men."

Hoffa himself likes to flourish this claim as an unbeatable argument. "Let the record speak for itself," he says.

Even if this were true, it would be no excuse for corruption, of course. But how true is it? How good are the contracts he gets for his men? Suppose we let the record speak for itself.

Early in 1959 we sent investigators out across the country to study and analyze the books of some big companies with Hoffa contracts. We talked with employers, Teamster officials, truck drivers and labor negotiators.

What did we find?

First of all, we discovered that Mr. Hoffa has made side deals with his friends in the trucking business throughout the Central Conference of Teamsters, deals advantageous to the management; he also has made sweetheart contracts with management in his home city of Detroit. And, worse, he has tried to bring down the higher standards of Teamster contracts in other parts of the country, where he cannot control the terms, to make them conform to his own.

143

Arthur Kaplan, one of our investigators, telephoned the office one day from Cleveland where he had been examining the records of the Glenn Cartage Company. In the files he had found a memorandum which contained shocking information. Written by a company official, it said:

George [George Maxwell, a Cleveland labor relations consultant] told me that in 1954 he made five separate deals with Hoffa concerning percentage pay rates for major carriers who are members of his association. . . . George further said that Hoffa is very tough in these open meetings, but you can talk to him in a closed private session. . . .

I had Kaplan get in touch with Maxwell. Maxwell came on to Washington, where he turned out to be one of the Committee's most important and straightforward witnesses. Born in India, the son of missionary parents, he came to this country after World War I to attend Princeton Theological Seminary, and was ordained a minister himself. Unable to serve in World War II because of a disability, he resigned his ministry to become an official of the National War Labor Board. In 1947 he went to work as a labor consultant in Cleveland. The majority of his clients were trucking companies engaged in hauling iron and steel. His testimony was important because as a labor relations consultant he had been in frequent contact with Jimmy Hoffa.

I had breakfast with him in the Senate cafeteria the morning of July 9, the day that he was scheduled to testify, and we reviewed what he was prepared to say. I realized that his appearance would be extremely damaging to him financially. Finally I said, perhaps because I had become cynical myself, "I don't understand it. You will ruin yourself, your business, if you testify like that." He answered quite simply, "I tell the truth, Mr. Kennedy."

Before the Committee he admitted that he had made numerous side deals with Jimmy Hoffa after labor-management negotiating committees had agreed upon a regular contract.

He explained it this way: "You negotiate a written contract with Mr. Hoffa and then you go behind the scenes and make a side deal."

Often, he said, the contract changes he obtained were never reduced to writing or even submitted to the rank-and-file membership for approval. Even when they were, it was only a gesture. The union members had no choice but go along.

I asked him: "With whom were those changes in the contract negotiated?"

MR. MAXWELL: In nearly every instance negotiations terminated at least with Mr. James Hoffa.

MR. KENNEDY: Isn't it a fact that the negotiations themselves in changing or altering the terms of the contract were conducted with Mr. Hoffa?

MR. MAXWELL: In a majority of instances they were conducted only with Mr. Hoffa. But in all instances they required his approval before they could be made effective.

Maxwell admitted that this procedure put the survival of all the companies who had Teamster contracts in Hoffa's hands. If a company was friendly with Hoffa and obtained a helpful "modification" to the contract, that firm did well. If Hoffa was unfriendly and they could not get the contract change they desired, it could mean economic disaster.

The man must have realized that giving us such information cut off any future possibility that Hoffa would deal with him, but he pulled no punches in telling us of his association with the Teamster chief. He testified, for instance, that Hoffa once called him and said he understood that a driver for one of Maxwell's clients was a Negro, and that he was driving a truck into Detroit, and thus came within Hoffa's jurisdiction. Hoffa said he didn't like "over-the-road drivers of the colored race coming into Detroit." He told Maxwell to tell the truck owner to keep Negroes out of his area, otherwise they would get hurt. The driver, Ross Hill, an extremely intelligent man, confirmed that he was told not only by his employer but by representatives of Local 299 that they wanted nothing to do with Negro over-the-road drivers. We heard similar testimony from other Negro drivers.

Hoffa denied discriminating against Negroes. Well then, he was asked, had he ever told George Maxwell that a Negro over-the-road driver coming into Detroit would be hurt? "I don't remember," said Hoffa.

The Committee had not been used to witnesses like Mr. Maxwell.

145

As I said to someone afterward, Diogenes with his lantern need look no further.

Special side deals by Hoffa were not restricted to Ohio. Let us examine another case.

Transamerican Freight Lines of Detroit, Michigan, is one of the nation's largest interstate trucking companies. Its drivers are, of course, all Teamsters. In 1955, Transamerican signed the regular Central States Conference union contract with the Teamsters. But Hoffa made a side deal with Transamerican. He allowed the company to give the drivers a cent-and-a-half-a-mile pay increase in lieu of fringe benefits such as holidays, layover, vacation and breakdown provisions. The Transamerican drivers were told to keep complete records, and if their records showed that the fringe benefits would have amounted to more money than the cent-and-a-half deal, they were to file a grievance with the company and would be paid what they had lost. It was at once apparent to many of the drivers that they were going to lose money, and would have to become bookkeepers to collect what they had coming. They objected.

The deal went into effect February 1, 1955, without approval of the membership—but the protests were so numerous that Hoffa called a special meeting February 13 in Detroit for representatives of all Transamerican drivers. There he acknowledged that the drivers were dissatisfied. However, he said, let's give the arrangement a tryout. If the men had problems they could file grievances, and the company would pay within ten days. He would meet again in ninety days with the drivers' representatives, he promised, to see how his deal was working out.

So the representatives went back to the rank and file and sold them on the idea that they should trust Jimmy Hoffa.

Ninety days passed—but there was no meeting. Four months passed, five months, six—a year. No second meeting. There never was a second meeting. When Hoffa was asked about it, he said, "I'll call it when I'm good and ready to."

Members found they lost money on this cent-and-a-half deal. They started filing grievances—but Mr. Hoffa and Robert Gotfredson, president of Transamerican, worked out a second side deal which bypassed several steps in the usual grievance procedure, and routed complaints directly from the local board to the Central States Drivers Council in Chicago, which was under Hoffa's direct control. Then, deeming even this procedure too hazardous, they decided to send all grievances directly from the local union level to Detroit, where they were decided by Roland McMasters and Frank Fitzsimmons, two of Hoffa's underlings in his own Local 299.

Gotfredson was asked about his deals with Hoffa.

"Is there any place either in the contract, the Central States contract, or in the separate grievance agreement which you have which provides that a representative of Local 299 should handle your grievance?" he was asked. He answered, "No, sir."

I asked: "Was the separate grievance procedure ratified by the membership?"

Mr. Gotfredson: "No, it was not."

When we called on Hoffa to answer questions about his deals with Transamerican, at one point he referred us to Roland McMasters. McMasters came down the aisle to the witness stand and Hoffa stood up and stepped away. As the two men passed, Hoffa gave McMasters a signal with five fingers: "The Fifth," he said. It was the old procedure of taking the Fifth Amendment by proxy.

McMasters sat down and to all questions after his name and address he declined to answer "on the ground that a truthful answer might tend to incriminate me."

What happened to the rank and file under these side deals made by Hoffa?

Scott Pickett of Indianapolis, a craggy-faced, wiry little truck driver for Transamerican, put in for a grievance with the company claiming $1,400 covering vacation, layover and other fringe benefits. Six months later he finally heard from the company. With the approval of Teamster official Frank Fitzsimmons, they offered him 40 per cent of what he claimed.

The Indianapolis driver told our Committee: "I called Frank Fitzsimmons. I sent him proof, and I mean it was proof without a doubt, that I actually had the money coming, the full amount, and that I would not accept anything else.

"He gave me an argument. . . . I made four individual trips to Detroit to see the man and was unable to see him. I was unable to see Mr. Dennis [a company official]. I called him and I couldn't even talk to him. He refused to talk to me and referred me to the local terminal manager. The local terminal manager wouldn't commit himself either way."

So he hired a lawyer, Kirkwood Yockey. Yockey called the company lawyer, who referred him to Fitzsimmons. Mr. Yockey told us that he informed Fitzsimmons that he was not going to settle for 40 per cent. He was going to file suit. Fitzsimmons then asked him to delay going to court. Hoffa would talk to him.

Then, Yockey testified, he received a call from Chicago. "This is Jimmy Hoffa," a voice said. He told Yockey to have his client accept the 40 per cent settlement and that if he did so, Hoffa would have it in cash the following morning in Chicago.

Yockey replied: "Well, Mr. Hoffa, it is hard for me to understand how you can represent these men in the Teamsters Union and recommend that a man take forty per cent of his vacation pay for two years or forty per cent of his hotel bill or forty per cent of items like that. . . . I can't see how you can represent a man and conscientiously recommend that he take forty per cent of those items. . . ."

What was Hoffa's answer? Yockey told us: "He said this man might have stayed with his aunt and didn't spend that much. . . ."

Yockey asked: "Will you just give me one good reason why this man should take 40 per cent?"

The caller said: "Because I said so."

The lawyer replied: "Mr. Hoffa, that is not a good enough reason as far as I am concerned, and if that is the best you can do, I will recommend that we file a suit."

Yockey filed suit; the company quickly settled and Pickett, the Indianapolis driver, collected $1,200.

Pickett left Transamerican because he lost his truck for a shortage of money and was working as a mechanic for another firm when Walter Sheridan, our investigator, got in touch with him. The business agent of Pickett's Teamsters local immediately told him not to talk to Sheridan. Pickett told the Committee that when he defied this order, his boss told him that at the union's request he had to lay him off. Perhaps it was a coincidence that just prior to our hearings he was rehired.

Another driver, Gilbert Curtis, tall and bespectacled, said some drivers lost as much as $2,000 a year on the cent-and-a-half agreement and that a number of them filed grievances, but the company and Fitzsimmons invariably attempted to get them to take a small percentage of what was due.

He told us: "Some of the boys didn't want to lose their jobs and so they wouldn't press them."

MR. KENNEDY: . . . it is common information that when you put your grievances in and tried to press them, you would lose your job?
MR. CURTIS: That is correct.

Curtis should know. The company laid off drivers with less seniority in order to get rid of him. Then Hershell Hinkley, the terminal manager of Transamerican, told him that the company would pay his grievance, give him a letter of recommendation and rehire the other drivers if he would resign. Curtis agreed to do so.

Hinkley admitted all this to Walter Sheridan. But when he came before the Committee he was obviously torn by an inner emotional struggle. It was truth versus security; fear of perjury versus fear of his company's officials. And his attorney did not seem to help.

One of the first questions I asked him was about Curtis:

MR. KENNEDY: You had been trying to get him?
MR. HINKLEY: Yes, sir.
MR. KENNEDY: Had you been laying off the drivers that had less seniority —do you want to give him some legal advice? [The witness conferred with his counsel.]
MR. HINKLEY: Mr. Kennedy, we weren't trying to fire him or get him.

Senator McClellan pointed out that he had given one answer under oath, and then, after talking to his attorney, had completely reversed himself. But when I asked him again if he had tried to get Curtis or have him fired, he repeated his denial.

A document Walt Sheridan had found in the files of Transamerican was shown to Hinkley. Once again the importance of investigative work was demonstrated. The memorandum began: "One of the actions taken by Mr. Dennis in his recent campaign to get former driver G. Curtis out of our employ was to . . ."

I then asked him again: "There was a campaign to get Mr. Curtis out?"

MR. HINKLEY: Yes, sir.
MR. KENNEDY: You did have a campaign to lay them [other drivers] off in order to get to Mr. Curtis?
MR. HINKLEY: Yes, sir.

By the time Mr. Hinkley left the stand he was in tears.

The cent-and-a-half deal never did set well with the drivers of Transamerican and in 1958 Hoffa was sent a petition signed by more than 90 per cent of the Transamerican company drivers—including all of the company drivers in Hoffa's Local 299—requesting that the arrangement be thrown out.

It read:

As you know we have repeatedly voiced our objections to the cent and a half arrangement with this company and we have been assured that when the present negotiations are concluded we would be out from under this cent and a half business . . . copies of petitions [are] signed by both company drivers and owner-operators who are very much opposed to the cent and a half arrangement . . . we would like for you to place us under the regular Central States loads contract under which the competitors of Transamerican are operating.

Nothing was done. The drivers asked for strike sanction from the Teamsters International, and received it conditionally; but were forestalled when McMasters arranged to visit the various depots, with a company representative, to see if the strike could be settled before it began. The company claimed that when meetings were held in the summer of 1958 the drivers overwhelmingly approved the cent-and-a-half agreement, but the dissident rank-and-file Teamsters insisted to the Committee that no such approval was ever given. Certainly in mid-1959 we found tremendous dissatisfaction among drivers over the whole arrangement.

At this time the company was switching over to new Mack trucks.

150

For a driver to get a new truck he had to approve the cent-and-a-half agreement. To further pressure the drivers, the company refused to repair old trucks. It was a choice of sign or lose your job and seniority. The drivers had no alternative, no way to fight back or defend themselves. And it was Jimmy Hoffa—the Teamsters Union leader who gets "good contracts" for his men—who put them on this spot. Not one of his underlings, not a gangster he had placed in power, but Jimmy Hoffa himself.

When the scandals involving Dave Beck were made public, Jimmy Hoffa used to proclaim widely that he never accepted entertainment from employers. And yet he and some of his Teamster friends from Detroit have been known to accept the "hospitality" of Richard Riss, president of Riss & Company, one of the nation's largest trucking firms, at Riss's lodge in Ontario, Canada. Both admit they are personal friends—and their closeness shows in the way Riss treats his Teamster workers, without union interference. Here again, as in the case of Transamerican, the testimony showed, it was a Hoffa side deal that sold out the membership.

Riss & Company had signed the regular Central Conference contract with the Teamsters in 1955. Section 5 of that contract provides that there will be "no new riders or supplements . . . negotiated by any of the parties hereto." But, in 1956, Riss went to see Hoffa and they agreed to let Riss pay his drivers the cent and a half, just as Transamerican was doing. This agreement was never submitted to the membership. It was never even put in writing. It was simply a deal between two friends.

In 1958 Riss's drivers were told that the company wanted them to own their own trucks, rather than drive company equipment. The idea was, of course, that they should buy them from Riss. Riss's trucks were ones he had bought from General Motors some four years earlier for approximately $13,000 each. Complaining that they were defective—in a letter to the company dated October, 1956, he said that in his judgment they were then worth less than $3,500—in January, 1957, he collected from GMC $3,000 on each one—a total of $1,500,000. By 1958 the trucks had been depreciated on the books of his company to $1,600. Yet that same year, for these same trucks,

Riss charged his drivers $14,800.

When the drivers, naturally, protested to their local unions, Hoffa and Riss found a way to silence them. All the Riss drivers, no matter what city was their base of operations, were transferred into Hoffa's own Local 299 in Detroit. Thereafter, any driver who wanted to complain had to go to Detroit to see Hoffa to do so. The locals in their own cities could no longer handle their grievances. This was, of course, impractical if not impossible. But there was nothing the drivers could do. Who was there to help them? A number of the men, in order not to lose their jobs, entered into the purchase agreement with Riss. More than half of these were unable to meet their payments, and lost all the money they had invested as well as their jobs and seniority. The trucks reverted to Riss, who sold them again at inflated prices.

This was one of the times I really became angry at a hearing. The callousness of the deal between big labor and big business was so infuriating that I lost control of my temper, as the following excerpt shows:

MR. KENNEDY: I am talking about the fact that these trucks, these same trucks that you stated were reconditioned by the end of 1955, according to your own testimony, that in October 1956 you stated that they were only worth $3,500 at the most.
You then sell them to these same union members for some $14,000 or $15,000, two years later; then when the union members tried to bring grievances in connection with this, all of the union membership all over the United States were transferred into Local 299 even though they had to work in their regular depots.
I say that this is all because of your friendship with Mr. James Hoffa that this has been possible and nothing else.

Riss, who pulled all kinds of strings to avoid testifying, justified his treatment of his drivers by saying that he was simply making the best deal possible for himself. He did add: "We don't feel too proud about the deal. We are not too happy about it."

Nevertheless, I have seen no indication that he has been pained into action about it.

On the day we questioned Mr. Hoffa about his deal with the Riss Company, his answers were filibusters which made no sense at all.

152

Asked whether Riss was paying money into the pension and welfare fund, Hoffa launched out:

"No, sir, let me explain that. Riss and Company does not operate equipment. T. M. & E. [a Riss-owned company, formed in an attempt to circumvent the terms of the contract] operates the equipment. . . . Under the law when you lease a piece of equipment other than driver-owners as such, you cannot, and if you try to read our contract we specifically accepted in here, you cannot take and have two checks for drivers who are not driver-owners as such, but where you have a fleet operation and it is in here, sir, right in here—"

I tried to interrupt him but Senator McClellan said: "Let him finish." Hoffa rambled on:

"Let me read it to you, without reading it all. It starts: 'owner-operator section 1,' at the bottom it states: 'Note where the owner-driver is used in this article it means owner-operator only and nothing in this article shall apply to any equipment leased except where owner is also used as a driver. . . .' "

By this time the Committee was completely and hopelessly lost but Hoffa continued:

"This means, sir, where there is a fleet operation, and T.M. & E. is an equipment fleet operation, it does not come within the scope of this contract where you have two equipment checks. If we can get the employer voluntarily to do it, fine, but if we try legally to enforce the issue we have been advised that we can find ourselves in a problem, as Mr. Goldwater stated a while ago, of antitrust and monopoly. We recently went all the way to the United States Supreme Court on this particular provision and the United States Supreme Court ruled after we had lost in all the lower courts that this was a legal provision in our contract because we recognized our inability to negotiate for a profit return and rather only the basic minimum returns to operate a piece of equipment and that the drivers' earnings were protected. This was the United States Supreme Court ruling out of Ohio, ACEF I believe is the case."

If this answer was designed to shed any light on his relationship with Riss, its significance escaped me. However, Hoffa made an attempt to enlighten me in private. When we took a recess he approached me with a man I had never seen before, and in a surprisingly friendly manner he said: "Bob, I want you to meet a management man who can tell you that this deal of Riss selling these trucks to the drivers is not so bad after all."

I said: "I don't want to talk to you about it. You sold out the membership. You're going to have to live with it and there's nothing more to be said." I walked away.

We also went into the contract of the Chi-East Company of Chicago, which, of course, is under Hoffa's Central Conference of Teamsters. The drivers belong to Local 710, which is headed by John T. O'Brien, one of Hoffa's International vice presidents. Chi-East drivers are covered by the Central States agreement. Mr. Harry V. Mattson, president of the company, was a Committee witness.

MR. KENNEDY: Mr. Mattson, the employees that work for you, the drivers, do you pay them union scale?

MR. MATTSON: Union scale?

MR. KENNEDY: Union scale.

MR. MATTSON: This year I am not, no.

MR. KENNEDY: Do you pay them any lay-over?

MR. MATTSON: No.

MR. KENNEDY: Do you pay them any breakdown?

MR. MATTSON: No.

MR. KENNEDY: Do you pay them any meal allowance?

MR. MATTSON: No.

MR. KENNEDY: Do you pay them any lodging?

MR. MATTSON: No.

MR. KENNEDY: Do you pay them any holiday?

MR. MATTSON: No, only when they ask.

MR. KENNEDY: . . . Has the union complained about the fact that you pay no lay-over, you pay no union scale, you pay no breakdown, you pay no meal allowance, you pay no holiday when it is specified in the contract?

MR. MATTSON: No.

Two drivers told the Committee they had complained to the company and to the union about the nonenforcement of the contract— and were fired. The union did nothing to help them. One hopeful but misguided driver even wrote to Hoffa for help. What did Hoffa do? Going through the correspondence file of Local 299, we found the letter. Hoffa had forwarded it to O'Brien for his attention.

O'Brien, who draws a salary of some $90,000 a year plus expenses from Local 710 (he gets a commission on all dues paid), took the Fifth Amendment on every question.

When Hoffa appeared on the witness stand, he grew red-faced and angry when confronted with the testimony regarding his failure to enforce union contracts. The drivers who had testified he sold them out were "disgruntled," he said. At one point he complained: "Let us not talk about cheating on this contract because it is not true. This burns me up. It is not true. I don't think this record has a right. It goes all over the United States, headlines that Hoffa sold the workers."

Senator McClellan replied drily: "All we know is what has been sworn to."

Mr. Hoffa said: "I appreciate that but the world does not know that. . . ."

Not content with selling out the Teamsters in his own domain, Hoffa, as his power increased, worked hard to persuade Teamster officials outside his immediate sphere of influence to lower the terms of their contracts to conform with those he negotiated. The drivers for Midwestern trucking companies whose operations extended into the Eastern states often, of course, lived in the East and belonged to Eastern Teamster locals, and thus benefited from the better contracts negotiated outside Hoffa's area.

From Patrick J. O'Neill, assistant to the president of one of these firms, Anchor Motor Freight Lines of Cleveland, and a close friend and ardent admirer of Jimmy Hoffa, we heard this testimony:

"I would say, Mr. Kennedy, that our drivers in the East have a greater opportunity to earn—that is they can earn more dollars in a given period than our drivers that are under the Central States Conference contract."

So in 1955 there were negotiations to "uniformize" the contracts.

I asked O'Neill if he was trying to bring the Eastern contracts down to the level of those in the Midwest.

His answer: "That would be our objective, yes, sir, because competitively we would be in a better position obviously."

LaVern Duffy, digging into the files of Anchor Motor Freight, had discovered a memorandum that created great excitement among the

155

staff members; for it showed that Hoffa himself had worked with the company to accomplish precisely that result. O'Neill identified this memo as a report of a meeting that had occurred June 7, 1955, between Hoffa, O'Neill, his uncle F. J. O'Neill, who prepared the memo, and Carney Matheson, Hoffa's lawyer friend and financial partner who heads management's negotiations with the Central Conference of Teamsters.

First of all, the memo showed that Hoffa got a copy of the demands from the Eastern Conference of Teamsters—before the company got them. Then Hoffa took them to the company and went over them with Anchor officials—before Eastern Conference officials could submit them to Anchor. The memo said that Hoffa thought the Eastern Conference "demands were ridiculously high," and that he "had a personal interest because he did not want the Eastern Conference to get out of line with the national conference."

According to the memo, Hoffa was confident that he could control the situation, because if the Eastern Conference tried to strike, the International union would not grant strike sanction without his (Hoffa's) approval. Unauthorized strikes could occur, of course—but again, the memo said, Hoffa would be called into the picture.

This document said that Hoffa advised the company to "move slow" in their negotiations. It also stated: "Hoffa thought it would be wise to use Carney in negotiations."

Before the memorandum was introduced O'Neill had testified that he had not discussed the contract with Hoffa, and he had denied that Hoffa had ever recommended that the company use Carney Matheson in its negotiations with the Eastern Conference. Confronted with documentary proof that his original testimony was untrue, O'Neill suggested that he might have been out of the room when the discussions took place. However, he admitted that his firm did hire Carney Matheson to conduct the negotiations and that his company and another paid Matheson $20,000 apiece, or a total of $40,000, for his work.

Mr. Hoffa's betrayal of the union rank and file in favor of Anchor did not end with the 1955 negotiations. The following year he and the International backed up the company and forced on a Teamster local in Yonkers, New York, a contract that the membership had previously voted down. Again, in 1958, the same local took an even worse beating at the bargaining table with Anchor when, matters having reached an impasse, Hoffa personally assumed charge of negotiations. This was testified to by the secretary-treasurer of the local, and confirmed by O'Neill: "The contract that was accepted by the union was essentially the terms that we had offered."

The business agent of a Baltimore local had a similar story to tell. He estimated that the contract forced on his local cost each of the truck drivers in his area $2,000 annually.

And so management spokesmen and labor officials both confirmed that when Jimmy Hoffa intervenes in negotiations it is the Teamsters who drive the trucks and load the freight who are likely to get hurt—and the companies that are likely to get helped.

Actually Hoffa's efforts to "uniformize" Teamster contracts date back to 1954, when he made a brazen attempt to undercut the power and influence of the then sixth International vice president, Thomas Hickey of New York.

In the area-wide negotiations with the trucking companies that year the union locals had banded together to make a single front, and were solidly behind Tom Hickey, who headed their bargaining committee. Joseph L. Adelizzi, executive secretary of the Empire State Trucking Association, was the chief spokesman for management. At the beginning the union asked for a fifty-cent-an-hour increase. The companies offered ten cents. The negotiations stretched out. Finally Hickey, on Dave Beck's advice, dropped his demand to twenty-five cents—and stood pat. Management dug in its heels, and a strike became imminent.

At this point into the arena—the Henry Hudson Hotel in New York—walked Jimmy Hoffa, heading a group of vice presidents sent in by Dave Beck to help settle the dispute. Tom Hickey was removed as chairman of the union's negotiating committee, and John O'Rourke, an eager supporter of Jimmy Hoffa (now one of Hoffa's International vice presidents), replaced him. It was obvious that Jimmy Hoffa had dictated the maneuver and was somehow in control.

Honest Tom Hickey walked away from the hotel in disgust. He

157

knew Hoffa and his New York underworld friends, whom he referred to contemptuously as "the mob." Moving immediately to counteract Hoffa's intervention, he started private negotiations for his own eleven-thousand-member Teamster local on the basis of a twenty-five-cent-an-hour contract.

Jimmy Hoffa was moving too. He was anxious for a quick settlement to make Tom Hickey lose face. He made it plain that O'Rourke was negotiating chairman in name only—and that Jimmy Hoffa was taking over. He met behind closed doors with Mr. Adelizzi. He told Adelizzi he could arrange a settlement for eighteen cents an hour with a seven-cent raise the second year. Adelizzi turned him down. Hoffa then offered seventeen cents an hour with an eight-cent increase the second year. Both offers would have made a tremendous economic difference to the companies. Nevertheless, Adelizzi and his fellow truckers rejected Hoffa's terms and signed a contract with Tom Hickey for a twenty-five-cent an hour increase.

When Adelizzi appeared before the Committee in July, 1959, we asked him why the truckers had refused Hoffa's offer. His testimony was a breath of fresh air in a hearing room where too often we heard from management officials who sold out their principles and their employees to get a "good deal" from Hoffa.

"Well, back in 1954," he said, ". . . there was strong suspicion on the part of the unions in New York and some of the employers that a move was afoot to take over control of the labor situation in the New York–New Jersey area. . . ."

MR. KENNEDY: Was it also felt by some of your colleagues that if you signed on this basis [with Hoffa], even though it was more profitable to you, that it would, in fact, be turning over the trucking business and the trucking industry to the underworld, or to the mob?

MR. ADELIZZI: There was a strong suspicion of that; a strong fear of that . . . for that reason we came to the support of Mr. Hickey and the leadership of [Hickey's local] 807.

Constantly in the background of the discussions, Adelizzi testified, was the lurking presence of Johnny Dio—"He was always in the hallways of the hotels or wherever we were meeting."

A story in the *New York Times* on October 12, 1954, took sharp notice of Dio's presence. The article said:

The day's events came to a curious end with the appearance on the second floor of the hotel where the negotiations took place, of John Dioguardi, convicted garment industry extortionist who until recently was a power in the United Automobile Workers-AFL.

Dio warmly greeted Mr. Hoffa, the Teamster vice president from Detroit, asked to speak privately with him for "two minutes," and announced he was looking for a job.

Mr. Hoffa, who appeared to know Dio well, said at this point, "Well you always know where you can find one."

The prospect of carrying on collective bargaining with Johnny Dio had little appeal to members of the trucking industry of New York. Mr. Adelizzi made this plain.

"I haven't done business with him so I can't speak with direct experience," he said, "but I understand, based on what I have heard and what I have read, that it is much cheaper to do business with people like that than it is with Mr. Hickey or any of these people who try to conduct an honest union."

Adelizzi's testimony was supported by John Strong, Hickey's successor as president of Local 807. Hickey could not testify because at the time of the hearings he was in a hospital having an infected leg amputated. But I had conferred with him many times and he had appeared as a witness in 1957. He is a strong, tough man of whom the labor movement and Teamsters can be proud.

It was not only the Teamsters who suffered from Hoffa's talent for making bad deals. In September, 1957, when I was in Detroit on an investigation, I found there a local of the International Union of Retail Clerks that Hoffa had literally stolen. It was owned and controlled lock, stock and barrel by the Teamsters, to whom it paid dues, and Hoffa actually negotiated and signed its contracts with various wholesale grocery companies. These contracts, we found, were frequently substandard. And not surprisingly, though the Retail Clerks International Association is an honest organization, we also discovered wide-scale misuse of the local's funds.

I called Sol Lippmann, the Clerks' general counsel in Washington, and told him what was happening to their local in Detroit. Shocked, he sent out an auditor immediately to go over the union's books, and came out himself to wrest the local from Hoffa's control and place it in trusteeship.

The next day he walked into our Detroit office, white and shaken. He sat down to talk to me and he could hardly speak. He had just come from seeing Jimmy Hoffa, who had sent for him as soon as he learned what was happening. Hoffa, Lippmann said, had met him with a screaming torrent of blasphemy and foul abuse and threats that went on for twenty minutes.

"You won't get away with this," Lippmann reported Hoffa had shouted. "I won't let you get away with it. Don't you know I could have you killed? Don't you know I could have you pushed out this window? I've got friends," he threatened, "who would shoot you in your tracks someday while you are just walking down the street."

"If I did it," he added in an obvious reference to the fact that he had recently been acquitted of bribery charges in Washington, "no jury would even convict me. I have a special way with juries."

I asked Lippmann if he would testify before the Committee at our next hearings. He was still upset. "I couldn't do it," he said. "It would jeopardize my position."

Because the Retail Clerks union had been a help to our Committee and because, looking at Lippmann, I felt that he would have difficulty withstanding the strain if forced to testify, I did not insist.

During the 1958 hearings I asked Hoffa about his conversation with Sol Lippmann. He shrugged it off, denied that it ever occurred. At the noon hour, I telephoned Lippmann from my office and asked him to testify and refute Hoffa. There was a long silence.

Then, "I can't," he said. "The Retail Clerks depend on the Teamsters in many ways. We have to get along with them in the future."

He said he would like to help. But he just couldn't.

I told him: "Sol, with that attitude, the Teamsters will own you in five years."

That was the end of that.

Hoffa's own attorney, Edward Bennett Williams, in talking to newsmen, has made no secret of the fact that he has no illusions about Hoffa.

Martin O'Donoghue, head of the monitors, was once the attorney for the Teamsters. He has been a highly respected labor lawyer for many years. When he first went in as a monitor, he seriously questioned the position that our Committee had taken regarding the Teamsters and Hoffa; he had an idea that we were too critical. Two months later he called me on the telephone and said: "You are absolutely right. This is the most corrupt, dishonest leadership that I have ever seen. It is a deep-seated corruption. The Teamsters will never be cleaned up as long as Jimmy Hoffa remains the International president."

George Meany, president of the AFL-CIO, has called Jimmy Hoffa organized labor's No. 1 Enemy.

I am the first to admit that the record we uncovered is only a portion of the evil wrought by Hoffa, his men or associates. But what we did uncover shows clearly that the Teamster membership has been betrayed; democratic processes have been stifled; money, including pension and welfare funds, has been misused to the tune of at least $9,500,000; Hoffa and some of the men around him have got fat off enterprises they promoted with union backing. Perhaps worst of all, this potentially great institution, the Teamsters Union, has been turned over to the likes of Johnny Dio and Joey Glimco and Bert Brennan and Babe Triscaro and Sam Goldstein, and others who have spent their lives shifting in and out of the Teamsters and in and out of trouble with the law.

In 1957 Hoffa promised to clean up the Teamsters if he became president. In 1958 he said he had not had time to do a complete job. In 1959 he said the Teamsters were clean. Hoffa has abandoned any pretense that he will clean up. He has not—and because of the men around him, he cannot.

The Teamsters Union is the most powerful institution in this country—aside from the United States Government itself. In many major metropolitan areas the Teamsters control all transportation. It is a Teamster who drives the mother to the hospital at birth. It is the Teamster who drives the hearse at death. And between birth and burial, the Teamsters drive the trucks that clothe and feed us and provide the vital necessities of life. They control the pickup and deliveries of milk, frozen meat, fresh fruit, department store merchandise, newspapers, railroad express, air freight, and of cargo to and from the sea docks.

Quite literally your life—the life of every person in the United States—is in the hands of Hoffa and his Teamsters.

But, though the great majority of Teamster officers and Teamster members are honest, the Teamsters union under Hoffa is often not run as a bona fide union. As Mr. Hoffa operates it, this is a conspiracy of evil.

PART II

Chapter 9 / INVESTIGATORS AT WORK

I HAVE WRITTEN of the essentials of our inquiry as it concerned Jimmy Hoffa before describing the organization of the inquiry, the staff, our methods of work and our problems because I did not wish to interrupt the continuity of the Teamster story—even though we never for a moment stopped to give all our attention to that one union. But a Congressional committee hearing doesn't just happen —it is made to happen. Now I'd like to go back to the men, the work, the machinery that made it happen, and then into other investigations that ran concurrently with the Teamster investigation.

Most of our hearings were held in the spacious caucus room just off the marble stairway on the third floor of the Senate Office Building. This stately chamber, with its vaulted ceiling and red carpets, its arching windows, marble pillars and glistening chandeliers, is steeped in tradition.

Here in 1912, in the first use of the room, the Senate conducted its hearings into the sinking of the *Titanic*. Here Albert Fall, the Secretary of the Interior in the Harding administration, was exposed as corrupt; here Tom Thumb, in a famous play for publicity during an investigation, once sat on the knee of J. Pierpont Morgan; here the star of Senator Joseph McCarthy rose and fell. And here in this room the McClellan Committee—more properly called the Senate Select Committee on Improper Activities in the Labor or Management Field—conducted its public hearings in an effort to learn more about a menacing enemy within our national economic framework —an enemy that is the shame of our nation.

Hearings were conducted over a period of two and a half years and included over five hundred open hearing sessions. During this time we heard 1,525 sworn witnesses (343 of whom took the Fifth Amendment) give testimony that filled fifty-odd volumes and totaled more than fourteen million words.

When the Select Committee was first established there were only six investigators from the staff of the Permanent Subcommittee who were available to come to work for us. They were all good men, but we were swamped with work almost before we were in business.

Overnight our office was turned into a state of confusion. Complaints of improper labor-management practices began pouring in from all over the country. Suddenly we were receiving six hundred letters a day, most of them requesting far-flung investigations; already our staff was filing daily reports on Dave Beck from Seattle; on Teamster links with vice from Portland, Oregon; on Teamster violence from Scranton, Pennsylvania; and on the Teamsters' "paper local" election from New York. There were daily meetings with Senator McClellan; there were daily interviews with prospective (and badly needed) staff investigators; there were important sessions to arrange for co-operation with the FBI and the Justice Department, the Internal Revenue Service, the Bureau of Narcotics; newsmen sought hourly interviews on the work of the new Committee, and often suggested possible leads (our investigations in Portland, Scranton and Tennessee began in just that way). The phone rang hundreds of times a day; the days were not long enough, our work never seemed done. Our office space was cramped and inadequate and often it seemed as though staff workers, newspapermen and visitors were standing on top of each other.

Senator McClellan and I set out immediately to enlarge the staff. In six months we put together the largest investigative team ever to operate from Capitol Hill: thirty-five investigators, forty-five accountants from the General Accounting Office, twenty stenographers and clerks—a staff of more than one hundred persons in all.

166

Our Committee staff office was in Room 101 below the street floor of the old Senate Office Building. This was to become the nerve center of the network of investigative machinery that spread quickly across the country.

The McClellan Committee lasted three years. We were working in one of the most sensitive areas in public life. Yet there was virtually no criticism of the staff, its procedures, techniques or methods.

I am confident that we were able to put together such a good staff because, first of all, we were selective. We had an overwhelming number of applications from people who wanted to join as investigators. We accepted only one in a hundred. Every man finally employed as an investigator was interviewed, first by me and then by Senator McClellan.

We looked for people to fit the job. We were not searching for lawyers or policemen (although we accepted both), but rather for men who were alert and intelligent. Men who were willing to work long, tedious hours. We wanted men with experience—but not so experienced that they were cynical; men with initiative and a sense of responsibility; men with curiosity who at the same time were objective, and mature enough to know when and how to keep their business to themselves.

The job of an investigator for the McClellan Committee was never easy. Sometimes it was dangerous.

Joe Maher is a tall fellow with a pleasant way about him. He has had experience with the FBI and served with the Navy during the war. He was decorated for bravery. In 1958 he walked into the Teamsters Building to serve a Committee subpoena on Roland McMasters, one of Mr. Hoffa's chief henchmen in Detroit. McMasters, who stands six foot five and weighs 245 pounds, grabbed Maher by the throat and drove him against a wall.

There were about ten of his Teamster colleagues in the office and they swarmed around the two men, jeering. Joe Maher struggled to edge near the stairway in the building. Suddenly he brought up his elbows and loosened McMasters's grip. Before the Teamster official recovered his balance, Maher was down the stairs and out the door.

Jim McShane is a former police detective from New York. He has been decorated seventeen times for bravery and received the Medal of Honor, the highest award that the Police Department can bestow. He has been in a number of gun battles. He has been shot at, and has himself shot two men.

During the juke-box investigation in 1958, we were trying to subpoena one of the Chicago underworld figures. McShane, through an informant, finally located him. Late one night, he telephoned the gangster's apartment and, disguising his voice, learned that the man we wanted was at home. McShane climbed three flights of stairs and knocked at the apartment door. When it opened he was looking into the muzzle of a gun.

"Take one more step and I'll kill you," the man said.

Beads of perspiration were standing on the racketeer's forehead. His hand was shaking from fright. McShane had his credentials in his hand. He showed them and said, "Put down your gun. I'm here from the Senate Committee."

The man collapsed in a chair. "I thought you were coming to kill me," he said.

LaVern Duffy, not only one of our younger staff members, but one of our three or four best, had been in the Marines, and was badly wounded in the fighting in the Pacific. He was in charge of investigating the dynamitings and violence in Scranton, Pennsylvania.

It was in the early days of the Committee. Several times Duffy answered the telephone and the voice on the other end warned: "You'd better leave Scranton, mister, or we're going to kill you."

Joe Maher subpoenaed Roland McMasters; Jim McShane subpoenaed the witness for our juke-box hearing; LaVern Duffy did not leave Scranton.

We told our men that we expected them to work long hours; that their success in developing cases for presentation before the Committee would depend on their own hard work. When they were in the field they learned that this was no exaggeration. They worked seven days a week, regularly—and at least until eleven o'clock at night. On more than one occasion, investigators worked from twenty-four to thirty-six hours without stopping.

I recognized that this schedule would be a tremendous hardship on our staff members—particularly since all but one had a wife and family. But never in those three years did I receive a single complaint. Once when I was walking down the corridor from a hearing, the wife of one of our men approached and introduced herself. She wanted to know when her husband would be able to come home. She wasn't complaining, she was simply concerned about him.

And it was a matter of concern to me—but I knew and they understood that we had to get the work done, and the greater part of that work was not in our Washington office—it was in cities and towns across the United States. During the course of three years, we traveled more than two million miles on Committee business.

While we expected hard work from these men, their complete devotion to the work was often moving. I am confident that most of them joined us not simply because this was a job (indeed, such men can always find jobs) but because they felt that it was a worth-while cause.

John Bartlow Martin, writing in *The Saturday Evening Post,* had this to say about the staff:

> They have few interests outside their work. They are irreverent, unimpressed with power. They have the moral certitude, the fervor and lust for a better world that goes with youth. . . . These men condemn wrongdoing unequivocally. . . . There is something a little chilling about their moral certitude and zeal.

Not surprisingly, perhaps, some of the people we were investigating were occasionally tempted to test the strength of this zeal. One of our investigators looking into a union in New York was told by the union official that he, the official, would be retiring in a few years, and that he would like to turn over the union to a young, vigorous man like our investigator. He said that between the two of them he felt they could straighten out any improper procedures or practices within the union structure.

On another occasion a company official told one of our accountants that there was a great deal of accounting work to be done for the company and he was looking around for a bright young man to handle it for him.

Max Raddock,[1] the grossly overpaid writer and publisher of a book on William Hutcheson, of the Carpenters Union, told our investigator, Paul Tierney, who was looking into his affairs, that he would like to have Paul come to work for him and write detective stories.

A far more difficult approach to handle is when a company hires a big-name attorney, someone prominent in politics. If the leading Democrat of a state or section of the country comes to your office and says, "You don't want to call this official. I have known him all my life and he is absolutely honest and he's got many, many friends in my section of the country," you know the pressure is there.

But I was only amused when, during 1956, a New York racketeer whom we were investigating hired a Boston lawyer to try to arrange for him not to be called before the Committee. The Boston lawyer, who was a well-known criminal attorney, got in touch with my father, my brother and me to see if something could be worked out. The hearings of the Permanent Subcommittee on Investigations were suspended at that time, before we had heard all the witnesses, so this man's client was not called. I learned indirectly later that word was out in the underworld that hiring this lawyer meant you could "fix" the Committee.

In 1957 we subpoenaed one of the biggest gangsters in New York. He went to Boston for the same lawyer. I suspect to his surprise, and clearly to his displeasure, he was, nevertheless, called as a witness, and took the Fifth Amendment. The records showed that the lawyer was paid $10,000 to represent him. Some of my colleagues remarked on how nervous the lawyer looked, sitting next to this tough, burly killer. Ten thousand dollars was a large sum of money. It was paid to accomplish a certain result, and I am sure it was not paid out lightly. I do not know what finally happened, but I certainly would not have liked to be that attorney.

Early in 1959, when I was in Milwaukee making a speech, I was asked about what pressures we were subjected to, and specifically whether any threats or promises of political support for my brother,

[1] See Chapter 10: Bread and Yachts

Senator John F. Kennedy, had been made in connection with any investigation. I replied that there had been, and that in several instances I felt the offers had been made in a serious vein, although for my part I did not take them seriously. I was asked whether I had reported them to the Committee. I said that I had not; I had never considered them that important, and they had never affected the work of the staff.

My reply caused considerable furor and some criticism. Karl Mundt said this was the most shocking thing that he had ever heard. Although he was inclined to exaggeration, a meeting of the Committee was called to consider what to do with the chief counsel. I enumerated the instances when pressure had been attempted. For example, the time that Abraham Teitelbaum, former attorney for Al Capone, who was involved in the Chicago Restaurant Association, came to see me before he was to be put on the stand and said that he had some very influential friends who would help my brother if I did not call him as a witness. Or the time Eddie Cheyfitz asked me, very possibly in a jocular vein, why I didn't lay off the Teamsters—didn't I know that Jimmy Hoffa could be talked into supporting my brother in 1960? There were quite a few similar incidents. In a number of other cases, the threat or offer was veiled—merely a suggestion. I didn't take any of the proposals seriously, then or ever. I doubt very much if there is a policeman or district attorney in the United States who hasn't been similarly approached. These things go on continuously. You simply go about your work and pay no attention.

The Committee decided, however, that from then on any approach made to a member of the staff should be brought to its attention. My brother and Senator Church suggested that it should also be reported if an approach of this kind was made to any member of the Committee. However, Senator Mundt was against this and it was left that only approaches to the staff were to be reported. Approaches to the Senators were to be kept confidential. There must be a distinction but it was too subtle for me.

The men who work as investigators for Congressional committees generally take it for granted that they can expect little or no support from the members of Congress on whose committees they serve. They feel that the committee members are unwilling to put themselves out

171

on a limb for a staff member; that they consider themselves too busy to be bothered about the plight of an investigator; that they are too interested in their own survival to risk their political futures for his sake.

There is the fear also, based on experience, that if it is politically expedient a member of a committee will use a staff member in a political fight—or misuse the evidence he has gathered in a political way. This, of course, may win a political battle for the Congressman —but it can destroy the staff member. Beyond that is the accepted possibility that a staff member's first mistake may well be his last. Often, they feel, extenuating circumstances or honesty of intent are not taken into account.

These fears are not unjustified. The record will show that, aside from Senator McCarthy—one of whose greatest mistakes was that he was loyal beyond reason to Roy Cohn and G. David Schine—Congressional committee members as a rule have been unwilling to stand up and be counted on behalf of a staff member who meets with difficulties. While this is understood and accepted by the investigator, it puts him under tremendous pressure from the start—aside from whatever strains the job itself may impose. I know a number of bright, energetic, honest investigators who have left Government service bitter and disillusioned after being caught in the middle of a political committee fight.

The result is that the caliber of staff investigators on Capitol Hill is often not of the highest. Added to all else, you have the problem of political appointees whose jobs are based on whom they know, not what they know. You have some men who, aware of the risks of being involved in a controversial subject, figure very early that the way to keep one's job is to do nothing—just keep out of sight and don't stir up anything or anyone. Then you have the crusader who will dynamite everything in sight to get over his point. There is little room left for the professional dedicated public servant.

The fact that we had no interest in the party affiliation of our investigators is, I believe, a main reason we were able to gather a superior staff. Also, if an investigator made an error in judgment, and it was an honest error, he knew he would receive our full support.

In return they gave us their complete and uncompromising loyalty. This combination is unique in the operations of Congressional investigation committees.

The men who came to work for the McClellan Committee came from various walks of life and contributed a wide background of experience. Most of them were young, but they were professionals. Some of them I have already mentioned, like Carmine Bellino, the soft-spoken, kindly veteran accountant who, probably more than any other staff member, was responsible for the over-all success of our work. I dislike singling out one individual from so many who did such outstanding work, but Carmine made a singular contribution. He has a tremendous abundance of a characteristic that is absolutely essential for an investigator—patience. He worked longer hours than anyone on the Committee staff; I doubt that there were fifteen days during the two and a half years, including Saturdays and Sundays, that he left the office before midnight. He is the best investigator-accountant in the United States. This fact is known and recognized by people in the business. He has the greatest knack for knowing when something is wrong, and where the error lies that I have ever seen.

Even those he investigated came reluctantly to respect his ability. During hearings when we were questioning Jimmy Hoffa, and Carmine Bellino would get up to obtain some records, I could see Hoffa's eyes immediately shifting to follow him around the room. Bellino's work was of tremendous concern to him. One time when Hoffa was going through his own records to get a paper, I asked him if he would like Bellino to help him. His reply was quick and to the point. "No, all Bellino does is get me in trouble."

His penetrating brown eyes seem to have an unsettling effect on witnesses. Francis Flanagan, who used to be chief counsel for the Senate Permanent Subcommittee on Investigations, told me a story about an attorney who came in and complained that Bellino was mistreating his client. After a half-hour of talk, Flanagan finally said to him, "Exactly what did he say to your client?" The attorney replied, "It's not what he said, it was the way he was looking at him."

Jerry Adlerman, our assistant chief counsel, was the "old man" of the staff, a short, pleasant-looking man who always seemed to be on a diet. He is an experienced lawyer who has served on the staff of Congressional committees for thirteen years, beginning with the old Senate Investigations committee, and we all leaned heavily on his advice and judgment. Whenever an investigation was exceptionally difficult and needed sound organizational work, Jerry was the one I called on to straighten things out.

The first investigator to join our staff after we became a Select Committee was Pierre Salinger, a former newspaperman who had written many stories on the Teamsters. Inquisitive and indefatigable, he was of great help in getting the Committee started.

Walter Sheridan, a slight, quiet, friendly-faced man, was one of our best and most relentless investigators. His almost angelic appearance hides a core of toughness, and he takes great pride in his work. In any kind of fight, I would always want him on my side.

Walter May, calm and pleasant-looking, had been a Navy pilot during the war, later worked for the FBI and then as circulation manager of a Boston newspaper. His judgment was excellent; I knew that when he said he had the facts he had them. Through patience and persistence, he seemed able to get material from witnesses that would have eluded many others.

Eddie Jones had been with the Crime Commission in New York and had innumerable contacts in law enforcement agencies across the country. He could find out things that no one else could.

Al Calabrese was a big, tough-looking, utterly uncompromising man of about forty who had been captain of football at Catholic University. An outstanding investigator of complete integrity, he was to handle some of our biggest cases.

Paul Tierney, a lawyer in his early forties, was another of our investigators who had been with the FBI. He worked with me on the Senate Permanent Subcommittee on Investigations and was primarily responsible for the investigations of the New York paper locals and the Carpenters Union. He is extremely loyal and hard-working, and his integrity is written across his good-looking face.

John Constandy is a big husky young man who came to the Committee from the District Attorney's office in New York. We had done a considerable amount of work with him when he was in that office and we were all impressed with his intelligence and judgment. He knew the situation in New York as well as anyone in law enforcement. His good judgment and his ability to obtain information from unusual sources made him invaluable.

Arthur Kaplan handled the juke-box and coin-machine investigation in Chicago, where he did an outstanding piece of detective work. He found that the owners had established an association in order to keep a monopoly of operations in the city. Furthermore, he found that the syndicate gangsters had put in a man by the name of Red Waterfall to run the association. Nobody seemed to know who Red Waterfall was, but Kaplan was determined to find out.

Waterfall did not live at the address he gave in his application for office; he did not have the background he gave for telephone service; the banks he gave as a credit reference did not exist. He seemed never to have had a picture taken, and only the most meager description of his physical appearance could be obtained from the operators themselves, who were obviously afraid in any way to point a finger at the man who was extorting thousands of dollars from them.

Nose to the ground, Art followed his trail from Chicago to Miami Beach to Texas to Fort Wayne, Indiana, to Little Rock, Arkansas, to Hollywood, California, to many other places. By tracing hunting licenses in Louisiana, applications for telephones in Chicago, reservations in a Texas hotel, insurance applications for a Chris-Craft cruiser, he finally was able to prove that one Hyman Larner, a prominent, well-dressed, sophisticated businessman in Chicago and Miami Beach, was also Red Waterfall—a long-time henchman of Dutch Vogel, Al Capone's associate and the undisputed boss of gambling in Chicago and the outlying areas.

Kenny O'Donnell, an old friend who was football captain at Harvard, and who had been wounded during the war, joined the Committee as administrative assistant, and helped co-ordinate the work of the staff in the field.

Kenny has the best memory of anyone I know. He remembers names and details with fabulous accuracy. While reviewing telephone toll tickets in the middle of 1958 he might spot a number and come into my office and say that he remembered that the same number had been called by a gangster in the middle of 1957. As he read the memos of all the investigators, he was often invaluable in piecing together the work that Eddie Jones, for instance, was doing in Chicago with work that Ralph Mills was doing in Miami. The significance of the fact that calls were being made from Detroit and Cleveland to the same barbershop in Miami, Florida, could only be realized if Kenny O'Donnell was able to correlate the information when it was reported in memos that came across his desk.

We hired three former policemen from New York. Two of them, Jim Kelly and Sherm Willse, having worked as special agents in the Narcotics Bureau, had an invaluable backlog of experience investigating people in whom we were to become interested. The third was Jim McShane, one episode in whose career as a Senate investigator I described earlier.

A few of the men we employed were lawyers; two of them were accountants. Two others, George Martin and Ralph Mills, had done some work with the Kefauver Crime Committee.

As for me, I had gone into Government work by way of the Justice Department, which I entered directly from law school. After an interval in 1952 during which I handled my brother's senatorial campaign against Henry Cabot Lodge, I returned to Washington and went to work for Francis Flanagan, a former FBI man who was then general counsel for the Senate Permanent Subcommittee on Investigations. About the same time Senator McCarthy, who was chairman of the Committee, hired Roy Cohn as chief counsel. It was a confusing situation, with three of us working for Flanagan and all the rest of the staff working for Cohn. When Cohn took complete charge of the staff in June, 1953, I left.

I told McCarthy that I disagreed with the way the Committee was being run, except for the work that Flanagan had done, and that the way they were proceeding I thought it was headed for disaster.

In February, 1954, after about eight months with the Hoover Commission, I returned as minority counsel of the Committee at the request of the Democratic members. Most of that year was devoted to the Army-McCarthy hearings, and when the Democrats took control of the Senate in January, 1955, I became chief counsel. Two years later, as I have explained, the Select Committee was set up and the investigative and clerical staff expanded.

It made a major difference in the effectiveness of our work that we all got along well. Often on Saturday afternoons and Sundays we would meet at my home ten miles outside Washington; investigators who were working on the same case in various cities would be called in and we would review their material together. During a hearing the men whose cases were being presented frequently came out to the house for dinner, to relax and discuss the hearings that were to follow. And once a year at Christmastime we had a meeting of the entire staff and office force.

During the whole life of the Committee the advice and help that J. Edgar Hoover gave to me personally and to the Committee were absolutely invaluable. We also received generous assistance from Harry J. Anslinger, Commissioner of the Bureau of Narcotics, as well as from Joseph Campbell, the Comptroller General of the United States, who at the outset made available ten accountants from the General Accounting Office; as the workload increased, we eventually drew altogether forty-five of his men. They played key roles in some of our major investigations.

Most of the cases in 1957 I was able to supervise myself, discussing interviews and procedure with the investigators, either in person or by telephone. Whenever I possibly could, I worked with the staff in the field.

At the beginning, a new staff member would be sent out with Al Calabrese or Paul Tierney or any one of the investigators we had acquired from the Permanent Subcommittee. After he had seen how an investigation was run and how a hearing was conducted, he was sent out on his own.

By the end of 1957 we had offices in eight cities and about fifteen major investigations going at once. By 1958 our work had evolved into a systematic operation. New investigators were now ready to handle cases, in whole or in part, on their own. They knew what was needed and the degree of proof that was demanded, when an investigation would be finished and the case ready for hearings, whether a case

177

was worth pursuing or whether they would do better to look into something else. They had little or no direct supervision—they were on their own.

If a crucial point arose or if they felt there might be some trouble, we would talk. When Duffy and McShane were in Chattanooga looking into the affairs of a judge, word spread that if they persisted, the judge would have them arrested and thrown in jail. Duffy and I consulted. They continued to investigate the judge and managed to stay out of jail. Except for such problems as this, I might not hear personally from investigators for perhaps as long as a month. They simply went ahead conducting their interviews, getting their material, examining their documents, until they were ready to prepare for public hearings.

Investigations for the most part were made up of countless interviews, detailed reviewing of hundreds of thousands of checks, bank statements and financial records, careful scrutiny of thousands upon thousands of telephone toll tickets, hotel and plane reservations.

Let us say, for instance, that A is under investigation. He telephones long distance to B. We subpoena B's telephone toll tickets. Immediately after the telephone call from A, B called C. In a complex investigation, the information gained by following this trail can bring a major break in the case.

Or take another example. Employer A goes to New York City. We know that, because examining his bank account we find a check made out to the Biltmore Hotel in New York. We go to that hotel and subpoena his records during his stay. We find from an examination of his account that he paid the bill of Y who was in the hotel at the same time. We subpoena Y's records. He is a union official, heading a union which has a contract with A, the employer. This is suspicious, but perhaps there is an explanation. Did Y repay A? Was it by cash or by check? Is this the only transaction between them? Examine this contract. Is it a sweetheart? If it's a good contract, is it being enforced? If it's not being enforced, whom can we get to testify to that fact? *All* these leads must be run down.

This is why every case took so much time from the moment it came to the Committee as a lead until it was ready for open hearings. When the public read about a hearing or a gangster's taking the Fifth Amendment, all they were getting was the last chapter. It is difficult to realize the amount of work and sweat that had gone into the case, how many dead ends and heartbreaks we had before we were able to put the puzzle together.

One telephone call busted the Carpenters case wide open. One check and a telephone call set off our investigation of Hoffa's fraudulent land scheme at Sun Valley, Florida. It was slow, tedious, boring work that took months and months of an investigator's time, but the results made it well worth while. Documents make the difference in a case. A witness can change his story or lie. A document never does.

The Akros Dynamics case was a prime example of how a study of bank records, plane and hotel reservations, and toll tickets paid off, leading to evidence that the Teamsters Union was prepared to give financial support to an airplane company involved in smuggling arms to the Dominican Republic. The same records proved that Jimmy Hoffa was personally concerned in the deal.

A counsel's examination of witnesses has been vastly overromanticized by a movie-conditioned public, but we could sometimes persuade a balky witness to tell the truth by sheer persistence. The Akros Dynamics case afforded one such occasion when I was questioning Alvin Naiman, who was the "key" figure in that investigation.

He had privately admitted to me in my office that at the request of Hoffa's Detroit lieutenant, Babe Triscaro, who was also involved in the deal, and in order to protect him, he had predated a certain check to make it appear that it had been written several weeks earlier than it actually had been. This was a crucial point. However, when he testified before the Committee he took a different position.

MR. KENNEDY: But isn't it correct, Mr. Naiman, that you dated the check June 1, at the request of Mr. Triscaro?
MR. NAIMAN: No, he never requested that; no, sir.
MR. KENNEDY: Didn't you have conversations along those lines?
MR. NAIMAN: Only along the lines to be sure that no expenses incurred by him should be paid by him on my behalf.
MR. KENNEDY: Isn't it correct that after you met with me in New York, that you had a conversation with him and he suggested or requested that you date the check back to June 1?
MR. NAIMAN: He never made no statement like that, sir.
MR. KENNEDY: Why would you take a check that you would write on

179

June 20th or any date thereafter and date it June 1st? What would be the reason for it?

MR. NAIMAN: It could be that maybe I was holding it in my pocket for a while, too.

MR. KENNEDY: You said you didn't make it out until a week ago.

MR. NAIMAN: No, I said I gave it to him a week ago.

MR. KENNEDY: Mr. Naiman, didn't you tell me downstairs just several hours ago that the reason you dated it June 1st was because of the request of Mr. Triscaro?

MR. NAIMAN: I wouldn't say that.

MR. KENNEDY: Didn't you state that down in the office?

MR. NAIMAN: No. You asked me that.

MR. KENNEDY: And didn't you say, "Yes"?

MR. NAIMAN: No, sir.

MR. KENNEDY: Mr. Naiman.

MR. NAIMAN: No, I didn't.

MR. KENNEDY: What did you say, then?

MR. NAIMAN: I didn't answer that.

MR. KENNEDY: Mr. Naiman?

MR. NAIMAN: I didn't answer.

MR. KENNEDY: What?

MR. NAIMAN: I didn't answer that question.

MR. KENNEDY: You didn't answer it?

MR. NAIMAN: No, sir.

MR. KENNEDY: And I let it go?

MR. NAIMAN: No. You kept insisting that he had asked me to date it June 1st. But he never did ask me.

MR. KENNEDY: Did you deny it?

MR. NAIMAN: I didn't deny it and I didn't affirm it.

MR. KENNEDY: Didn't you say "yes," Mr. Naiman?

MR. KENNEDY: Mr. Naiman, didn't you say "yes"?

MR. NAIMAN: No, I didn't.

MR. KENNEDY: Mr. Naiman, didn't you say "yes" to me when I asked you that? You are under oath.

MR. NAIMAN: I can honestly say—

MR. KENNEDY: You are under oath now, Mr. Naiman. Didn't you say "yes" to that when I asked you that down in the office less than two hours ago?

Mr. Naiman hesitated for a long moment, looked off into space in an agony of indecision. Then—

MR. NAIMAN: I did say that.

With that answer I felt as if a tremendous weight had been lifted from me.

Sometimes, too, witnesses trap themselves, and I recall one time when it gave me great pleasure to watch one do so. This was during the 1959 hearings when we were discussing with Hoffa his proposed alliance with Harry Bridges, whose West Coast Longshoremen's Union had been expelled from organized labor for following the Communist line.

I was reading out loud excerpts from the Teamster magazine editorials which attacked Communist infiltration of the labor movement. Hoffa wanted to know who had signed them, and I told him Dave Beck. Hoffa scoffed. "That answers it," he sneered.

Then I read another excerpt: " 'If Communist unions ever gain a position to exercise influence in the transport lanes of the world, the free world will have suffered a staggering blow.' Who do you think wrote that?"

"I am not interested in politics and philosophy," Hoffa said, "I am interested in workers."

"Do you agree?" I asked.

"No," said Hoffa, "I don't agree."

"Do you know who made that statement?"

"I don't know," Hoffa said. And then he added contemptuously, "Probably Beck. It sounds like him."

"Mr. James Riddle Hoffa," I told him.

Hoffa nearly tore the roof off the ceiling. "Let me see it," he shouted. "Don't read it out of context. Let me read it. I know what I write and what I don't."

But to have the facts to do this kind of questioning takes hard investigative work.

For every witness who was called before the Committee we interviewed at least thirty-five. For every hour a witness testified on the stand before the Committee, he was interviewed on the average of five hours. For every document that was introduced, five thousand were studied. For every hearing held, there were approximately eight months of intensive investigation, with two investigators from the staff and six accountants from the General Accounting Office.

Sometimes an alert and persevering investigator can develop a case from the most unlikely clue. Walter Sheridan, for example, during the course of his work on Hoffa's strong-arm man, Barney Baker, ran across a harmless-looking staff memorandum in our files. It was a complaint by a driver for "State Cab Company" of Indianapolis, which we had found to involve only a practical joke played on the cab driver by a relative.

In reviewing this "closed case," Sheridan noticed that the memo mentioned that David Probstein, a lawyer and owner of the cab company, had disappeared. His curiosity aroused, Walt investigated further and learned that just before Probstein's disappearance he had talked to a friend, who described him to Walt as a "scared man," and had told him that "he was in great danger and that he had become involved with some people he considered dangerous and that he was going away on a mission he considered dangerous." More curious than ever, Walt Sheridan called on Probstein's wife. She said that following her husband's conversation with his friend she had driven him to the train. The next night he had telephoned her from St. Louis and said he was driving East with some companions. It was the last time she had heard his voice.

Mrs. Probstein supplied Sheridan with a list of long-distance calls Probstein had made shortly before his disappearance—and here Sheridan's curiosity paid off. For David Probstein had telephoned James Hoffa in Detroit on April 29 and again three days later. On May 3 he telephoned a lawyer associated with Allen Dorfman in Chicago. Three days later he telephoned Jimmy Hoffa's accountant. He also called accountants for Hoffa's firm, Hobren, on two different occasions.

David Probstein, missing person, suddenly became of tremendous interest to our Senate Committee, and we launched a full-scale investigation. We wanted to know how a man in such financial straits as Probstein was reported to be in could afford to start a cab company.

As Sheridan kept digging around, we finally learned that Jimmy Hoffa, through the Hoffa and Brennan owned firm of Hobren Corporation, was the money behind David Probstein and the State Cab Company. The proof was two checks for $10,000 each and another for $8,000 issued by Hobren Corporation and endorsed by Probstein. We learned in addition that Probstein wasn't permitted to keep his cab company for long. Two of Hoffa's henchmen stepped in to take over its operation—and Barney Baker was also in Indianapolis about that time. According to the testimony of Barney's wife, Mollie, he had told her that he had to go to Indianapolis "to take care of a shyster lawyer for Jimmy Hoffa." (Baker denied ever saying this.)

Shortly afterward Probstein disappeared.

When Jimmy Hoffa took the witness stand, I asked him about his relationship with Probstein. He said he had loaned him $8,000, of which Probstein had repaid $7,000. I asked: "Did you have any interests in any of his financial affairs?"

In the light of the two checks for $10,000 apiece, I was shocked to hear him say no. He had had nothing further to do with Probstein, he said. This, of course, couldn't be true, and the record was sent to the Justice Department for perjury action.

There the matter rests, and although we fitted almost all the bits of the puzzle together, one piece is still missing—David Probstein.

Good leads, as I mentioned earlier, can come from anywhere. A Senator once told me that when he received an unsigned letter of complaint he automatically threw it into the wastepaper basket; if a person didn't have the nerve to sign his name, he said, his letter wasn't worth considering.

My experience has been quite to the contrary. A number of very important and interesting leads came to the attention of the Committee through anonymous letters. And some of them developed into cases. I found that unsigned letters often came either from people afraid to sign their names or from people who, dreading embarrassment, did not want to become personally involved. The mortgage fraud that ultimately toppled Dave Beck from power was first outlined by an anonymous correspondent; and our investigation of the Textile Workers Union was set in motion by an anonymous letter. So was the investigation that revealed that the Detroit *Times* was keeping a union official on its payroll in order to avoid labor trouble.

Sometimes the leads we received were as fruitless as they were promising. At one time, for instance, Jim McShane and I visited a prisoner in Joliet in connection with our juke-box investigation. He told us that he had participated in the shooting of a local newspaper-woman who had been opposing the activities of certain racketeers in the Joliet area. He said that they had buried her in lime in a field some miles away.

I arranged with Warden Regen for the prisoner to be released temporarily; then, taking some picks and shovels, we drove to the field. He told us where to dig and we dug. The farmer who owned the field came out from his house and our prisoner friend warned us to be careful, because the farmer knew about the murder. When the farmer asked what we were doing, Jim McShane, ever resourceful, implied we were from the State of Illinois, and hinted we were looking for a special kind of rare metal. After we had dug in vain for some time, the prisoner took us to another spot and said, "She is definitely buried here."

I was tired of digging. He swore he was telling the truth and blurted out this quaint oath: "May I have syphilis of the eyes, and may my mother be a whore, if she isn't buried here." I know little about the man's mother or his eyes, but Jim McShane and I both know, after hours of digging, that the woman's body was not there.

At this juncture, the farmer came out again, this time with three very husky-looking sons, so we took off across the fields.

In another city where we had found large numbers of the Teamster records missing, our method of investigation involved unusual cruelty to an innocent person. A soldier reported to his commanding officer that he had been out with the maid of the wife of a former Teamster official and that she had boxes of records hidden under her bed. We got in touch with the soldier and asked if he would do his duty and take the maid out again and see what more he could learn about the records. He explained to us that though he would be willing, he would be making a great sacrifice, for he had found upon reflection that the maid was quite ugly.

A double date was eventually arranged. Our investigator was invited to the house where the records supposedly were hidden. The maid drank too much, our investigator crawled under the bed—no records.

On another occasion we learned more than we cared to know about a man's "private" life. Having received information that a trucking company executive was making pay-offs to certain of the Teamster hierarchy, I sent two investigators to review the firm's records. They examined over 200,000 checks covering a two-year period before they came upon some $35,000 made out to cash, with no supporting vouchers.

When interviewed, the president of the company said that in violation of the ICC regulations, he had bought another trucking company and had disguised the transaction so that the ICC agents would not discover it. Upon investigation, we found that while he had, in fact, bought the other trucking company, he could not have used the cash in question for that purpose.

The next day he came back, saying he wanted to make a clean breast of it, and made an appointment to meet our investigator in his hotel room that evening. He arrived with a young lady whom he introduced as his mistress. He was a married man, he said, and had used the unaccounted-for money to keep this lady in coats, jewelry and other luxuries. His mistress confirmed the story.

Finding us, to his surprise, still skeptical and still inquisitive—for his confession by no means accounted for all the money—he came up with another admission: He had used the money to obtain abortions for two other girl friends of his. He offered to bring in these ladies for an interview. Our investigator said this was not necessary, and we found upon checking that the man had been telling the truth. Further, we found that this respectable business executive had established a charge account with a considerable retainer in a house of prostitution for his various clients. We decided we had had enough. We took an affidavit from him encompassing the above facts, and attesting that he had paid no money to any union officials, and left town.

Inevitably, we all made mistakes—sometimes during an investigation, sometimes in evaluating evidence, sometimes in the conduct of a hearing. During one of the Hoffa hearings I made a mistake in connection with seating arrangements that had unfortunate consequences. I let Hoffa sit directly behind a witness whose testimony he knew could hurt him.

The witness was a former boxer named Embrel Davidson, in whom Hoffa, at a previous hearing, had admitted having once had a financial interest. At the same time he had sworn that no Teamster money had been used in connection with Davidson's career.

Davidson, a bright, alert young man with one of the nicest, widest smiles I ever saw, had not wanted to talk when our investigator, Jim Kelly, finally traced him to Youngstown, Ohio. He had a job, he had recently become engaged, he was enjoying life, and he was not anxious to tangle with Jimmy Hoffa.

"That little man is mean," he said earnestly to Kelly. "I don't want any of his people coming after me, for I'll wind up in the bottom of the river wearing concrete boots."

But Jim Kelly is a convincing man, and Davidson finally talked. Contrary to what Hoffa had previously told the Committee, Davidson said he had indeed been supported by Teamster money while fighting under Hoffa's (and Brennan's) management; in fact, he had been on the Teamster welfare fund payroll as an investigator at $75 a week, though doing no union work. And Hoffa, he said, had known of the arrangement. If this was true Hoffa had committed perjury before the Committee.

But when Davidson testified, he said nothing at all about this. Later in my office, I asked him why. He told me frankly that he'd been afraid to. As he had entered the Senate chamber he had seen Hoffa, and all the way across the room Hoffa had stared at him. When he was called to testify, Hoffa turned to his lawyer and swore. Throughout his testimony Hoffa, sitting directly in back of him, had continuously emitted a low cough. This had upset him and he just didn't want to talk about his former manager.

Later, Davidson made amends by sending the Committee a sworn affidavit stating that he had been on the Teamster payroll with Hoffa's knowledge—but I never again allowed Jimmy Hoffa to sit behind the witness chair.

As I hope I have made clear, our investigation had its moments of disappointment as well as triumph. It also had moments of tragedy. There was the day a man who had been called before the Committee walked into the office accompanied by his son-in-law and his attorney. At her desk just inside the door, Lena Heck, a stenographer who had been with the Committee for only a week, was busily pounding away at her typewriter. As she looked up, she saw the man apparently trip. He fell forward over the top of her desk, then slipped to the floor, dead from a heart attack.

Fortunately, our work was not without its lighter moments. There is an office building on Fourteenth Street in New York City whose tenants include a number of labor unions. Knowing that some of these unions were under investigation, and suspecting that perhaps the building was owned by a racketeer or perhaps even by "The Mob," Walter May, Paul Tierney and Bellino checked the records. They were shocked to learn who owned the building.

It was my family.

When the subpoena was served on the superintendent, he looked at the document and said, "I take my orders from the father, not the boys."

The serving of subpoenas was a problem that frequently challenged the ingenuity of the staff. One of our investigators, Count Langenbacher, after a succession of unrewarding tries, finally had to disguise himself as a postman in order to subpoena a particularly elusive and notorious character in Detroit.

Sometimes, when gangsters involved in labor racketeering were avoiding subpoenas, we served their wives or associates. On a number of occasions, this produced the gangster himself.

The wife of a man we were searching for in the Johnny Dio case in New York said she had no idea where her husband had gone, he had just disappeared. We subpoenaed her telephone toll tickets and found that she frequently called a particular apartment in another city. We staked out the apartment and several days later out of the door came her husband.

It always interested me that some of the most hardened criminals whom we investigated appeared to have no personal animosity toward

187

what we were doing. Dick Kaminetsky is a notorious gangster in New York, and one of Tony Ducks Corallo's chief lieutenants. Although he was not a union official, we knew that he was in charge of the affairs of certain Teamster locals in the New York area. An investigator of the District Attorney's office finally located him and, although he insisted that he was not Kaminetsky, subpoenaed him. During the hearings, however, we found time would not permit our calling him as a witness, so Walter May telephoned him to tell him that his appearance was being postponed. Kaminetsky told May he had been watching the hearing on television. As May recounted it, he said: "You fellows are doing a wonderful job down there. It's very exciting and I'm sorry I can't be a part of it. If you ever want me let me know." He was very cheerful. May and I were somewhat taken aback.

Then there was a well-known burglar who broke into a union headquarters in Detroit. He was caught, and the union officials, thinking he was a representative of the Committee sent to steal their records, hung him upside down outside the tenth-floor window and questioned him for three hours; then they turned him over to the police. The police captain who went to pick him up told me this man actually ran to him yelling: "Tell them I'm a thief—I've been a thief for twenty years—and I have nothing to do with that Senate Committee!"

I also like to remember the witness in New York who, ordered by subpoena to appear at once in Washington, answered: "I can't go down there today. I've got to wash the dog."

And our work had its leveling influences. One day I received a letter from a young lady who spent seven paragraphs praising the work of the Committee. I was greatly enjoying reading the letter until I reached the eighth paragraph, when she said she had been watching the hearings on television and the only trouble was she didn't understand any of my questions. She went on to say, however, that she didn't feel badly about it, for she could see that the witnesses didn't seem to understand them either.

On another occasion, I was having breakfast in Detroit when a gentleman came up to me and told me what a wonderful job I was doing. I bowed my head modestly and then he said, "I want to shake your hand. It's the first time I've shaken the hand of a United States

Senator." After I recovered he said, "Senator Kennedy, there's one thing that puzzles me. That fellow who sits next to you, the counsel of the Committee, do you know he looks exactly like you!"

Finally—I was going into New York from La Guardia Airport when the cab driver turned around and said, "I know who you are. Now, let me see—" He thought for five minutes or so and just as he was about to let me out he said, "I know who you are—you're Roy Cohn!" I felt I had arrived in more ways than one.

Chapter 10 / BREAD AND YACHTS

1. BAKERS

IN OCTOBER, 1956, I was traveling with Adlai Stevenson during his campaign for the presidency. While he was in San Francisco, he was invited to address the International convention of the Bakery and Confectionery Workers Union.

This union, founded in 1886, had a rich and deep heritage in the trade union movement of this country. It was a relatively small organization in 1956 with only 150,000 members and 319 local unions. But over the years we have depended on its members to supply our daily bread and, incidentally, our cakes, pies, cookies, candy and ice cream.

I recall that when the invitation from the Bakers Union convention came to Governor Stevenson, there was some discussion among his advisers about whether he should accept, for it was common knowledge that the union was in the throes of a bitter intra-union squabble. He did accept, however, and I went with him to the hall.

James G. Cross, the president of the International Union, presided at the session we attended. Although I did not realize it then, Cross during that convention destroyed some of the last vestiges of democracy within his labor organization. He instigated major and vital changes in the union's constitution, changes that were designed to give him dictatorial power.

I learned about this just four months later, in February, when Curtis Sims, the International Union's secretary-treasurer, came to my office in Washington to tell me Cross had stamped out democratic procedures in the union and that an investigation would show vast misuses of union funds by Cross and International Vice President George Stuart.

We were caught up at the time in a number of other investigations. But such charges coming from the Bakers Union International secretary-treasurer demanded attention. I told Curtis Sims I would assign investigators at once to look into it.

Shortly after our talk, reports that we were going to investigate the Bakers Union appeared in the newspapers. I was irritated because it looked as if Sims might be attempting to use the Committee and the publicity of an investigation in an intra-union fight with Cross. I was prepared to call off the investigation, and telephoned Sims and told him so. He came to see me with his attorney, Henry Kaiser, a straightforward, honest lawyer. They assured me that Sims was against Cross only because of what Cross had done to the union. It was no petty union jealousy, Sims said. We ironed out the misunderstanding.

I assigned George Kopecky, a former FBI man and one of our accountant-investigators, to the case. Basing our work on information Sims supplied, we made immediate progress. Kopecky found that Cross, during that 1956 convention, had moved in a number of directions to seize dictatorial control of his union.

1. Formerly International officers had been elected by secret ballot of the entire membership of the union. Now Cross arranged for them to be elected on the convention floor by the delegates.

2. Cross did away with *Robert's Rules of Order* to settle questions before the convention. He told the delegates: "Parliamentary procedure was made for Senators, not for bakers."

3. Formerly the local unions received a complete report every three months on the International Union's finances. Now they would receive only a summary report once every six months.

4. Formerly the money of the International Union had been deposited only in banks approved by the executive board. Now President Cross was to decide where the union funds would be deposited.

5. Cross was given power to select and remove all International representatives of the union.

6. Formerly the salaries of the president and the secretary-treasurer —Cross and Curtis Sims—had been set by the full convention. Now the salaries of these two chief executives were to be set by the union's executive board.

Immediately after the convention a special meeting of the executive board was held and Cross's salary was increased from $17,500 to $30,000. Sims was given a pay boost from $15,000 to $22,500. Cross reciprocated by instituting pay raises for the board and all International organizers, whose salaries he, in turn, determined.

One Friday afternoon in the spring of 1957, I boarded a plane for Florida, sat down, opened a manila envelope and began going over the memoranda George Kopecky had prepared on the Bakers and Cross. I had not noticed the gentleman sitting next to me, but apparently he had been looking over my shoulder, for he announced: "You had better understand something. I am James Cross."

Most of that flight to Florida was spent conducting a preliminary interview with Mr. Cross based on the information Kopecky had developed.

The story of corruption in the Bakers Union is basically the story of this one man, Jimmy Cross, whose ability and initiative were quickly recognized by his union. But by the time he became International Union president in 1952, he was closer to the executives and officials of the companies that employed his union men than he was to his own membership. His initiative and ingenuity had deteriorated. He had developed rich tastes.

Prior to our investigation he had reported to the NLRB that his total compensation in 1956 was $17,500. The Committee showed that this figure was short of the truth by some $40,000. At least $25,000 went for entertainment, dinners, birthday parties and personal expenses—all union business, he said, but there were no vouchers to show it. On an eleven-day jaunt to New York he once spent $4,000 of Bakers Union money. A six-day trip to Miami cost the union $3,890—not including $1,079 he charged the union for driving his automobile from Washington to his home in West Palm Beach. In 1956 he and his wife and daughter went to Paris and London, an outing that cost the union $4,200. He spent $962 in two days on a trip to Portland, Oregon. A second visit to Florida in early 1957 set the union back $4,431, of which $331 went to provide a hotel room for Miss Kay Lower, his girl friend. But this $331 was only a drop in the bucket of union money that was poured out for this woman; the total amount we ultimately traced was approximately $10,000. Miss Lower, pretty, slim, brunette, had a long police record which included charges of grand theft, residing in a house of ill fame, drunken driving and offering, but she had never been convicted.

When it became obvious that the evidence warranted hearings on Cross and his union, I spoke to him and his attorney about the problem Miss Lower presented. I explained that I had no wish to go into Cross's relationship with Miss Lower if it could be avoided. I felt that his personal life was his business—except when it involved union funds. It had been our policy to avoid such situations, where possible, simply by acquiring during the hearing an admission from the union official involved that the union funds had been used improperly on "personal expenditures." This made the record clear that a misuse of funds had occurred and obviated the necessity of revealing a personal scandal.

When I suggested this to Cross, he insisted that Miss Lower was an organizer for his union and that there was nothing improper at all. Thus we had no choice but to go into the situation. We found that, at his instructions, Miss Lower had been placed on the payroll of Local 37 in California, from which she had received approximately $1,000. Cross said this was for work she had done while the union was organizing Vandekamp Bakery.

We asked Albert Barker, manager of the offices of Local 37 at the time she was on the payroll, what she did to earn the $1,000.

MR. KENNEDY: Did you ever know of any work that she did for the union?
MR. BARKER: No, sir, I did not.

Miss Lower took the Fifth Amendment on most questions. She did tell us about her work in organizing the bakery. She visited the place once or twice, she said, and talked with the head baker, whom she described as "a very good friend of mine."

I asked: "Can you give us his name?"

Miss Lower: "I can't even remember. He is a Mexican fellow. He is married to a woman named Margie. That is all."

Cross, we found, maintained almost constant contact with Kay Lower by long-distance telephone. These calls cost the union $2,500.

When we raised this matter, Cross told us that he had reimbursed the union with his personal check for $2,500. But why in the world, the Committee wanted to know, would he reimburse the union if this woman actually was a legitimate union organizer?

In martyred tones, he answered: "The daily newspapers had already smeared me with a relationship which was not true. Rather than have the organization exposed, I remained silent, took the blame and returned the check."

Cross also found it necessary to confer with her frequently in person. These conferences took place in hotels all across the country, and always at union expense.

But the most serious situation we found in our investigation of the Bakers Union concerned the relationship between Cross and certain employers. Specifically, the Committee looked into loans of $113,600 which he had received through the family of Martin Philipsborn, who owned a major financial interest in Zion Industries, Inc., a company with which the Bakers Union had contracts.

Cross, the Committee found, had borrowed $57,600 from the Philipsborns to buy a Washington home, $40,000 to buy his home in West Palm Beach, and $16,000 to buy a home in Chicago. He claimed the elder Philipsborn loaned him money because of a "paternal fondness." But the company in which the Philipsborn family had big-money interests got major contractual concessions through Cross and without any approval from local union officials.

George Stuart, an International vice president, also figured in our investigation. He called on a number of local unions to contribute $500 a week to what was to be a "quiet campaign" to organize the Salerno Biscuit Company of Chicago. It was such a "quiet campaign" that nobody ever knew anything about it and the money ended up in the personal savings account of George Stuart. We found he charged the union for such expensive gifts as earrings, an air conditioner, a necklace and other items, including $7,500 worth of camera equipment. When he appeared before the Committee, he took the Fifth Amendment. He later was indicted and convicted of embezzlement in Chicago.

Cross did not seize dictatorial control without a struggle from courageous men inside his union. Curtis Sims was one. Another was husky, plain-spoken Joseph Kane, the fearless president of Local 525 in New York. At the 1956 convention, Kane stood up and fought.

One morning during the convention, Kane told us, he was visited in his hotel room by a delegation composed of President Cross, Vice President Stuart, and two of their supporters. Stuart, he said, had a pistol. Kane was helpless against such odds. They beat him, then marched him at gunpoint to the rooms of other foes of Cross, who also were beaten.

On the witness stand, Cross denied that he took part in these beatings. "I was asleep in my room," he said. He was indicted for perjury. The judge dismissed the case on the ground that there was not a legislative intent in questions concerning the attacks.

The San Francisco County grand jury in San Francisco investigated the beatings. It returned no indictments, but issued a report that said: "We were of the opinion that Cross, contrary to his statement, was in Kane's hotel room when the argument and beating took place."

Curtis Sims brought union charges against Cross for the collusive deals with Philipsborn; the use of union funds for a prostitute; the activities of Vice President Stuart and the beatings in San Francisco.

The executive board heard the charges and cleared Stuart and Cross. It suspended Sims on the grounds that he had preferred charges in bad faith; had used the public press to air intra-union matters; and had put the board to the unnecessary expense of a special meeting.

Actually the board had made up its mind before a hearing was ever held. The document that suspended him was originally typed on March 6, 1957—the day before the board heard the case and "decided." The date, "March 6," was inked over so as to read "March 8," the date of his formal suspension.

The AFL-CIO ousted Cross and his union from the legitimate body. Curtis Sims and others who opposed Cross headed a new union chartered by the AFL-CIO. As of this writing in the fall of 1959, Sims's union has some 90,000 of the 150,000 Bakers Union members. The new group constantly is winning out in elections across the country.

In 1958 I again had occasion to fly to Florida from Washington. Most improbably, there on the plane was James Cross. This time we did not sit side by side or talk.

At the airport he was met by a red-haired woman who drove off with him in a flashy automobile. I checked the license plate. It was owned by a Washington, D.C., rental agency—and all the bills for the car were being paid by the rank-and-file members of James Cross's ousted Bakers Union.

2. OPERATING ENGINEERS

When a labor union has a history of corrupt leadership at the International level stretching back over a quarter of a century, it is no simple matter to clean up. For a rank-and-file member who tries, it can be a frustrating, frightening, life-or-death struggle. It was just that for Roy Underwood, of Philadelphia, a member of Local 542 of the Operating Engineers.

He became a friend of mine. I first met him when we were preparing our case on the Operating Engineers. He came to my office in Washington and we sat and talked about the long campaign he and his friends had waged against the leadership of his union. He was a big man with a round, pleasant, intelligent face, deeply devoted to his union and ashamed of what men like International President William E. Maloney and the notorious Joey Fay had done to ruin its reputation.

His Philadelphia local had been placed under trusteeship in the 1930's. For many years it was part of the territorial dictatorship of racketeer-labor leader, Joey Fay. Fay had as his main base of operations Local 825 in New Jersey, but from there he exerted wide influence over many locals in the New Jersey–New York–Philadelphia area. He went to Sing Sing for extortion in 1947. His conviction grew out of charges that he had taken more than $700,000 in shakedowns from employers.

Roy Underwood told me something of Joey Fay's reign. Membership meetings were rare in those days, and when Fay held them he permitted no objections from the rank and file about the way the union was being run. He shouted down questions and had strong-arm men on hand to back him up. A special 3 per cent assessment was levied on the salaries of members, and it went into the pockets of union officials, not into the treasury. Sweetheart contracts were the rule. But in 1948, with Fay behind prison bars, Roy Underwood formed a "committee of liberation" which succeeded in obtaining the release of his local from International trusteeship.

Underwood told me that when the trusteeship ended he found most of the local's records had been destroyed. There was no evidence of how the union's money had been misused. Before he and his supporters could take control, they were required to pledge that no charges would be brought against any preceding union leader. From 1948 until 1952 they built up the union treasury; there were regular meetings of members; contracts were enforced as they were written.

But in making employers abide by written contracts Roy Underwood ran into trouble. Powerful contractor-employers had strings tied to International President William E. Maloney. They let Maloney know of their displeasure with Underwood. And when the strings were pulled, Maloney moved. In 1952 he clapped the local back into trusteeship. Under the union's constitution Underwood and his friends were helpless. When they opposed Maloney's action, in came the strong-arm boys to crack them into line.

We heard testimony about Ray Dawson, a friend of Roy Underwood:

"There were several who would gang around him and surround him while the ones on the inside would beat him and get down on the floor and put their feet on him. . . . He seemed to be very badly beaten. He was covered with blood. . . ."

Then there was T. C. McCarthy, who spoke out in favor of barring all nonmembers from the meeting. He was escorted onto the elevator by a dozen strangers, and while the elevator went up and down they beat and kicked him into a bleeding hulk. Some of his attackers were prosecuted, convicted—and fined $200. The union paid all their expenses.

Sam Morris, an elderly man, was another who was backing Underwood. He was slugged and his jaw is wired together today as a result of the blow.

It became very difficult for Underwood's backers to get jobs. Many of them had to move away from Philadelphia to find employment.

After our 1958 hearings I hoped that Roy and his friends would be able to get for their union the decency they deserved. But there was prolonged litigation. The courts, though they ruled in Underwood's favor, were of little help. Legal proceedings are expensive and justice moves slowly sometimes; always some legal technicality held things up. Finally Roy Underwood lost hope.

On the morning of April 3, 1959 he told his son: "Never get in a fight with the rackets. You can't win." It was the last advice he ever gave the boy. He sat down and wrote his wife a letter, then walked out to his garage. They found his body a short time later. The gun was nearby.

I feel that we failed Roy Underwood. He was a man of rare courage. But corruption in his union was an overwhelming thing. It is not true that he cared too much about what happened to his union. The truth is that others cared too little.

There were reports that Joey Fay, even after he went to Sing Sing, remained the dominant figure—the man to see—in the Operating Engineers. If this is not true, it should have been. For the union continued to pay him—although his membership was revoked when he was convicted. From the time he was imprisoned until his release in 1956, his wife received $67,800. What did she do to earn it? Joey Fay appeared before the Committee and told us: "She was always ready and willing to do whatever the President . . . asked her to do in visiting the sick and doing things she had done all her life."

After he was convicted the union paid $63,000 in legal fees for Joey Fay. We were unable to determine how much had been spent on his actual defense, but it was a substantial sum. Out of Sing Sing, Fay was reinstated in the union—with the approval of International President Maloney. Today Joey Fay is an automobile salesman and also receives a special annual pension of $12,600 from the Operating Engineers.

Peter Weber, his lieutenant in the New Jersey local, took over where Fay left off. Weber, who appeared before the Committee with a patch over his eye, ran the union with the ruthlessness characteristic of Fay's day. Weber went into four separate businesses, each one with contracts with his union. His business partner told us that whenever there were labor problems he simply called one of Weber's underlings in the union, "who of course were mindful that he [Weber] had an interest in the company." In 1950 Weber's stock in one of these companies was worth $671. Today it is worth $108,000.

We found that the evils that prevailed in the Fay-Weber regime of the Operating Engineers stretched from coast to coast.

On Long Island, New York, Local 138 was run by William C. DeKoning, Sr., and by his son after he was sent to prison for extortion. The son, William C. DeKoning, Jr., was convicted for extortion in the same case in 1953 and was barred from holding office in a union for a year. But when that time was up he resumed his command and it was a ruthless, undemocratic reign. Those who opposed the DeKonings—men like Lou Wilkens and Peter Batalias—were "tried" by a union court and barred from membership for as long as five years. This cost them their employment. Some who objected to the DeKoning way of running the union were beaten up.

The situation in the DeKoning local became so critical that a committee of Long Island ministers conducted their own investigation in 1955. Reverend John W. Van Zanten, pastor of the Presbyterian Church in Roslyn Heights, New York, told us: ". . . We discovered a great deal of fear in the working community; they were afraid they would lose their jobs. Some of these men have said to us when we discussed it with them—'I have a wife and children. I cannot stand up against this.'

"We don't like the fact that men are afraid to speak their minds. We feel there is dictatorship involved."

On the West Coast we went into the operation of Local 3, which has headquarters in San Francisco. This is the largest local in the

U.S., with a membership of 24,000. The corruption here revolved around three men—Pat Clancy, the president of the local, who claimed he was too dumb to be crooked; Porter E. Vanderwark, treasurer, a Harvard graduate, who claimed he was too smart to be crooked; and Victor Swanson, business manager, who claimed he was not dishonest because the other two were. All three had faced an indictment in a California land scheme in which it was charged that they and others defrauded the union of some $45,000.

They spent money like water—$120,000 in union funds on a yacht and an airplane, for example. Clancy claimed that as union president his only obligation was to spend two hours once a month presiding over meetings. The boat they bought was for Swanson and his friends, not for Clancy, he said.

"I got sick the first time," he said. "I didn't get no pleasure."

However, he was pilot of the union's airplane. And, we learned, he controlled the plane in just about the same way he controlled the union. One day he had a little trouble coming into San Francisco airport. I asked him about it:

MR. KENNEDY: You landed in San Francisco Bay?
MR. CLANCY: With the gear down. That is the problem. . . .
SENATOR GOLDWATER: You were short of the runway?
MR. CLANCY: I was a little bit low, sir, yes, I got a little bit low.

Then he said to me: "I put it in with the gear down. If you think that ain't a pretty good piloting job, Bob, have at it."

This "pretty good piloting" job cost the union $32,000 for repairs.

We were more interested in another airplane trip taken by Clancy, the man too dumb to be crooked, and Vanderwark, the man too smart to be crooked. They had with them five checks of $2,000 each. They flew to Washington, Montana, South Dakota, Minnesota, Colorado and Nevada getting this $10,000 in checks cashed so that it would appear to have been used on union business.

I asked Clancy about it:

MR. KENNEDY: Why did you go to a lot of different cities to cash the checks? So that it would appear that you were doing work in the various cities?

200

MR. CLANCY: I presume.
MR. KENNEDY: What?
MR. CLANCY: I presume it was.

On their return to San Francisco, Clancy said, they turned over the cash from the checks to Brother Swanson.

"I know we got hell," Clancy said, "he [Swanson] figured we spent too much money."

Clancy saw nothing improper about his check-cashing jaunt.

"I was just working there," he said.

He and Vanderwark placed the blame for most of the union's problems on Swanson, and there was no denying that he was the dominant personality within the local. He also was an International vice president and a bitter foe of International President Maloney. But this did not make him an honest labor leader. There was rank-and-file opposition to Swanson, Clancy and Vanderwark and they hired an ex-convict to try to find out who was behind a membership publication that criticized them. Swanson was convicted of forging a death threat in a letter in an effort to get the FBI to investigate the rank-and-file members who were against him. He was given two years' probation for this Federal offense.

Swanson, for the most part, was a candid witness. He told me that originally he had planned to take the Fifth Amendment, but was infuriated when Clancy and Vanderwark tried to put all the blame for the union's corruption on him. So he testified, and denied getting the money that Clancy and Vanderwark said they got on their $10,000 check-cashing jaunt.

He was frank in discussing the lack of democratic procedures in elections. After one election, he confessed, ballot boxes were placed in an automobile and the officers all drove out to a cabin the union owned some 150 miles from San Francisco. They sat around and had a few drinks. There were some 2,000 or 3,000 votes. They counted about 500 of them and felt by then a "trend" was established; it was not necessary to count any more. The tally sheet Local 3 sent in to the International gave friends of Victor Swanson over 16,000 votes. Those with whom he was not friendly received only 300 votes. Victor Swanson excused padding the vote on the grounds that the other In-

201

ternational officers, particularly William E. Maloney, the International president, would do the same thing.

I said on this point: ". . . The only way to combat that, your group thought, was to stuff the ballot boxes, too?"

Swanson said, "That is correct."

We found many of the nationwide problems in the Operating Engineers traceable to lack of democratic procedure. Out of 270,000 International members, less than 50 per cent are allowed to vote in any election. The members often have no control over their local officers or their International officers.

A forceful, honest figure at the head of the International Union could have done a great deal to control the coast-to-coast corruption. But the International president was William E. Maloney. During the period of his rise to the top of the union, beatings and bloodshed and killings were prevalent. In the days when he was a local union leader in Chicago and was trying to snare control of the union machinery in his home town he was opposed by a man named Dennis Ziegler. One day on his way home from work Dennis Ziegler was shot to death on the sidewalk. Maloney made friends with racketeers and hoodlums and courted management contractors with whom he negotiated. Information developed before the Committee showed that he sold out his membership in a variety of ways. He studiously worked to keep two Chicago locals in trusteeship for twenty-nine years, so that he could keep check on the contracts they negotiated with his management friends, particularly with the S. A. Healey Company. (Healey, the president of the firm, took the Fifth Amendment when we questioned him about his arrangement with Maloney.)

Such activities paid off. From 1950 to 1956, for example, Maloney reported an income from salary and expenses of $388,000. Our investigation showed that this figure was short by $354,000. He actually received $742,000. At least $182,000 was double or triple expense payments he charged to his local, to the International, and sometimes to a third agency.

He was paid expenses for meetings across the country that he never attended. He had at least ten lock boxes in various banks—and he refused to let us look into any of them.

Out of the union's treasury we found gifts going to Maloney that included air-conditioning units, TV sets and cars (among them, four Cadillacs) for his personal use. He and one of his Chicago underlings, Andrew Leach, let the union pay for purchases so ridiculous that they compared with those Dave Beck made through Shefferman. The union spent $250 to raise birds at a Sportsmen's Club, and paid for twenty pounds of almonds, twelve French pastries, twelve artichoke bottoms and twelve goose livers. There were two cases of champagne, and parrot liquor. Our investigators discovered many things, but we never found out what parrot liquor is.

The union members knew nothing of all this fancy or foolish buying. There was no way they could know that the Cadillacs Maloney's wife drove had been bought and paid for by the union. They did not know that $35,000 of union funds were used to purchase a yacht for Maloney and his friends, and to pay the captain's salary and all the boat's expenses. They did not know that Maloney was clothed at union expense, or that his race track membership, his apartment, his maid and a $1,250 platinum wrist watch all were paid for by him out of union dues.

Maloney never appeared before our Committee. Neither did Anton Imhahn, an International vice president involved in the Committee's investigation. They claimed they were too ill to appear. As a result of the hearings, however, Maloney, Imhahn and some lesser officials resigned—Maloney on a $50,000-a-year pension.

The new president is Joseph J. Delaney of New York. We conducted an investigation of him when he succeeded Maloney, but found nothing to suggest that he was anything but a labor leader interested in trying to run a proper labor union. He has taken some necessary preliminary steps toward cleaning up the union and it is hoped that the Operating Engineers will have a cleaner, more stable administration under his leadership.

3. CARPENTERS

During the seventy-fifth anniversary celebration of the founding of the Carpenters Union in 1956, Maurice Hutcheson, president of the union, was invited to the White House to meet President Eisenhower.

Secretary of Labor Mitchell, of course, was present for the meeting. So was Max Raddock, then considered a harmless labor publisher who was handling publicity for the Carpenters' celebration. I later heard from Secretary Mitchell how Raddock seized on this moment to tell President Eisenhower about a wonderful fellow—"my friend Mr. Hoffa." Raddock suggested that the President should meet Mr. Hoffa. "You'll really like him," he said.

Secretary Mitchell, following that meeting, left word that Max Raddock was never again to be allowed at the White House.

Raddock had not changed when he appeared before us. He had a smooth, glib tongue, a quick mind and utter gall. With his brazen, oily approach he tried to fast-talk his way through our hearings in the same way he tried to fast-talk the President of the United States.

Raddock was the publisher of a periodical, *The Trade Union Courier,* which shook down employers for ads. This is a newspaper that has for many years been sharply criticized by legitimate labor as well as the Federal Trade Commission and the Better Business Bureau. It was therefore eye-opening to discover in the records of the Carpenters Union huge payments to Raddock which over a period of three years totaled $519,000. There was $82,000 for handling the union's seventy-fifth anniversary celebration alone. What he had done for this sum of money was a mystery.

The most extraordinary amount was a total of $310,000 which had gone to Raddock for the writing and printing of 68,000 copies of a book on the late William L. Hutcheson, who had been president of the Carpenters until he handed the job over to his son Maurice in 1952. It was Maurice who had authorized the writing and publication of the book about his father.

Our investigation of the Carpenters started with the book. I assigned Paul Tierney and Bob Dunne to the case and immediately we ran into trouble with Raddock. He would not co-operate. We couldn't get him to turn over his records. He blocked us from talking with his employees in his World Wide Press plant where the books were supposed to have been printed. We couldn't get straight answers from

Raddock himself. The few people in his organization who at first were permitted to discuss the matter with us were as devious as Raddock himself.

As far as we could find, not many copies of the book existed, although Raddock had been paid to produce 68,000 of them. So I suggested to Senator McClellan that we call him and some of his associates in the World Wide Press for questioning under oath in executive session. Raddock, smooth and verbose, gave us some long-winded answers and charged that this was a political investigation of him because he was a Republican, but we got no concrete information. From Julius Terkeltaub, his production manager at World Wide Press, we received sworn testimony that was outright lies.

I pinned Terkeltaub down that day as best I could about how many of the books he had produced year by year at Raddock's plant:

MR. KENNEDY: How many were printed in 1955?

MR. TERKELTAUB: Several thousand . . . 2,000 or 3,000. I don't know the exact figures. . . .

MR. KENNEDY: How many were printed in 1956?

MR. TERKELTAUB: It ran into thousands. I couldn't say.

MR. KENNEDY: Were there another couple of thousand in 1956?

MR. TERKELTAUB: I would say it probably would be 10,000, 15,000 or 20,000—somewhere in that area.

From our preliminary investigation we knew that this was a bald-faced lie. As of the time he appeared in executive session before our Committee on February 19, 1958, only 18,000 of the 68,000 books had been printed—and not one of them had been turned out by Terkeltaub at World Wide Press.

It was infuriating to see such men under oath use half-truth and untruth, and be unable to prove it. The hearing lasted three hours and the arrogance of Raddock and Terkeltaub made this as unpleasant a time as I ever spent in a hearing room. When it was over I called Tierney and Dunne to the office to talk over the investigation. All of us were burning mad.

"We know they are lying," I said, "and we are going to prove it. Find out where and when and if they ever got their paper for these books; when and where they got their ink and material. Check the delivery dates of the material. Check every person in that plant that will talk to you whether Raddock likes it or not. Look at every record you can get your hands on. We are going to beat this."

Four months later the investigation was complete.

Now we held open hearings. On Friday, June 6, 1958, Julius Terkeltaub appeared and again swore to tell the truth. This time he told the truth because he knew we had evidence to prove him a liar.

He sat down in the witness chair and was a picture of humility as he read an opening statement:

> At the Executive Session held on February 19, 1958 I testified that 2,000 to 3,000 books, "Portrait of an American Labor Leader: William Levi Hutcheson" were printed in 1955 and between 10,000 and 25,000 books in 1956. . . .
> I wish to correct the aforesaid testimony which is erroneous. . . .
> No books were printed at the World Wide plant in 1955 and 1956.

Once our investigation had got under way the presses at the Raddock plant had suddenly come to life as he tried to catch up on the books he was in default to the union. But by the time of the hearings in June he was still 9,900 copies short.

He had perpetrated a fraud on the Carpenters Union and there was no question but that the leadership of the union permitted it and even co-operated with him. Raddock had entered into the contract with Maurice Hutcheson late in 1953. The original agreement required him to turn out 6,000 copies of the book for $25,000. He was to deliver them in November, 1954, to the Carpenters Union convention.

"We will be burning the midnight oil for the next eight months," he wrote Hutcheson. He predicted that he would have the book out on time "God and the elements willing."

By May of 1954 he was having problems, although there was no indication that either the Almighty or the elements had interfered. He got another $25,000 advance. Came November and the convention —but Raddock had not produced the book. Hutcheson apparently had growing faith in Raddock for at this point the union ordered 50,000 more books and agreed to pay Raddock the fantastic price of $200,000 more for them.

On November 30, 1955, about two years after the original agreement for 6,000 books, Raddock finally turned out 5,000 books. He had received a quarter of a million dollars from the union—and was 51,000 books behind schedule. It would seem that at least at this point somebody with the Carpenters Union would have wondered where their money was going—and for what.

But as fantastic as it may seem, on February 24, 1956, the union paid Raddock another $50,000 for an order of 10,000 more books and still later 2,000 more were ordered and Raddock got another $10,000—the last of the $310,000 he was to receive.

The company that printed some of the books told the Committee that they could have handled the whole lot of 68,000 for $75,000 and still made a profit. Allowing $50,000 for writing and research—at least five times more than was justified—the Carpenters still were over-charged by some $185,000.

And the book, called *Portrait of an American Labor Leader: William Levi Hutcheson,* was a technical and literary mess. Senator McClellan pointed out during our open hearings that the copy he was furnished had the index inserted upside down.

The "writing" of the book was the greatest Raddock farce and fraud of all. Much of the actual wording was stolen from Dr. Robert Christie, a college professor of history who in 1953, as a candidate for Doctor of Philosophy at Cornell University, had written his thesis on the history of the Carpenters Union.

The day Max Raddock testified in open hearings he did not know that Dr. Christie was in the Senate Office Building waiting to follow him to the stand. Raddock was as full of himself that day as he had been when he suggested that President Eisenhower should get to-gether with Jimmy Hoffa. He was poised and superior as we started discussing his literary talent.

How did he describe his writing accomplishment?

"Eloquently," he replied, "as immodest as it may sound."

Did he copy the material from others, and present it as his own?

"I personally, by my lonesome, little ol' me, wrote the book and I gave proper and due recognition to all who asked and sought recognition. . . ."

Did he have help from outsiders? He had "excellent aid" from colleagues and researchers on his staff, he said.

And then for the first time he hedged as if he were growing sus-picious.

". . . Some others who are not directly part of my staff but work elsewhere in the literary world," also had assisted, he said.

MR. KENNEDY: I just want to ask you about some of this. . . . On page 68—I am not going to read the whole book through—

MR. RADDOCK: I wish you would, Mr. Kennedy, and perhaps it might lead you in some noble directions.

Then I read him a passage from his book. It was identical with a passage in Christie's thesis. He did not catch on at once. He said:

"First of all, may I say that I enjoyed it, and I enjoy your reading, Mr. Kennedy."

MR. KENNEDY: Thank you.

MR. RADDOCK: Your diction is excellent.

He claimed full credit for that paragraph. I read another plagiarized paragraph. Now he was not quite so cocksure.

". . . To the best of my recollection, every word in that paragraph is mine, and with the aid of researchers who helped me with the book," he said.

There were other identical phrases, sentences and paragraphs. I read a passage describing how John L. Lewis punched William Hutcheson at the 1935 AFL convention. The book described the blow as "timed with the careful precision of a choreographer pirouet-ting his dancing partner on stage."

"Is that you, Mr. Raddock?" I asked.

Raddock knew by now that he was caught; he weakly suggested he might have "borrowed the expression."

We then called Dr. Christie. Raddock almost stumbled out of the witness chair. What did Christie think of Raddock's book?

He told us of that first time he read it.

"It was like living in a dream. . . . I kept seeing myself in the pages. . . . This is a Brinks robbery of literary plagiarism. It is an enormous steal. . . ." he said.

Dr. Christie estimated that between five and eight thousand words had been stolen directly from him and not attributed to his work. And parts of at least five other books had been stolen verbatim and no acknowledgment given.

As history, Dr. Christie said, the book was valueless.

Max Raddock loved the sound of his own voice. So I know it must have made him sad to have to take the Fifth Amendment when asked whether he had helped fix a case in Indiana in which Maurice Hutcheson and two other officials in the Carpenters Union were charged in a land scheme conspiracy.

Hutcheson and his fellow officers Frank Chapman and O. William Blaier, paid $20,000 for land in Lake County, Indiana, near Gary, and sold it several months later at a $78,000 profit to the state for a proposed highway. Part of the profit allegedly went to an Indiana official who reportedly had given Hutcheson, Chapman and Blaier information on where the highway was going.

In 1957 all of this had been gone into by a Senate committee headed by Senator Albert Gore (Democrat—Tennessee) and it was presented to a grand jury in Lake County, Indiana. The Carpenters officials were anxious to keep from being indicted in Lake County, where they feared they had no political friends. There, the Committee found, Max Raddock seemed to enter the picture.

Paul Tierney discovered that during the time the grand jury case was hanging fire Raddock had called Gary, and talked to a man listed on the telephone toll ticket as "Sawaka." This man, it later developed, was Mike Sawochka, the secretary of Local 142 of the Teamsters in Gary—and a man with political influence in Lake County. We found other interesting telephone calls from Raddock to a lawyer named Joseph Sullivan, Sawochka's lawyer—who also was an assistant in the office of Prosecutor Metro Holovachka where the case was prepared for grand jury action. Raddock, we learned, traveled at Carpenters Union expense during the period the Lake County grand jury was investigating. He registered at the Drake Hotel in Chicago as a representative of the union. His bills were signed by Hutcheson. We found that Hutcheson had made a call to James Hoffa in Detroit during this time and following that there was a flurry of activity that involved Sawochka in Gary.

After all this there was a startling announcement from the prosecuting attorney, Metro Holovachka, that Lake County lacked jurisdiction to indict Hutcheson and Chapman and Blaier. However, Marion County did indict—but as this is written some three years later, the case has not come to trial, despite the efforts of the prosecuting attorney.

We found that shortly afterward Sawochka paid a Gary company $40,000 for some property worth only $18,000. The company in turn bought a piece of property in which Holovachka had an interest. And this property had liabilities that were greater by four to one than its assets.

On the witness stand Raddock, on grounds of self-incrimination, would not tell us whether he knew the Gary Teamster leader, Sawochka, or whether he had tried to fix the case for Hutcheson or the other Carpenter officials. Sawochka also took the Fifth Amendment.

As was Committee policy, we did not ask Hutcheson about the matter for which he was under indictment. Questioned about the fix, he refused to answer questions, "on the ground that it relates solely to a personal matter not pertinent to any activity which the Committee is authorized to investigate, and also it relates or might be claimed to relate to or aid the prosecution in the case in which I am under indictment and thus be a denial of due process of law."

Obviously aware of the AFL-CIO ethical practices, Hutcheson insisted he was not invoking the Fifth Amendment. The Committee Chairman then ordered him to answer questions. When Hutcheson still refused, Senator McClellan recommended that he be cited for contempt. He has been indicted and the matter is now before the courts.

Prosecutor Holovachka was invited to appear as a witness, but declined. Dick Sinclair, an able accountant on loan from the General Accounting Office, had worked on some of Holovachka's financial dealings and was convinced that this was only one phase of Holovachka's activities that warranted our attention. Before he finished we had had some further hearings on Holovachka's activities with the result that he was removed from the prosecutor's office.[1]

[1] See Chapter 12: Organized Crime.

Although Maurice Hutcheson is president of the Carpenters Union, Charley Johnson, the vice president of the International, and in command of the union in the Eastern sector of the U.S., is perhaps the most important figure in the organization.

Johnson is one of those Hoffa had particularly in mind when he asked Cye Cheasty to search the Committee files to find out what information we had on certain people. He was involved with Maurice Hutcheson in the Indiana land scheme. But beyond that a number of his other activities interested the Committee. For instance, we found that Yonkers Raceway, in the midst of a jurisdictional labor dispute, paid him $37,000 for serving as a "labor consultant" and helping solve the problem between two unions and the race track. Labor elements involved in this matter thought Johnson was acting for them and were shocked to learn he was being paid such a sum by management. In the years 1955-56-57 Johnson and his family received a total of $450,000 from the Carpenters Union—but we found he was also a salesman and part owner of Penn Products, an outfit which sold oil and oil products, and 90 per cent of his accounts in this business, which paid him $96,000 from 1950 to 1957, came from construction companies such as Merritt-Chapman and Scott and Walsh Construction Company. These firms needed his good will as a Carpenters Union official, and the Committee charged, their dealings with Penn Products were nothing less than pay-offs to him. His partners in this project were the Weiss brothers—Ed, Emanuel and Philip. Phil Weiss is a close associate of Frank Costello, and another good friend of Jimmy Hoffa. The Committee described him as a "fixer."

The success of men such as Charles Johnson, William Blaier and Maurice Hutcheson depends, of course, on their successful portrayal of the role of the labor leader who is interested solely in the concerns and aims of the working man. It is unfortunate that some of them are such good actors.

4. OTHER UNIONS: CONCLUSION

The labor movement in America is a huge, living, human machine. It is subject to human error. But with a few exceptions, the men who run our great labor unions in this country are honest, dedicated men.

We have mentioned a few who betrayed their trust—Hoffa, Cross, Joey Fay, Maloney, Johnson. There are others. We uncovered corruption in the Hotel and Restaurant Workers Union; in the Sheet Metal Workers Union; in the Mail Deliverers Union in New York.

Max and Louis Block, who ran the Amalgamated Meat Cutters and Butchers Workmen's Union in the New York area were prime examples of labor officials who misuse their position for personal enrichment and power. They had a different twist. For instance, they owned a country club, and forced employers with whom they had contracts to lend them money or join the club. They used their positions with the union to get stock in some big food and grocery concerns.

Lloyd Klenert, secretary-treasurer of the relatively small United Textile Workers of America, and Anthony Valente, the union's president, used the UTWA's comparatively small treasury to buy luxurious homes for themselves. They had an ingenious explanation for their action: They were simply "hiding" the money so someone wouldn't steal it from the union.

What is a "golfer's lamp" that the union should spend $49.50 on it for Mr. Klenert? Someone suggested it was a lamp used to find golf balls at night. We never did learn. What did Mr. Klenert want with a milk stool? Why should the union spend $15 to buy him a sport cane? Or $92.60 for trampolin lessons. Quite apart from the cost of his house, we found that Klenert's sticky fingers in the UTWA treasury came up with some $65,000, which he spent on himself, his family and his friends. He paid for beauty salon visits, jewelry, girdles, petticoats, eleven sun shirts ($35), diaper service—all out of the money rank-and-file Textile Workers had entrusted to him.

He had a special fondness for the theater, and over a three-year period he spent $11,000 for theater tickets. *My Fair Lady* was an immense favorite of his apparently, for he bought $2,500 worth of tickets for that play alone.

But after our hearings, under pressure from the AFL-CIO hierarchy, Max and Louis Block got out of the Meat Cutters Union, and Klenert and Valente left the Textile Workers. I am confident their departures left the labor movement a cleaner, healthier, more wholesome area.

When our committee came into existence it was no easy decision for George Meany and the numberless other honest, dedicated labor leaders in the country to offer their support to our work. They knew that the labor movement, by the actions of a few, stood to be discredited. But because by and large they are honest men, from Meany down, they backed our investigations, at least initially, and took positive steps to correct labor union abuses.

George Meany and his associates in the AFL-CIO were sicker about the corruption our Committee revealed than anyone else in the country. Shortly after our work started I sat down to lunch one day in the noisy bustle of the dining room of the Senate Office Building with Mr. Meany, Arthur Goldberg, the labor lawyer and adviser, Senator McClellan and Senator Ives, the ranking party members of the Committee. The luncheon had been arranged so that we could explain to Mr. Meany the tremendous tasks we faced and so that we could try to understand the problems that our work would create for him.

All he asked from us at that meeting, or anytime, was that we be fair. Never did he ask us not to conduct an investigation, or not to call a particular witness. He never attempted to bring any pressure. Several times afterward he disagreed with what the Committee was doing, and said so. There is no question that we made mistakes, but his criticism was not always justified or based on fact in my judgment. It was understandable, however, that a union official, reading in his paper every morning for two years about the goons, thugs and crooks in the movement, and knowing they comprised only a small percentage of the labor officials in the country, would have his patience tried. Certainly I could understand Meany's disquietude.

In the three years of our work I had perhaps a half-dozen meetings with him about various problems that developed. He was courteous and co-operative. He had acted as president of the AFL before the merger with the CIO, and had tried to take steps to clean up the Textile Workers Union. He came before our Committee in connection with that case—the only time, as a matter of fact, that he appeared.

When it was announced that he was to testify, there was some speculation that Republican members of the Committee would try

213

to make things difficult for him. But nothing of the sort happened. Face to face, they treated him with respect and courtesy—and even docility.

He recognized that there was corruption within the labor movement, but said publicly that he had not been aware of 2 per cent of what the Committee showed existed.

At a time when the faces of Beck and Hoffa stood out in the public mind as an image of labor corruption, George Meany and some of those around him stood out just as clearly as symbols of what was right and decent and honorable at the head of the American labor movement. Meany is a gruff, stubborn man. It is my belief that he sometimes depends on people around him who give him only those reports that they feel will be best for themselves, or that he wants to hear. But he is incorruptible and the labor movement was fortunate to have him in an hour of crisis. So was the country.

Chapter 11 / THE RESPECTABLES

1. BUSINESSMEN

ONE DAY in the fall of 1958 I received an invitation to speak about the work of our Committee to an association of businessmen at a dinner at the Waldorf in New York.

A week before the dinner I received a second letter from the association. It read:

DEAR MR. KENNEDY:

. . . I am most embarrassed to be confronted with a situation which necessitates the withdrawal of that invitation. Our members have a very real and deep interest in the subject on which you were expected to speak. . . . They would very much like to hear you be the one to discuss it, but it now develops some of the members of the industry feel that the subject is one which probably should be discussed in a meeting of a more general character than a single industry meeting.

I am certain that you, too, realize, as do we upon reflection, that it might be a mistake for one single industry to sponsor a speech at this time by one in your official position. There is too much opportunity for misunderstanding arising therefrom. Such would not be so if the speech were delivered before a general meeting, such as the Chamber of Commerce or Association of Manufacturers, etc.

Accordingly it is necessary for me to ask you to disregard my letter of October 31 and to accept my apologies for having to withdraw the invitation.

Some otherwise honest businessmen look on the relationship between labor and management as a great power struggle in which "anything goes." In their anxiety to gain the upper hand in this struggle they resort to unethical and dishonest tactics on the mistaken theory that they must do this to win.

The great concentration of power that rests in some of the unions in this country should be a matter of concern, just as should the great concentrations of power in some companies and businesses in certain sections of the country. But the answer to the problem of powerful unions is not to be found in a breakdown of morality in the nation's business community. Unfortunately this is the answer too many businessmen are willing to accept.

I recognize that the majority of American businessmen are above crookedness and collusion in labor-management negotiations. But we found that with the present-day emphasis on money and material goods many businessmen were willing to make corrupt "deals" with dishonest union officials in order to gain competitive advantage or to make a few extra dollars.

Because of limited jurisdiction our Committee could not go into improper activities of business per se, but only where there was some direct connection with labor. Even thus restricted, we came across more than fifty companies and corporations that had acted improperly —and in many cases illegally—in dealings with labor unions. Here it was not a matter of an employer's being whipped into line by fear or fright or abuse. Such things happen, as in the case in New York, for example, where an employer was told that his children would be killed on the way to school if he did not give in to union demands. We found management representatives who were threatened and maltreated by union officials. Where this occurred the Committee did not find it difficult to understand that a man afraid for his life or for the welfare of his family might act unwisely. Such an employer deserves sympathy and help.

But in the companies and corporations to which I am referring the improprieties and illegalities were occasioned solely by a desire for monetary gain. Furthermore we found that we could expect very little assistance from management groups. Disturbing as it may sound, more often the business people with whom we came in contact—and this includes some representatives of our largest corporations—were uncooperative. For some it was a question of not wanting to involve themselves; for others, such as the writer of the letter mentioned above, it was a question of not having the courage to speak out—because "there is too much opportunity for misunderstanding."

We found there is often a thin line between bribery and extortion, shakedown and pay-off. Labor-management corruption is a crooked two-way street. That is why company officials who conspire with union officials won't talk. They have bought something, just as the labor leader has sold something. And those management officials who aren't involved themselves are usually satisfied to let things go along with everybody happy. They don't want anyone to rock the boat.

Frank Hogan, the able New York District Attorney, told me of his difficulties in dealing with so-called respectable management people during his investigation into labor racketeering in the 1940's. Company officers even fled his jurisdiction and hid out in states beyond his reach.

Fifteen years later I found the situation had not changed—not even the faces had changed.

We called before the Committee S. A. Healey, owner of one of the major construction firms in the United States. He had hidden out from Hogan for over a year before he finally came in and admitted having paid $125,000 to "Big Mike" Carozza, the head of the Hod Carriers Union. We wanted to know about Healey's relationship with William E. Maloney, the International president of the Operating Engineers. But rather than discuss it with the Committee, he took the Fifth Amendment.

During Joey Fay's trial in the forties officials of the Walsh Construction Company in New York admitted having made a pay-off to him. In our hearings in 1959, the Committee found this same company had awarded a contract to Charley Johnson of the Carpenters Union under circumstances that made it clear that this too was a pay-off.

By and large, little or no accurate information came to us from the business community. We received 150,000 complaints during the Committee's life. Seventy-five per cent of them came from representatives of organized labor, mostly rank-and-filers. Some came from people outside the labor-management field. Only a handful came from people in the business world. Certainly no investigation was touched off by any voluntary help we received from management. And this was not because management had no information to give. I believe 90 per cent of the corrupt deals between business and labor could be eliminated if business officials would simply talk to proper authorities.

It was encouraging to see the AFL-CIO move against certain unions—notably the Teamsters and the Bakers—as a result of corrupt practices found within the unions. But not one management group or association has made a single move to rid itself of members who were found to be involved in collusive deals. Not one firm has been barred from any business organization for wrongdoing that officials of the firm often admitted existed. These corrupt businessmen are still sitting down to luncheon and dinner meetings with business groups across the country, and they are getting encouragement and admiration—not censure.

Often we found that corrupt deals involving management were handled through attorneys who played the role of "middleman" or, as we came to think of them, "legal fixers" or "legal prostitutes." More often it was the labor relations consultant who played the "middleman" role. And America's most notorious middleman was Nathan W. Shefferman, some of whose activities we discussed earlier in connection with Dave Beck.

As our investigations moved from Beck and the Teamsters into other areas we ran across Shefferman and his operatives repeatedly— most often where a company was resisting unionization. One of his assets as a labor relations consultant was, of course, his friendship with labor leaders, which he used to get favorable treatment for his management clients in their negotiations with the unions. (Naturally the favors were reciprocal.)

His methods of rescuing a firm from the dreadful prospect of legitimate unionization were various and devious. We discovered in his files an outline of what must have been one of his favorite methods of attack (judging by the frequency with which the pattern cropped up) when dealing with labor leaders who could not be bought. This was his advice to one company that was facing organization:

"Don't dignify them. Call them bums and hoodlums. Cheap common bums. Don't argue wage differential. Don't answer it. Stay away from it. Ridicule leaders."

He urged his client to find an employee who would work with a lawyer to organize an anti-union group:

"Find lawyer and guy who will set up 'vote no' committee. Give American Legion material we have and let 'vote no' committee get it from American Legion."

The memo continued: "Material to use: Communism, un-Americanism, destroying our country . . . Attack them and pin them down when they get closer to an issue. Hit leaders toward last. . . ."

One of Shefferman's clients was Sears, Roebuck, which paid him approximately $250,000 during the period from 1953 to 1956 alone.

Sears, Roebuck officials were amazingly frank. Wallace Tudor, a vice president of Sears, Roebuck & Company, admitted to the Committee that:

Many of the activities engaged in by Labor Relations Associates and certain company personnel acting with them were inexcusable, unnecessary and disgraceful. A repetition of these mistakes will not be tolerated by this company. . . .

Mr. Tudor said the relationship with Shefferman had been terminated in 1957. He could not explain why it had not been broken off earlier.

His attitude and forthright admission blunted the sharp criticism the company might otherwise have received from the Committee. As a practical matter, when someone says that mistakes have been made, asks for no sympathy and pledges in good faith that the errors will not be repeated, it is difficult to be critical.

As we went into the efforts of other companies to stave off unionization, or to get a union that would "deal" with them, the same pattern was apparent again and again. At times our investigators would spot the Shefferman imprint almost immediately. One interesting case involved the Morton Frozen Food Company in Webster City, Iowa.

When the United Packinghouse Workers started an organizing drive there in June, 1955, immediately a "spontaneous" opposition group called "We the Morton Workers" sprang up. From the outset, union

219

officials were certain that the company was supporting this group financially, but could not obtain proof.

Looking into the case, we found that their suspicion was justified. A middleman lawyer, a man named Stewart Lund, hired by the company's regular attorney, had worked with a Shefferman representative in the usual way to defeat the union. When first interviewed, Lund told Pierre Salinger that all he ever received by way of compensation was a set of steak knives from the grateful "We the Morton Workers"; later—after we proved that he had been well paid by the company's attorney—he admitted that he had lied. He excused his falsehood on the grounds of a "confidential relationship" with the company.

I recognize the real need for a bond between lawyer and client. But, as we pointed out at the hearing, if Mr. Lund felt that by talking to Salinger he would have been betraying this relationship, he should have said so, instead of lying to him.

The hearings showed that for keeping the union out, Shefferman got $12,000. The next year, 1956, he got $8,000 for bringing a union in. During the year Morton Frozen Foods had become a division of the Continental Baking Company. Continental's general counsel was George Faunce, a close friend of James Cross of the Bakers Union. So with the help of a Shefferman operative, Cross and his Bakers Union took over, in an "organizing drive" that was more a conspiracy against the employees than a legitimate organizing program. The officers of the new local were chosen in the office of the general manager of the Morton Company, and the contract was drawn up and signed in Shefferman's office. It was a very bad contract. It did away with the wage incentive and contained no seniority provision. But the members were not consulted, and only parts of the contract were read to them.

We asked George Faunce about this, and he said: "I think you normally make a contract with a union leader. You don't make a contract with a mob of people."

Nevertheless, in order to give the contract some appearance of legitimacy, Shefferman's man, James T. Neilsen, alias James Guffey, had wanted the new union to go through the farce of a negotiating session. Merle Smith, a field organizer for the International, and a legitimate union leader, had objected.

"These people are not that stupid," he told Guffey.

At the hearings the Continental Baking Company had swarms of public relations men all over the hearing room. They had employed Tex McCrary's publicity firm and there seemed to be more of their people around than there were witnesses. After George Faunce made his remark about "the mob"—a reference to Morton workers—McCrary's public relations men seemed to double. They put out a new statement every hour in an effort to kill the bad publicity the company was getting.

In my estimation the Morton firm showed bad judgment in not following the example of Sears, Roebuck and admitting what the facts clearly proved. Their failure to do so made their position much more difficult before the Committee.

We also found Shefferman's muddy footprints at the Whirlpool Company in Ohio, which was being organized by the UAW. "Spontaneous" anti-union committees handed out literature paid for by the company; lists were made of pro-union employees, and workers were bribed to vote against the UAW.

At one point during this investigation, we drew up at the request of several Committee members a complete list of Shefferman's clients. Shortly thereafter, John Herling, an outstanding Washington labor reporter, obtained a copy and printed it. Senator Goldwater and several other Republican Senators exploded, mistakenly holding me responsible.

One of Shefferman's agents, George Kamenow, was extremely close to Hoffa and other union officials. Many of his clients were able to avoid unionization. However, the middleman who turned up most often in deals where Hoffa was concerned was Jack (Babe) Bushkin, the Detroit labor consultant. During the period that Hoffa controlled the Detroit local of the Retail Clerks, Bushkin was able to get substandard contracts with them for a number of his clients.

A year after the Committee had exposed Bushkin's operations and he had pleaded the Fifth Amendment before us, we found some of the most reputable firms in Detroit—Federal Department Stores, Cunningham Drug Stores, the ACF Wrigley Grocery chain—still had him on their payrolls as a "consultant" and they had no intention of getting rid of him. While this would have been disillusioning for me in 1957, by 1959 it no longer seemed surprising.

On the role of the "middleman" in labor-management affairs, Senator McClellan, after listening to accounts of the activities of Shefferman, Kamenow, Babe Bushkin and others, had this to say:

> THE CHAIRMAN: I am compelled to observe that I see nothing wrong in seeking counsel and employing legal counsel, and employing even experts in labor-management relations . . . but it looks to me like we are developing a pattern of what amounts to a payoff to union officials to have them disregard the rights of the workingmen or to be reluctant, if not to refuse, to press any drive for unionization. . . .

The labor relations "middleman" was not always a necessary ingredient in the deals some companies cooked up with unions. Sometimes management officials acted for themselves without a "consultant."

In 1955, Food Fair Stores, the sixth largest food chain in the country, created an affiliate to be known as Food Fair Properties, Inc. Bonds and stocks were issued the latter part of 1955 and "stock rights" were given to all those who already owned stock in Food Fair Stores. Holders of the stock rights had preferred treatment in the purchase of a debenture bond and eleven shares of stock.

Mr. Samuel Friedland, Chairman of the Board of Food Fair Stores, made 136,000 of his own "rights" available to twenty individuals who otherwise would not have been entitled to them. Of the twenty, four were labor officials, who received as a gift a total of twelve thousand "rights," which at the time were worth approximately $9,000. This enabled them to purchase for $30,000 units that actually were worth $42,000.

In addition to the units, common stock was issued, for which a tremendous demand built up. The offering of 650,000 shares became greatly oversubscribed. Nevertheless, through the courtesy of Mr. Lou Stein, president of Food Fair, twenty labor leaders were permitted to buy 12,100 shares of this already oversubscribed stock for $12,000—though at the time of purchase these shares were actually worth $48,000. Altogether, Food Fair officials made available to labor officials for $42,100 bonds and stocks worth $90,400.

Some of the major stock rights went to Max and Louis Block of the Meat Cutters Union. In a nice *quid pro quo,* Food Fair was granted an eighteen-month grace period before having to pay into the union's pension and welfare fund in New York. This saved the firm a tidy $142,000. The two major competing firms in its area were not similarly blessed.

To Ben Lapensohn, a union leader of Local 107 of the Teamsters, Stein made available—in addition to the Food Fair stock—$15,000 worth of stock in another company of which he was a director. This cost Lapensohn only $10,000.

When I asked Stein why he wanted to favor Mr. Lapensohn, he said, "Because if anyone is in business, and you know that a person stands well in labor circles, you don't try to incur any ill will. If it did not mean anything to me, and he came and asked me for a favor, certainly I ought to try to do it for him, because that is human nature, and that is the way business is done, not to get any benefits that you are not entitled to . . . but merely to be sure that you don't create ill will but try to get good will of people insofar as your business is concerned."

Good will, the Committee found, is what Mr. Stein got—approximately $300,000 worth—when in the contract negotiations with Lapensohn's local in 1954 Food Fair was given extremely advantageous terms regarding the unloading of merchandise that were not granted to its competitors.

Although I thought I had become case-hardened, I discovered I still was not shockproof when I studied the results of our investigation of the A & P—the Great Atlantic & Pacific Tea Company. This is the largest retail organization in the world, with 4,500 stores in the United States and Canada, and an income of approximately $4,700,000,000. For many years, a number of different unions had tried to organize the A & P employees and for many years the company had fought the unions off—and in the process had several times been found guilty of unfair labor practices. Eventually, however, the Meat Cutters and Butchers Union succeeded in organizing the people in the stores' meat departments.

But, for the company, the real D-day came when in the summer of

1952 the Safeway Stores signed a contract with the CIO Clerks Union calling for a forty-hour week. This put the heat on the A & P, because it was obvious that in the next negotiating session, at the end of the year, the Meat Cutters would demand a forty-hour week for its members. It was also obvious that when some union succeeded in organizing the rest of the A & P employees—a day that could not be far off—it too would demand a forty-hour work week.

So, the Committee found, representatives of the A & P got together with the Meat Cutters' Max Block to see what could be "arranged." The A & P, the giant of big business, secretly agreed to turn over to the Meat Cutters some ten thousand of its unorganized workers—in return for a five-year contract with a forty-five-hour week.

Walter May and George Martin, our investigators on the case, suspected from the beginning that a secret agreement had been made, though both company and union officials denied it. All copies had been destroyed—they thought. But digging into the union's files, May found a copy of it. It extended the previous two-year contract an extra three years. And in the A & P files we found a memorandum showing that the five-year deal saved the company at least $2,000,000 a year. The company thus got what it wanted.

The union got ten thousand new members—and $500,000 a year in dues.

The employees of the Atlantic & Pacific—the hapless new members of Max Block's union—got virtually nothing, and lost the chance of legitimate representation.

They were told only that a two-year contract had been signed; nothing was said about extending the present forty-five-hour work week for another five years in all.

Senator Ervin and Senator Church made their feelings plain when they questioned Charles A. Schimmat, attorney for the A & P Company.

SENATOR ERVIN: In other words, you agreed with him that it was all right, since your company got such a big advantage out of it, it was all right for him to conceal, and that you would assist him in concealing it, the knowledge of the five-year agreement from the very persons who were to be bound by the five-year agreement?

MR. SCHIMMAT: May I point out to you that the International name was also on that document with Max Block's name on it.

SENATOR ERVIN: That does not change it. You tell me that your conscience would approve conduct like that . . . ?

MR. SCHIMMAT: That is what we did in this case.

SENATOR ERVIN: Yes, sir; you sure did.

Senator Church pressed the point.

SENATOR CHURCH: You would think then when representatives of the labor union ask you to keep certain terms of the contract concealed, that since it is their responsibility to expose the terms of this contract, you can enter into such an agreement and your hands are not soiled by doing it; is that right . . . ?

MR. SCHIMMAT: I did not see anything wrong with it, sir. . . .

SENATOR CHURCH: Well, I do. . . .

It is not possible here to relate in detail every corrupt practice that our investigation placed at the doorstep of the so-called respectable business community, but these self-serving deals cropped up constantly from the very beginning of our investigation. I have already shown, for example, how the power of Dave Beck induced Anheuser-Busch and other companies to deal with him; how Martin Philipsborn enabled James Cross to profit personally at the expense of his union members; how a number of oil companies made mutually beneficial arrangements with Charley Johnson's Penn Products; and there were many other cases. The Niagara-Mohawk Corporation of New York, for example, paid $93,000 to Ben Lapensohn, the Teamster official and labor "fixer" from Philadelphia, supposedly for ads in a yearbook he was publishing. Lapensohn, we found, raked off $84,700 of the $93,000, though corporation officials told us they thought the money was going to the New York state labor federation. Then there was Harold Roth, the New York businessman who loaned or arranged for more than $200,000 in loans, some unsecured and interest free, for Milton Holt, a Teamster official with whom Roth interests had contracts. Mr. Roth told us he saw nothing wrong with the loans—but admitted he would not make them again.

In addition, we found many small businesses that made deals with racket locals simply to keep their workers in line and to keep legitimate

225

unions out. This was true especially in New York City, where the likes of Johnny Dio and others were allowed to come in and "organize" the employees.

More often than not these were illiterate Negro workers, or Puerto Ricans who could neither speak nor understand English. There are tens of thousands of them living in squalor, sometimes on as little as $32 a week. The ones we interviewed could not understand what was happening to them. They only knew they were faced with severe hardships and that providing food and clothing for a family on less than $40 a week was nearly impossible in New York, or in any other industrial community.

We heard from one witness, Miss Bertha Nunez, who told of a woman who contracted pneumonia and lost a child because of the coldness of the plant where she worked. Miss Nunez was an attractive and intelligent Puerto Rican who knew that she and her fellow workers were being exploited. But she was helpless to do anything about it.

2. LAWYERS

No one could listen to the testimony before our Committee, or read the record, and not be deeply concerned and badly disillusioned about the practices some attorneys engaged in while representing labor and management. From the first, we found lawyers who considered that their clients were not the rank and file but the union officials who held the purse strings.

I have already mentioned some, but consider also the attorneys who represented union officials in the following cases—again just to take a sampling from the many in our files:

Lou Berra, a Teamster official in St. Louis who paid for his house with union money, was indicted for income tax evasion. Some $35,000 of union funds were used to defend him, with the argument that he had embezzled the money and embezzled funds do not constitute income. The attorneys who made this argument knew their fee was coming from union funds.

Similarly, the attorneys defending Jimmy James, a vice president of the Laundry Workers Union, who was charged with taking over $600,000 from the pension and welfare fund, and was indicted for income tax evasion, argued their case on the same grounds, and accepted their compensation from the union.

Even more disturbing was the behavior of the attorney for Hoffa's own local, George Fitzgerald. He got $100,000 Teamsters loan for a construction firm in which he had a major interest, and a $135,000 loan to go into the insurance business.

But what really concerned the Committee was his connection with a land development company in Michigan. He had recommended that the Teamsters lend $1,000,000 to a group of land speculators known as Winchester Village Land Company to develop some property on which the union held a mortgage. But the borrowers, with Fitzgerald's approval, invested so much of the money in a quite different plot, in which the Teamsters had no interest, that the whole deal turned into a financial bust which cost the union at least $600,000.

We found that Fitzgerald and his law partners received a $35,000 fee from the Winchester Village Land Company for arranging this loan from the Teamsters.

Hoffa told the Committee that he never knew that George Fitzgerald had shared in this fee of $35,000.

Fitzgerald, questioned about the propriety of his action, said: "Hindsight is better than foresight. If I knew this inquiry was going to be made about it, it would have made a difference."

A different kind of situation is that which concerned Carney Matheson of Detroit, the chief negotiator for the over-the-road truckers. He wields immense power and has been remarkably successful in obtaining favorable contracts for those he represents. Albert Matheson, his brother, was also in the trucking business. Both of them have performed legal work for Hoffa for which they have received no reimbursement and Carney Matheson has been in a number of financial deals with Hoffa.

Just as this kind of operation is improper for Hoffa, so is it improper for the two Mathesons.

The Committee was also highly critical of lawyers who accepted payment from the union treasury while representing officials who refused on the ground of self-incrimination to answer questions about the misuse or misappropriation of union funds. It was perfectly proper for them to represent these men, but they should have received their fees from the individual officials, not from the union members' dues.

I think that bar associations have a strong obligation in cases such as this. Leading members of bar associations across the country are eloquent in denouncing the corruption within the labor unions and the betrayal of trust by certain union officials. But they are silent about the betrayal of trust by their fellow lawyers. And while the AFL-CIO has taken action against the union leaders whose corruption we exposed, the bar associations have done virtually nothing about attorneys whose duplicity we also exposed. One exception is the Bar in Tennessee, which sought to disbar a judge who had been impeached.

But William Langley, a former district attorney in Portland, Oregon, whom our Committee showed was working hand in glove with the city's gangster elements, is still a practicing lawyer.[1] It would also seem that the Bar Association of Indiana might look into the situation regarding Holovachka, the former prosecuting attorney of Lake County, Indiana.

Time and again the Committee was disillusioned to discover that lawyers had lied to our investigators. In New York, while investigating the Teamsters' connection with the Akros Dynamics firm, we ran into a father-son team of lawyer and accountant in Herbert and George Burris who were certainly less than truthful. When our investigators asked Herbert about a certain important document related to the case, he denied that it ever existed. When we produced it, he said, startled: "I thought it had been destroyed."

The Committee also showed that Martin J. Quigley, a businessman in Washington, D.C., and a member of the Bar of the District of Columbia, knowingly accepted union funds to make payments on two houses for officials of the Textile Workers Union. In order to hide these transactions from the trustees of the union Quigley, on two separate occasions, wrote completely untruthful letters to conceal the real use to which the money had been put.

However, labor has been fortunate enough to attract the active assistance of many wise and skillful lawyers, men like Arthur Goldberg, counsel for the AFL-CIO, who have been drawn to the growing labor movement by a sense of idealism and a dedication to the cause of

[1] See Chapter 12: Organized Crime.

economic justice and a better way of life for the working man. They are men of high principle, who recognize that their profession carries with it certain responsibilities and obligations; they are completely loyal to the best interests of their clients—within the bounds of sound professional ethics.

Jim Rowe, a Washington, D.C., lawyer, comes to mind as one of these. For a time, he represented James Cross, president of the Bakers Union. At first he was convinced that the Committee's investigation of Cross was inspired only by the complaint of a faction within the union, and that the hearing would simply air an inter-union rivalry. But before we opened hearings he came to my office and, complimenting the staff on its work in the case, told me he was withdrawing as Cross's counsel. He did not tell me why; I did not ask him. Mr. Rowe, I knew, had done substantial preparatory work before the hearings; but as we later found, the union's records showed that he did not charge a fee for his services.

Another man who gave his time and talent was Abraham Freedman of Philadelphia, who represented Roy Underwood and his followers in their fight against the corrupt leadership of the Operating Engineers. Mr. Freedman knew that his clients were men with little money. He acted as their attorney at a personal sacrifice, because he hoped to achieve for Underwood some measure of justice. Dave Rabinovitz, the UAW attorney, was another whose ability and integrity have contributed greatly to the labor movement.

We did not meet Asher Schwartz, of New York, the general counsel of the Mail Deliverers Union there. We went into this union's activities and discovered corruption among some of its leaders. Mr. Schwartz resigned his job and gave up a substantial retainer rather than represent officials of the union who took the Fifth Amendment on questions pertaining to a sellout of the union members. He believed in the cause of his clients—and as he saw it the clients were the rank-and-file union men whose dues made up the treasury that paid him his retainer. Any other course, he felt, would involve him in a conflict of interest.[2]

His was a rarely found point of view, in our experience.

[2] When the leadership of the union changed, Mr. Schwartz resumed his connection with the union.

In 1934 Supreme Court Justice Harlan Stone gave a speech at the University of Michigan in which he referred to lawyers of that day who were serving large corporations:

I venture to assert that when the history of the financial era which has just drawn to a close comes to be written, most of its major mistakes and its major faults will be ascribed to the failure to observe the fiduciary principle, the precept as old as holy writ, that "a man cannot serve two masters." . . . There is little to suggest that the Bar has yet recognized that it must bear some of the responsibility for these evils. But when we know and face the facts we should have to acknowledge that such departures from the fiduciary principle do not actually occur without the active assistance of some member of our profession; and that their increasing recurrence would have been impossible but for the complaisance of a Bar, too absorbed in the work-a-day care of private interests to take account of these events of profound import—or to sound the warning that the profession looks askance on these things that "are not done."

Now twenty-five years later, history has given us an interesting parallel. Though Justice Stone was talking about evils that had developed in corporations, not labor unions, his words are just as pertinent today.

I feel very strongly that our bar associations should deal with these problems. But as matters presently stand the bar associations are not meeting their responsibilities. And if they continue to ignore such practices as our Committee encountered, as well as the unethical tactics of some attorneys engaged in the practice of criminal law, they will simply be asking for stricter regulation.

The sooner lawyers face up to this situation, the sooner we will have a profession of which we can properly be proud.

3. THE PRESS

The high editorial ideals fostered by American newspapers do not alter the basic fact that to exist as great instruments of information, newspapers must be successful business enterprises. As such they are subject to the same economic pressures, the same financial pitfalls and the same management problems that confront other corporations.

This was forcefully brought home to the Committee—and to the press itself—in a series of hearings beginning in May, 1959, when it was disclosed that associates of Mr. Hoffa had practiced shakedown on management people engaged in newspaper distribution.

The papers were: the *New York Times,* the New York *Daily Mirror,* the Detroit *Times,* the Pittsburgh *Sun-Telegraph,* and *The American Weekly.*

Deeply involved in the pay-offs by the *New York Times,* the *Mirror* and *The American Weekly* was the Neo-Gravure Printing Company of Weehawken, New Jersey.

Strangely, this investigation began in Miami—far from the New York–New Jersey scene where the pay-offs occurred. We were investigating Harry Gross, the ex-convict-extortionist, who in October, 1958, many months after Hoffa had promised to clean up the union, had been given a Teamster charter in Miami. The union, Local 320, had only thirty-two members but Gross was receiving $14,000 a year in salary and expenses. The local was also paying for a red Thunderbird for his comfort. We found that Hoffa was sending International funds to the local to support him. Gross also maintained two Florida residences and one in New York, and seemed generally to have a limitless source of ready money.

During the course of his investigation, Walt Sheridan talked with a filling station operator who had had some dealings with Gross, and he mentioned that he had cashed a number of checks for him; some of them, he said, were from a printing company in New Jersey. Sheridan became curious. The operator said he happened to have one with him. It was this minor incident that broke the investigation wide open.

The checks were from the Neo-Gravure Company of Weehawken, New Jersey, and within a few hours Sheridan was on a plane north to discover what lay behind them. But the Neo-Gravure Company executives were wary and evasive. Yes, they said, Harry Gross was on their payroll. He was a platform foreman in their Shipping Department. He was worth his pay. They were satisfied with his work.

We could not possibly understand how a foreman for Neo-Gravure —with the record and reputation of Harry Gross—could earn his money on a New Jersey shipping platform while running a Teamsters local in Miami, Florida. Then a secret source who knew the inside workings of the company told Sheridan that a close study of the company's books would indicate that Mr. Gross was far more than a platform straw boss.

Placed under Committee subpoena, the company officials employed an attorney, former Governor George Craig of Indiana, who advised them to offer complete co-operation. I interviewed them in my office Monday, May 4, from 8:00 P.M. until nearly midnight.

The Neo-Gravure Company, it turned out, had been paying Gross over $1,000 a month to insure "labor peace" since shortly after his release from Sing Sing. At one time or another it had also had on its payroll Gross's two sons, a brother and brother-in-law. Over a period of a few years the combined salaries totaled $226,000. Gross, the company officials said, worked in league with Cornelius (Connie) Noonan, president of Local 1730 of the International Longshoremen's Association, with whom they had a contract.

"Had he received any other payments?" I asked.

Yes. From 1952 to 1958 he had been paid an additional $4,000 annually for "outside work."

What was "outside work"? In 1952 Neo-Gravure had started printing *The American Weekly* for the Hearst organization. However, a union jurisdictional dispute blew up and Hearst could not get its magazine delivered. Officials at *The American Weekly* asked the officers of the Neo-Gravure firm if they could do anything to help. Neo-Gravure in turn called on Harry Gross. Yes, he could fix it— for $4,000 a year for ten years, which he said he would spread around to the various labor officials concerned. *American Weekly* agreed, and the pay-offs were made through Neo-Gravure. Finally in 1958, acting on a request from *American Weekly* executives, Neo-Gravure asked Harry Gross if, in view of cost pressures, the payment could not be dropped. A few days later Mr. Gross agreed.

"Were there any other payments?" I asked.

In 1954 and 1955 they had made two payments to Gross of $2,500 each for settling a contract with Noonan's ILA Local 1730 platform workers at below-scale wage increases.

"Had any other pay-offs been made to Gross?"

"Yes."

In 1948 a Teamsters Union strike had hit the entire city of New York. But the *New York Times,* which then was having its Sunday magazine section printed by the Neo-Gravure Company, and the *New York Mirror,* which was receiving a Sunday supplement from the same firm, were able to obtain distribution.

That night in my office in the Senate we found out how.

Through the Neo-Gravure Company, these two newspapers made a $45,000 pay-off to Gross and Noonan in order to get their supplements delivered. Approximately $35,000 came from the *Times;* some $10,000 from the *Mirror.* Moreover, two years before, the same two papers had made a pay-off amounting to some $10,000 and for the same purpose. I could only think as I drove home that night of the little boy's reputed plea to Shoeless Joe Jackson in the 1919 World Series, "Joe, say it ain't so."

Several days later when we held our hearings, the Neo-Gravure people appeared as witnesses and deviated in no way from the story they had told in my office.

Senator McClellan told Charles Chenicek, vice president and general manager of the Neo-Gravure Printing Company: "What it actually amounted to is that you acted as agent, in a sense of go-between, between *The American Weekly* and the racketeers; is that true?"

Without flinching Mr. Chenicek answered: "That is true."

Both Gross and Noonan took the Fifth Amendment when questioned. Between the two of them and Gross's family they had received $307,000 as pay-offs for labor peace.

Senator McClellan expressed his appreciation to the Neo-Gravure witnesses for their testimony. He said: "The time has come in this country, if we are going to stop this racketeering and rascality that is going on . . . it is going to require that businessmen, honest labor people, their leaders, all of us stand up and be counted in this thing."

After our conversation in my office that Sunday night, Jerome Adlerman and Walter Sheridan called on business officials of the *New York Times* and the *Daily Mirror.* From the outset the *Times's* business department co-operated. They furnished documents that we did not know existed, setting forth the details of the pay-off, which

233

the memorandum referred to as a "tribute." The man who had handled it was no longer alive and the *Times* could have pleaded ignorance. They chose rather, like the representatives of Neo-Gravure, to tell the truth.

Amory H. Bradford, vice president and business manager of the *Times,* appeared before the Committee and summarized the history of the 1948 strike. He said that had the magazine section not been delivered, the cost to the *Times,* because of advertising commitments, would have been $160,000. He admitted that a similar problem in 1946 had also been taken care of by a pay-off. Through Neo-Gravure, he said, Harry Gross had passed the word along that "Connie Noonan can reach the proper people."[3]

But he added: "This is not the kind of payment that we would make today . . . in order to obtain deliveries of this kind."

On the day after Mr. Bradford testified, the *New York Times* played the story on the front page of the newspaper. Objectively written by an Associated Press reporter, it gave complete details of the *Times's* involvement in the pay-off as exposed by the Committee. This, and the straightforward admission of error and co-operative attitude of the *Times's* representatives, helped us greatly to recover from the shock of discovering that a paper of the *Times's* reputation should have been concerned in such a deal in the first place.

When we questioned Joseph E. Fontana, business manager of *The American Weekly,* regarding their $28,000 pay-off to Gross, he insisted that he had never bothered to ask Neo-Gravure where the $4,000 was going each year. He just paid it. The Committee could call it payment for labor peace, said Mr. Fontana, but he was going to call it payment to assure delivery of *The American Weekly.* He did say it was an action that the paper would never repeat.

Warren Kelly, vice president and advertising manager of the *Daily Mirror,* testified that his company had paid $13,856 in shakedown money through Neo-Gravure at the same time the *Times* had.

[3] Gross and Noonan are under Federal indictment on charges growing out of the Committee's investigation. In December, 1959, Gross was convicted of income-tax evasion and resigned as president of Local 320.

Did he worry about who got his money as long as his papers were delivered?

"I did not," he said.

"Do you think that is the proper attitude for a business executive?"

"I think it is the proper attitude for an executive that wants to sell two million papers."

And if he held the same position today that he had had then, and the same situation arose, would he still pay a bribe in order to assure delivery of his paper?

Mr. Kelly: "That I would have to give more thought to."

Senator McClellan later raised the same question with him.

SENATOR MCCLELLAN: You know it is the wrong thing to do, do you not? Your paper editorially would condemn it in others just like that.

MR. KELLY: Exactly.

SENATOR MCCLELLAN: Don't you condemn it when you do it?

MR. KELLY: Yes, sir.

MR. KENNEDY: You wouldn't do it again if you were in the same position?

MR. KELLY: I would not.

In Pittsburgh, the Committee found that the *Sun-Telegraph* had on its payroll as a driver President Theodore Cozza of Local 211, one of Mr. Hoffa's union leaders, who had been convicted three times—of obstructing public justice, entering a building to steal, and operating a lottery. According to company officials, Cozza performed "very little" work for the money the paper paid him. Yet each week he pocketed a check for working fifty-six hours, plus the highest amount of overtime paid to any driver who really worked for the company. From January, 1950, until May, 1959, he received a total of slightly more than $100,000—including some $20,000 he was paid for a truck he rented to the newspaper.

Why had the payments to Cozza continued?

"I would say it was continued for fear of disturbing our labor relations and labor peace," said Mr. Poch, business manager of the paper.

A month before Mr. Poch testified, the paper had fired Cozza for roughing up its efficiency expert when he questioned Cozza's usefulness.

Cozza then called a strike and the newspaper was shut down. The strike was settled when the paper agreed to hire a substitute for Cozza, but with the understanding that he would actually work.[4]

The Committee also found that Cozza was getting a 5 per cent rake-off from the firm that leased trucks to the newspaper. This, the truck company said, was to "control drivers and prevent damage and abuse of their equipment."

In Detroit, Joe Prebenda, head of Teamsters Local 372, the union that handled delivery of the Detroit *Times,* was also serving two employers: the local and the *Times.* He drew substantial salaries from both.

Charles Obermeyer, business manager of the paper, said Prebenda did do "some work" for the paper, but only on Saturday nights. For this he drew a full week's salary, $36,000 over a five-year period. He received $14,000 a year from the union.

Mr. Obermeyer told the Committee that he planned to end Prebenda's employment with the *Times* immediately after the hearing. He was a quiet, soft-spoken man. It obviously disturbed him to have to admit that his company paid Joe Prebenda for doing little or no work.

Senator McClellan asked Mr. Obermeyer if he could construe the money paid to Prebenda as anything but a shakedown.

"I don't think so," answered the newspaper official.

"Do you think it is a proper payment?"

"Absolutely not."

As he got to his feet to leave the witness chair, I called for Joe Prebenda to appear. Walking to the table, he passed Mr. Obermeyer on his way out of the hearing room.

I saw him step directly in front of Mr. Obermeyer, and it was obvious even in the crowded hearing room that Prebenda had spoken sharply to him. When the Teamster took the stand and was under

---

[4] As this book is written, Cozza is under Federal indictment on charges growing out of our Committee's investigation.

oath, I asked: "What did you just say to Mr. Obermeyer as he left?" Joe Prebenda, unaware that he had been observed, hesitated. Then he grinned: "I just said, 'I think you made a mistake,' " he answered.

Before Mr. Obermeyer left the witness stand, Senator Ervin made this comment: "Your evidence indicates to me that the press in the United States is not quite as free as it is supposed to be."

It cannot help but be disquieting that gangsters like Cozza or Gross are in a position to shut down great newspapers merely because they are not receiving their pay-offs. It is an intolerable situation; for this is a power that the Constitution denies even to the Federal Government. I hope that the hearings aroused concern among people about the tremendous power presently wielded by such people; certainly we shall have to have a far different attitude than we have had in the past if we are to lick the problem.

The Committee was unhappy to learn during our investigation that besides the cases I have mentioned, Teamsters Union money had contaminated a few reporters, a few columnists, a few feature writers. We found that in a number of cases Hoffa's union had paid cash, or given gifts or "expenses" to get favorable press coverage. Nevertheless, these few cases were more than overshadowed by the integrity of the vast majority of the newspapers of the nation, and by the idealism of a number of reporters whose vigilance contributed in many ways to the work of the Committee.

Pulitzer Prizes were awarded to such men as Clark Mollenhoff of the Cowles Publications, who, more than anyone else, was responsible for the existence of the Committee; to Wally Turner and Bill Lambert of the Portland *Oregonian;* to Harold Brislin of the Scranton, Pennsylvania, *Scrantonian* for outstanding investigative reporting, which led in more than one instance to hearings by our Committee. And the assistance and advice of men like Ed Guthman of the Seattle *Times* and John Seigenthaler of the Nashville *Tennesseean* were essential in our investigation of bad situations in their areas. Columnists such as John Herling, the late Fred Othman, Fred Perkins, and

237

Victor Reisel frequently used their talent and space to raise significant questions.

And above and beyond the individual work of these and many others, the newspapers, national magazines, television and radio performed a substantial and constructive task in sifting the maze of day-to-day testimony and flashing it out across the nation, making the public aware of the enemy within.

Chapter 12 / ORGANIZED CRIME

"There'll be fifty-eight for tea, Mrs. Barbara."

IN NOVEMBER, 1957, at least fifty-eight men met on an estate in upper New York. They had come from all over the United States. Joseph Francis Civillo came from Texas; James Colletti, from Colorado; the Falcone brothers, from New York; Vito Genovese, from New Jersey; Russell Bufalino, from Pennsylvania; Santos Trafficante, from Tampa, Florida.

Fifty of the fifty-eight had arrest records, thirty-five had convictions. Eighteen had been arrested or questioned in connection with murders, fifteen in connection with narcotics, twenty-three for illegal use of firearms. The host, Joseph Barbara, had been the chief suspect in two murders.

They were also active in many so-called legitimate enterprises. Nineteen were involved in garment manufacturing; seven, in trucking; nine were or had been in the coin-machine business; seventeen owned taverns or restaurants; eleven were in the olive oil–cheese importing or exporting business. Others were involved in automotive agencies, coal companies, entertainment; four in funeral homes; one was a conductor of a band; *and twenty-two were involved in labor or labor-management relations.*

It was not a chance meeting. It had been well organized beforehand. Subpoenaed telephone toll tickets proved that they had been in close contact with each other for weeks before. Reservations had been made at the neighboring motels and lodges; huge amounts of food had been ordered.

This was the now famous Apalachin conclave at the home of Joseph Barbara, where some of the elect of the underworld met to plan strategy in the fields of gambling, narcotics and labor racketeering.

Subsequent testimony before the Committee revealed that the underworld was increasing its effort to seize control of legitimate businesses and unions, which they often used as "fronts" for their illegal activities. In some industries they actually had gained a monopoly control.

The results of the underworld infiltration into labor-management affairs forms a shocking pattern across the country. We found and duly proved that the gangsters of today work in a highly organized fashion and are far more powerful now than at any time in the history of the country. They control political figures and threaten whole communities. They have stretched their tentacles of corruption and fear into industries both large and small. They grow stronger every day.

We have seen how the Dio-Hoffa operation worked in New York, and how ex-convict Harry Gross shook down some of the country's leading newspapers; but let us look at a few further examples, of the many that the Committee examined, of how these people operate and how some businessmen work with them to give them their power.

The Monti Marine Corporation is one of the major ship repair companies on the New York waterfront. In 1953 the union, the International Longshoremen's Association, insisted on a "hiring boss." Monti Marine refused. The men were called out on strike.

Mr. Charles Montanti, owner and general manager of the company, hired a labor relations consultant called Carmine Lombardozzi. The company won.

Later, Monti Marine began having trouble with Henry "Buster"

Bell and Harry Kashin,[1] officials of the ILA. Again, labor expert Lombardozzi was called in. And again, peace was restored.

Who was Carmine Lombardozzi and what experience in labor-management affairs enabled him to settle this company's problems?

Lombardozzi has been arrested twenty-one times and convicted thirteen times, twice for disorderly conduct, four times for book-making, once for being a common gambler. (A charge of rape and abduction was reduced to disorderly conduct, and a charge of burglary was reduced to unlawful entry.) In 1944 he was sentenced to six months' hard labor after going AWOL and was discharged from the Army in November for "ineptness, inability to adapt and general misconduct." He was described as being "extremely high strung, hot tempered, undependable, a chronic drinker, and a user of marijuana."

He was one of those who attended the meeting at Apalachin in 1957, and thus became the subject of our attention. According to the testimony of Lieutenant Mooney of the New York Police Department, Lombardozzi was called to account for his activities in the juke-box field at the Apalachin meeting. He was "previously scheduled to be killed, but instead his situation was considered by a council made up of certain of the higher ranking individuals present at Apalachin." Lombardozzi "was not allowed to be present or to participate in the hearing, but was required to remain in Barbara's garage to await the verdict. The council decided to fine the offender [Lombardozzi] $10,000," instead of having him executed.

This is the man who could solve Monti Marine's labor problems. He was paid $125 a week but this was not his only compensation. In 1954, with the financial assistance of Montanti, Lombardozzi purchased a generator for $13,000. He then turned around and rented the generator to Montanti's company for $750 a week. This amounted to $15,375 in 1955, $15,425 in 1956, $11,225 in 1957, and $6,400 for the first half of 1958.

In 1958 Monti Marine purchased the generator from him for

---

[1] In 1931 Kashin was convicted of murder in the first degree and sentenced to be executed; in 1933 he was retried and acquitted. Bell has been arrested a number of times and convicted of impersonating a public official.

$15,000, making a grand total of $63,425 that Monti Marine paid Lombardozzi during a four-year period.

Montanti denied that this was a pay-off. Explaining why Monti Marine hired Lombardozzi, Montanti told a grand jury in New York: ". . . All I can say is that when we got into trouble with Buster Bell, and this fellow Perrone, he took care of it 100 per cent, and there aren't many people on the waterfront who can fight these people and come out on top."

The war that broke out in Westchester County in 1951 is another story. The Committee found the prize was a share of the fifty-million-dollar New York garbage removal industry. The stakes were high, the sides unequal, and the battle short and deadly.

On one side was Local 456 of the Teamsters run by two tough, honest union officials, Everett Doyle, president, and John Acropolis, secretary-treasurer. Local 456 had an agreement with the Rex Carting Company, which was owned by reputable businessmen.

On the other side was Local 27 of the Teamsters run by Joe Parisi, secretary-treasurer, a member of Murder, Inc., and Bernard Adelstein, business manager.[2] Local 27 had signed a secret agreement with the Westchester Carting Company which is operated by ex-convict Nick Ratteni and his friend Joey Surprise.[3]

With the help of Parisi and Adelstein, the Westchester Carting Company expanded its operations. Businessmen were threatened, equipment of competitors was burned and destroyed, and reluctant storekeepers were picketed.

When a Safeway Store in Yonkers switched from Westchester

[2] Parisi has a record of 11 arrests, 1 rape conviction; Adelstein a record of 5 arrests; a conviction for extortion was reversed.

[3] Ratteni, arrested for suspicion of burglary, grand larceny, assault and robbery, had spent seven and a half years in Sing Sing. He was one of Frank Costello's chief lieutenants and, according to testimony before the Committee, a handler of narcotics.

Joey Surprise had been arrested for felonious assault, homicide and murder in the first degree. On the latter charge (involving the killing of one policeman and wounding of another), he was convicted and sentenced to death. The conviction was reversed on appeal and, pleading guilty to manslaughter, he was sentenced from seven and a half to fifteen years in Sing Sing. He was on the company books of Westchester Carting as their "efficiency expert."

Carting to Rex Carting, Adelstein picketed all the other Safeway stores.

The public relations manager of Safeway explained to the Committee:

> After several days we had a rather serious problem with both the quantity of the refuse in the stores and the condition of the smell, and, therefore, the concern of whether the board of health might, possibly, close the stores.
>
> . . . After exploring all possibilities, it was decided that we had nothing to do but to try to make a deal with these people. . . .

At the Teamster state convention in Rochester in 1952, Adelstein and Parisi of Local 27 told Acropolis and Doyle of Local 456 that they had better stop giving them trouble and turn Rex over to them.

As Doyle reported it: "There were some pretty harsh words spoken. Adelstein said to Johnny [Acropolis], 'You are not that tough. Don't think you are too tough that we can't take care of you. Tougher guys than you have been taken care of.'"

Parisi spoke in similar terms: ". . . I am through arguing with you. I have a bad heart. I am not going to argue with you. There is other ways of taking care of you."

Three weeks after the convention, Acropolis was shot to death as he opened the door to his house.

A month later, Rex Carting sold out to Westchester Carting, which now had monopoly control of the garbage removal business in Westchester County. Their work done, Adelstein and Parisi abandoned their contract with Westchester, the Committee found, and allowed them to form a company-dominated union. The battle was over.

Garbage removal is used by gangsters as a vehicle of extortion. When there is a monopoly control, the refusal to remove garbage or waste can put a company out of business. Garbage which has not been removed will bring swift action from the Sanitary Commission.

Because it is comparatively easy to gain and maintain control, gangsters and racketeers have been attracted to the multimillion-dollar industry. Important in their organization is a friendly labor union which can act as an enforcing arm.

Gangster infiltration of the garbage industry is not confined to

243

Westchester. In 1955 the various garbage companies in the New York area formed an employer association. Soon afterward, the Senators learned, the underworld took control of this association and with the help of Adelstein's new union, Teamster Local 813, maneuvered to monopolize the industry.

The men behind the move were an interesting group. The top man was Jimmy Squillante, described as "a major source of supply for narcotics, as well as being a prominent racketeer." Squillante, a short, thin man with glasses, described himself as the godson (church records did not confirm this) of Albert Anastasia, the lord high executioner of Murder, Inc. He was sitting in the barber chair next to Anastasia when the former overlord of the New York underworld was murdered in the fall of 1957. The sergeant at arms of the employer association was Alfred Fazula, known as Pasta Fazula, whose police record included burglary, larceny, auto theft and vagrancy. But perhaps the most interesting executive of the group was Professor C. Don Modica.

I spent a considerable amount of time talking to the Professor in New York City. He admitted that as a young man he had had some difficulties with the law (six months in the Delaware State Prison for practicing medicine without a license; one conviction of grand larceny). A graduate of St. John's University in Brooklyn, New York, he was an instructor in philosophy of education at New York University. He also edited a garbage magazine called *The Hired Broom,* for which he coined such morale-lifting slogans as "Out of garbage, there grows a rose."

And in his spare time he tutored the children of such major underworld figures as Willie and Salvatore Moretti, Vito Genovese and Joe Adonis.

To add to this rather incredible group of people was a boy in his teens whom Professor Modica tutored in the office of the association. A witness before our Committee described him in action:

He had a blackboard and he had all kinds of symbols and numerals and different things. It didn't bother me at first, but after the third time I said to myself, "Who is this fellow?" I asked Beansie Fazula, "Who is this fellow?" and he turned around and tells me, "That is Albert's boy." I drew my own conclusions after that.

"Albert's boy" was Albert Anastasia's son.

It was understood that Modica was in the office of the cartage industry as a representative of Albert Anastasia to make sure that Anastasia's interests were being protected. To quote one of the witnesses: "I would say he was a watchdog."

Under constant pressure from the gangsters, the cartage companies found it advisable to take certain steps.

1. Join the union—though the union as run by Adelstein was little more than a racket. It did virtually nothing for its eighteen hundred members; its function was to act as the enforcement arm for Squillante and the association. Through the use of picket lines it helped obtain business for favored companies, even for some that had no union contract—like the one owned by Squillante's brother.

2. Join the association. Adelstein's union contract gave a discount to association members, demanding only a $25 deposit per company, as against a $300 deposit per man per company for nonassociation members. This provision helped Squillante keep the companies in line.

3. Stay in your territories. Once the company became a member of the association, it was assigned a territory outside of which it was not allowed to remove garbage. If the company broke this basic law, it had to appear before "Judge" Squillante (fines $3,000 to $5,000). A monopoly control for favored companies was thus established.

Besides his other duties, James Squillante decided how much the members of the association should bid on various contracts. With other underworld figures he formed a company to loan money to cartage firms in financial difficulties; then to consolidate his control completely he and several of his colleagues purchased the land where the garbage was dumped. When he got into difficulty with the tax authorities he raised a fund among the cartage owners "to defend ourselves." Fifteen thousand dollars of the money was used to pay his back Federal taxes and another $10,000 to pay his state taxes and attorneys fees. He also used some money to investigate the District Attorney who was looking into his activities.

On the basis of the revelations of the Committee hearings, Squillante was returned to jail for violating his parole. Subsequently he and Adelstein were indicted for extortion, convicted and sentenced to Sing Sing. As of October, 1959, they were out on appeal.[4]

Gangsters and hoodlums have also taken over much of the coin-machine business in the United States. In some five weeks of testimony we established that they are entrenched in most of the game and juke-box companies and making major inroads into cigarette vending companies. Invariably, as in the garbage industry, they work through an employers association and have their tame unions which they manipulate to tighten their control.

Milton Hammergren, vice president and general sales manager of the Wurlitzer Company, one of the largest distributors of juke boxes in the country, freely admitted that he had gone to the major underworld figures in various sections of the country to handle the distribution of his machines.

MR. KENNEDY: And the people that you found as a general rule—the only people that could get this distribution achieved—were these people with the underworld connections, as a practical matter?

MR. HAMMERGREN: Yes, that is true.

I asked him why.

MR. HAMMERGREN: They have connections, they were able to do things that the ordinary individual wasn't able to do in a big metropolitan area. They had unions and associations at their disposal.

Hammergren described in detail the force, violence and terrorism that frequently accompanied distribution.

MR. KENNEDY: Were company officials upset about the use of force?

MR. HAMMERGREN: Company officials, of which I was one, yes, we didn't like it, but we still had to sell juke boxes. We all knew about it, and we knew what the problems were. We tried to go along with it the best we could.

MR. KENNEDY: Even if it became necessary that somebody was killed during the course of it?

MR. HAMMERGREN: Well, that is pretty broad, Mr. Kennedy. I don't think we would condone that knowingly, no.

[4] In December, 1959, the Appellate Court reversed their convictions. Squillante and his brother Nunzio still face an indictment in Brooklyn, along with contractor Carmine De Cavala.

MR. KENNEDY: I mean if somebody, just in the course of trying to get your boxes distributed, if somebody was killed, that was taken as part of the trade?

MR. HAMMERGREN: That is one of the liabilities of the business, I would say.

He spoke of setting up the big gangsters in business—Meyer Lansky on the East Coast; Buster Wortman, in St. Louis: "Greasy Thumb" Guzik and Tony Accardo (the remnants of the Capone gang) in Chicago. Once in control of the operation, the gangsters are able to put pressure on local owners of taverns and bars to install their merchandise. When an outsider tries to compete with this more refined operation, the employers association has its union send pickets to any tavern or bar that accepts the competitor's machines. When any member of the association gets out of line, the same thing happens. If this does not work—violence.

However, if a new group of juke-box distributors moves into a community, and is powerful enough, it forms its own association and creates its own union. They send *their* union to picket the established association's locations. It is not unusual to have one union picketing another union's pickets. The results, naturally, are fights, arsons, dynamitings, beatings and death. To the underworld this means nothing, for if a monopoly can be established, the profits can run into millions of dollars.

It sometimes surprises people to learn that anyone, whether he had a criminal record or not, could form an international union. In most areas there were no background requirements, no standards that had to be met. He could then go on and form locals. No membership even was required.

When I asked representatives of one International where they met, they admitted quite frankly that their meetings, when they were held, took place in the back of the automobile of a friend. They had no office space.

Abraham Gilbert was a part-time carpenter. He was doing some work on the office of a local of one such International when one of its officials resigned. The president asked him if he would like to take over. As he told us: "I put down my hammer, climbed down from the ladder, and went to work."

Another International union with a total of eight members made the mailman secretary-treasurer, with the understanding that "he would do some organizing work for us while delivering the mail."

In all cases these unions were operated either for purposes of extortion or as an enforcement arm of an employer association. They had absolutely no interest in their members, who benefited in no way from their union membership. They were gangster-controlled and run for the benefit of gangsters.

Since these phony unions have no members, picketing has become a fairly profitable work. As some people grow up to become lawyers, doctors, cowboys, mechanics, bankers, engineers, so now we have the professional picket. I interviewed one of them in New York. He showed me his wallet, which was filled with the cards of some eight different unions. He said that sometimes when on picket duty he had difficulty remembering which card to show when asked for identification.

With few, if any, members, the financing for unions in the coin-machine fields comes from the sale of stickers for the machines; selling for approximately one dollar, a new sticker must be purchased every month. As a result, a company with fifty machines and only one employee would have to pay the union at least $50 a month. Some of the unions, with only a hundred members, have incomes of $50,000 to $75,000 a year. This allows a very nice cut for the gangster "union official" in charge of that part of the operation.

Charles Lichtman, who had been head of one of these locals in New York, explained his function quite frankly:

MR. LICHTMAN: You see, in the coin machine business, the operators get together and they form an association. This association is formed of members who were operating machines in various sections of the city. These operators want protection so they don't lose these locations. That is, when another operator who is not a member of the association takes the location, that they will use the union to secure the location back for the operator who was a member of the association.

SENATOR CHURCH: Through the device of picketing?

MR. LICHTMAN: That is right.

SENATOR CHURCH: In other words, these associations are formed just to divide up the spoils, so to speak, to divide up the city?

MR. LICHTMAN: To protect their members only.

About stickers, Mr. Lichtman had this to say:

MR. LICHTMAN: The purpose of the sticker was to see that the union had sufficient money which to use in going out picketing locations that members of the association had lost.

MR. KENNEDY: So this was just a way of financing the union so that the union could provide services; is that right?

MR. LICHTMAN: That is right.

MR. KENNEDY: Many of the people didn't know they were in the union, the employees?

MR. LICHTMAN: That is right.

The Gallo brothers helped operate an enforcer union in New York. The day they were to appear before the Committee, a man entered our reception room in Washington and started toward my office. Suddenly another man dressed completely in black sprang to his feet, approached the newcomer and searched him, running his hand professionally through all his pockets. The newcomer, flabbergasted, turned and rushed out.

Someone in the office asked the man what he thought he was doing. He replied: "No one is going to see Mr. Kennedy with a gun on him. If Kennedy gets killed now everybody will say I did it. And I am not going to take that rap."

And he was probably right. The man was Joey Gallo, the brother of Lawrence Gallo,[4] self-professed successors to Murder, Inc. Joey Gallo was one of the most extraordinary witnesses to appear before the Committee.

When he first strode into my office, dressed like a Hollywood Grade B gangster (black shirt, black pants, black coat, long curls down the back of the neck), he felt the rug and said: "It would be nice for a crap game."

Ten minutes later, he offered one of our secretaries a job, telling her that she could determine her own salary by "taking as much as you want from the till."

[4] Joey Gallo has a record of 17 arrests and 4 convictions; Lawrence Gallo, a record of 13 arrests and 4 convictions.

Joey Gallo was a labor-management racketeer and chief suspect in a murder where the victim was shot so many times in the head that facial recognition was impossible. Down in my office, before he testified, we asked him about his part in it and received a giggle and a shrug in reply.

The Gallo brothers had formed their own International union. Until 1958 they battled with four or five other unions on behalf of certain favored employers for control of the New York juke-box industry. Because of the havoc and confusion the rivalry caused, the underworld made peace in 1958 and all closed ranks behind a Sing Sing character named Joe DeGrandis[5] and a newly formed Teamster union, Local 266. Soon afterward pressure was put on recalcitrant operators to join up with the new DeGrandis-Gallo run union. There were threats, beatings and violence. A wave of fear spread through the industry.

Since DeGrandis would tell us nothing, we subpoenaed the Gallos, Joey and his brother Larry.

When it was their turn to testify, their dress, their swagger, their foxlike faces, and their "two-step shuffle" to the witness stand created a furor in the hearing room. Taking the Fifth Amendment on all questions, Joey Gallo rounded out his academy award performance by spilling two glasses of water and knocking an ash tray off the table.

When John Amalfitano, a partner of the Gallos in their union operation and a relatively small-time hoodlum, testified before the Committee, I remarked that he wasn't in the same category as the Gallos, pointing out that they were much more dangerous. Afterward Joey Gallo told our assistant counsel, John Constandy, who had been working on the case: "Mr. Kennedy is a better fellow than I thought he was. We really appreciate him saying that nice thing about Amalfitano. It shows he is very fair."

When Amalfitano came downstairs after testifying, Joey rolled up a newspaper, hit him over the head, and laughingly said: "You damn labor racketeer, you gangster, aren't you ashamed of yourself?"

---

[5] DeGrandis was arrested, convicted and sentenced to Sing Sing for receiving stolen property, was returned later as a parole violator and convicted for possession of an unregistered still.

He told Constandy that he really liked him and if there was anything he could do, either in the way of money or taking care of someone, he should call on him.

The Gallos, laughing, said that their mother was terribly upset about them: she couldn't understand how they could have so much money and "do no work." Their mother was wrong about one thing: they did work. And they did their work well.

Milton Green testified to the way their union was operated. Green was a juke-box distributor who opposed his association's signing up with the Gallo-De-Grandis local, feeling it was dominated by gangsters. He went to a meeting and voiced his opposition, even though he had been warned to keep quiet. His objections were overruled. On his way home, he said: "They came out with steel bars and they split my skull open for me and I was taken to the hospital."

When he appeared before the Committee, seven months later, Milton Green was a thin, wan, pathetic figure, still without full use of his faculties. He will never completely recover.

Sidney Saul was another juke-box distributor. He also ignored threats of bodily harm and refused to join the Gallo-DeGrandis local. He was badly beaten by three of Gallo's aides, who wanted Saul to cut them in on 50 per cent of the profits of his business.

MR. SAUL: . . . I started pleading with them, and it didn't seem to have any effect. The only remark was that I was an excellent actor. They kept saying to each other, "This fellow is an actor," because I was pleading with them to stop beating me. . . .

He kept pounding away at my head and face and it got to a point where I was just barely able to keep my head up. Every time I started to plead, Panarella would lift a napkin holder, a commercial-type napkin holder used in luncheonettes, with the open face on both sides, about ten inches high—he lifted it in his hand and said he would bash my skull in if I said anything else.

Finally, as he was losing consciousness, they brought coffee over to the table. One of them put on the juke box to drown out any noise, and the beating began again.

". . . I didn't know what to say, and I didn't cry, and I just went

251

along and pleaded with them and I kept pleading with them to stop beating me. . . ."

They ordered more coffee. With a wet towel one of them helped him wipe off the blood that was now pouring out of his nose and ears.

". . . Then he started the conversation again that he wanted to be a partner on the juke box. Finally out of desperation I said I would take them in as a partner."

Saul appealed to the District Attorney. Gallo's three henchmen were tried but it was a hung jury, eleven to one for conviction. The District Attorney in New York assured the Committee that they would be retried.[6]

When Joey Gallo left, he said we had treated him very nicely: "I'll line up my people for your brother in 1960." To prove this, he called five or six of his friends in and made each one pledge a vote for Senator Kennedy for President. I told him the second biggest favor he could do me was to keep his preference quiet—and the biggest favor would be to announce for my brother's opponent. He laughed and went merrily on his way.

The underworld set up the same kind of association-union operation in the coin-machine industry in Chicago. We discovered that even Al Capone's brother Ralph was active in it. The union in this case was Local 134 of the International Brotherhood of Electrical Workers, run by "Jukebox" Smitty.

Investigation soon showed that Mooney Giancanna, the gunman for the remnants of the Capone mob (with the help of his two chief lieutenants—"Potatoes" Daddano and "Crackers" Medino) was the motivating force here behind the underworld's infiltration of the union and the association. We searched for him for fifteen months and finally located him in Las Vegas. Giancanna told a reporter, Sandy Smith of the Chicago *Tribune*, how much he had enjoyed dodging the Committee's subpoena servers.

When Smith asked him how he had managed to stay out of the service during World War II, Giancanna said: "Who wouldn't pretend he was a nut to stay out of the Army? When they called me to the

[6] They have been retried and convicted.

board they asked me what kind of work I did. I told them I steal for a living. They thought I was crazy, but I wasn't. I was telling the truth."

Concerning the alleged crime syndicate, Giancanna said: "What's wrong with the syndicate? Two or three of us get together on a deal and everybody says it's a bad thing. Businessmen do it all the time and nobody squawks."

About investigations in general he said: "There's going to be a lot of crime if these investigations keep up. It will be worse than Capone."

What was the effect of this man and his lieutenants on legitimate businessmen?

Bernard Poss comes from Aurora, Illinois, just outside Chicago. He had been in the juke-box business since 1947. In 1956, Rocco Pranno, another of Giancanna's lieutenants, approached him about distributing gambling equipment. Poss turned him down, but after several worrying visits, agreed to go with Pranno to see "the boss."

MR. POSS: The man they introduced to me as "Joe." He said, "That is the boss." . . . Then he asked me how many machines I had, and I told him. He said, "We are going to be your partner."

He said, "We are going to make you a lot of money." He said, "We will run books and slot machines and everything."

I said, "I never ran a book," and he said, "We'll teach you."

And I sensed that the two men alongside of him looked like bodyguards, and with this driver and him I thought the odds were kind of bad. So I agreed to whatever he said, they are going to be my partner.

MR. KENNEDY: Why did you agree to bring them in as partners?

MR. POSS: These roads that I was being rode over I had at various times saw in the paper that bodies were hung over fences in those areas as I thought it would be better than having that happen.

MR. KENNEDY: You figured if you didn't, you would have been killed?

MR. POSS: I did.

Once safely back, Poss told Pranno the whole thing was off. Pranno answered: "The boss wouldn't like this."

Poss's telephone began to ring. They told him to get out of business—to sell out.

"One telephone call said, 'Now, I am telling you for your own good,' he says, 'we will take you out and beat you up with a ball bat and break your legs, and if you live you will be crippled for life.' "

They began wrecking his machines. Two men would enter his locations, one with a gun, the other with an ax. While the man with the gun held the people at bay, the other man chopped up the pinball and game machines.

Ralph Kelly, a friend of his in the vending business, came to see him. Poss knew Kelly's story. One day Kelly had been taken to Joliet, Illinois, where cement weights were tied to his feet. He was asked to make a choice—the river or a partnership with Rocco Pranno. He chose the partnership. When Kelly visited Poss he told him he had better sell out, too. Kelly was so terrified, Poss said, that he was contemplating suicide. He admitted Pranno "owned" him, and went on to tell Poss: "It is an order. I am sent here . . . I am sent here to tell you to get out of business."

Poss still refused.

Then his wife began getting telephone calls. With tears rolling down his cheeks, Poss said: "She was so nervous that I was fearful that she was going to go insane."

Mr. Poss went out of business.

Rocco Pranno is a big, husky, well-dressed man. Before testifying he came to my office and I asked him about Ralph Kelly. He snarled as he told me he wasn't going to answer any questions. I got mad. I told him he was a bully, and to get out of my office. Afterward, he told one of our investigators that the next time he came to Washington he was going to bring a lawyer to protect him from being mistreated by Mr. Kennedy. I thought grimly of Mr. Poss, his wife, and of Mr. Kelly.

When Pranno appeared before the Committee he took the Fifth Amendment and so did the unfortunate Mr. Kelly, who was too frightened to testify. His records indicated that he had turned over half of his business and received nothing for it. He was a little man, who looked absolutely petrified. Everyone present felt extremely sorry for him.

Mr. Ted Sipiora of Chicago owned a company that sold records to juke-box operators. In 1958 he began losing business, and asked the operators why they had stopped buying from him.

MR. KENNEDY: What kind of report did they give you?

MR. SIPIORA: Well, it was an element that would be rough.

MR. KENNEDY: How did they describe who was behind it?

MR. SIPIORA: Well, to put it point blank—

MR. KENNEDY: Just as frankly as we discussed it?

MR. SIPIORA: They said the hoods had gotten into the record business. That is the way they put it. . . . The operators told us that it came to a point where they could no longer buy from us, that the pressure was too great, the people behind it had forced them to leave us.

In short, the Committee found, under pressure from the underworld and "Jukebox" Smitty's Local 134, the operators had switched to the Lormar Distributing Company, although Lormar charged five cents more per record. Anyone who resisted was faced with labor problems or had his juke boxes wrecked.

The backers of Lormar, looking for more profits, hit on a plan to avoid paying royalties. They began copying records and counterfeiting the labels of major companies. The District Attorney later found they had copied at least 25,000 records, one of them appropriately entitled: "You Can Make It If You Try."

After the investigation, Chuck English, Giancanna's lieutenant and business partner, and one George Hilger were both indicted. The indictment against English was dismissed and Hilger was let off with a fifty-dollar fine. Furthermore, not one of the major companies whose records had been counterfeited sued Lormar!

Lormar Distributing Company, as of October, 1959, still controlled the record business in the Chicago area. Certain elements of law enforcement, the judiciary and big business have combined to permit these underworld businessmen to continue to operate.

Sometimes, as we have seen, the racketeers find a fertile field in the labor movement. Sometimes elements of the labor movement find a fertile field in racketeering, and sometimes it is mutual. In a majority of cases there is a breakdown of local law enforcement. That is what happened in Portland, Oregon, where the various elements joined forces to organize the vice rackets.

In our investigation there we had the invaluable help of the Portland *Oregonian* and two of the best and most courageous reporters I have ever seen, Wally Turner and William Lambert. For their work in exposing this sordid situation they both were honored with the Pulitzer Prize.

The case there centered around a key figure in the city's underworld: a racketeer named Jim Elkins, a slim, rugged-looking man with a rather kindly face and a very attractive and devoted wife. Elkins was one of the most interesting and controversial witnesses that appeared before the McClellan Committee. He was very guarded in what he said and to whom he said it. The first time I met him he was reluctant to talk. But the second and third and fourth time—and for many days after that—he talked freely. Once he made up his mind that he was going to co-operate, he went the whole way. He told me later that he had "checked me out," to see if I could be trusted.

I checked him out also. I learned that he had manufactured illicit whisky during prohibition, been given a twenty-to-thirty-year sentence for assault with intent to kill, a one-year sentence for possession of narcotics, and had been arrested several times on gambling charges (I also learned that he had performed some valuable services for the Army during the war).

Nevertheless, Jim Elkins was one of the three or four best witnesses the Committee ever had. Because his background was so unsavory, we checked his story up and down, backward and forward, inside and out. We found he didn't lie, and that he didn't exaggerate.

Occasionally, at the beginning, he would not answer a question. He would ask me to go on to something else. Later, as we came to know each other better, he would answer the question but tell me not to use the information. And sometimes when I pressed him for an answer, he would say, "You don't want to know the answer to that."

He was bright. He had a native intelligence. He was highly suspicious—and a fund of information. He never once misled me. He never once tried.

I never approved of what he had done and, perhaps, I would not approve of what he is doing now. However, I believed him when he said he had never participated in prostitution, or dealt in the peddling of narcotics.

Although one of the best, Jim Elkins was also one of the most difficult witnesses the Committee ever had. He never used proper names. It was always "he," "she," "we" or "they"—it was always "him" or "them": "They went visiting there and then he left and went over to the other place and met them."

By the time you had stopped his flow of conversation and discovered what he was talking about, an hour had passed.

When our investigation was finished—all leads run down, all data checked and rechecked, everyone interviewed whom it was possible to interview—and the case finally ready for a public hearing, I had Jim Elkins come on to Washington early. We locked ourselves in a little room away from my office and went over what he expected to tell the Committee. I spent more time with him than with any other witness, not only because of the tremendous amount of information he had, but because of the difficulty I feared that the Committee would have in understanding him. I needed to know the story almost as well as he did, so that I could clarify some of his complicated answers.

But nothing could keep Jim Elkins from being Jim Elkins, even on the witness stand. For example, before going into the story of the rackets, I questioned him about his arrests and convictions.

MR. KENNEDY: What was the first major difficulty or problem that you had?

MR. ELKINS: Well, I got twenty to thirty years in 1931 for assault with intent to kill. . . .

MR. KENNEDY: You received a pardon, did you, after four years?

MR. ELKINS: That is correct.

MR. KENNEDY: You had been in partnership with a policeman at that time, is that right?

MR. ELKINS: Well, let's say I was cutting a little money. . . .

MR. KENNEDY: And then you had a plan with him to move into a place, and as you came in he started to shoot you, is that right?

MR. ELKINS: Well, I believe he was going to shoot the boy that was with me, but I shot back.

MR. KENNEDY: Did you hit him?

MR. ELKINS: Not bad, no.

On another occasion, when he was picking up some slot machines under rather questionable circumstances, he went down a hill to put the machines in his car and then, according to him, this is what happened:

257

MR. ELKINS: Well, there were several people standing there on the porch watching us and one of them hollered at me something that attracted my attention and I looked around and he was hitting at me with a gun, and I turned around and hit him. He was bootlegging, too, and he had a fifteen-year-old boy with an old rusty Luger pointing at me. He started shooting about that time and shot me through the side. I am telling the boy that is driving the car, "Let's get away from here," and he said, "He has that thing pointed at me," and I said, "It is darn funny. He is pointing at you and he is hitting me."

THE CHAIRMAN: Let us have order.

Here is the Portland story as we had learned it and as Jim Elkins now related it on the witness stand during the very first hearings after the Select Committee was established:

In 1954 two Seattle underworld figures, Tom Maloney and Joseph McLaughlin cooked up an elaborate plot to take over vice in Portland. Involved with the two Seattle racketeers were top officials of the Teamsters Union, who could pull political strings and corrupt public officials, and Jim Elkins. Elkins was necessary to the scheme since he already controlled most of Portland's illegal gambling operations. Maloney approached him, he told us, and in return for his help in setting up a vice syndicate offered him a percentage of the profits.

(Although Frank Brewster and other Teamster officials were to deny any relationship with Maloney and McLaughlin, our investigation revealed that the expenses of the Seattle hoodlums while they were in Portland were paid with Teamster money.)

To carry out their plan, a friendly district attorney in Multnomah County (which encompassed Portland) was necessary. After talking with William Langley, a candidate for district attorney, they decided to support him. Clyde Crosby, a Portland Teamster official, swung the support of the union organization behind Langley and helped put him in office, over the opposition of all the other labor groups in the county.

After his election in 1955, Langley met Maloney to work out arrangements for pinballs, punchboards, card rooms and horse books; they also felt that Portland "could afford three or four houses of prostitution." Then they discussed who should take over the job of chief investigator in the District Attorney's office, and decided that

258

Clyde Crosby should visit the mayor and tell him to get rid of his chief of police, whom they suspected might be troublesome.

In the course of our investigation, we were able to get from the mayor, Fred L. Peterson, an affidavit stating that Clyde Crosby had indeed called on him in December of 1955 and told him he would lose Teamster support unless he disposed of the chief of police.

Maloney and McLaughlin now moved into a Portland apartment and set up their operations. They formed a pinball distributing company which immediately signed a contract with the Teamsters Union. Other major pinball operators were not allowed to join the Teamsters. Pickets sent out by the Teamsters brought cafeteria and bar owners into line with the threat that pickups and deliveries would be cut off if they did not use this company's machines.

The owner of one place reported to the Committee: "I couldn't get coffee, I couldn't get bread, I couldn't get meat deliveries." He capitulated, as did others.

Maloney and McLaughlin then concentrated on punchboards. Setting up a company with a respectable front, they repeated the pinball operation. Only the "syndicate" company would be allowed to join the Teamsters Union and picket lines would be placed in front of bars, cigar stores, cigarette counters, to cut off all pickups and deliveries unless the owners took the syndicate punchboards.

There was one small difficulty: punchboards were illegal. However, Clyde Crosby went to the City Council and succeeded in having an ordinance passed that made it legal to have punchboards on the premises.

At the same time there was a move to make pinballs illegal. Again Clyde Crosby proved useful. He approached Portland Commissioner Stanley Earl and told him that the Teamsters would oppose him when he ran for re-election if he voted to bar pinball machines. (Nevertheless, Earl voted for the ordinance and in 1956 received the all-out opposition of the Teamsters. Despite this opposition, he was elected.)

The syndicate next planned their move into the field of prostitution. The "houses" were to be operated by a woman named Ann Thompson and two "madams" known as Big Helen and Little Helen.

At this juncture, Elkins balked. When he refused to have anything to do with prostitution, the syndicate's carefully laid plans began to fall apart.

Elkins's break touched off a no-holds-barred underworld struggle in Portland. He told the Committee he realized that, because of his reputation, he was up against all the power of the Teamsters, gangsters and the District Attorney's office.

At one point, he testified, he was threatened by Frank Brewster when he went up to Seattle to complain about what McLaughlin and Maloney were doing in Portland. Brewster got mad because Elkins was interfering. As Elkins told it: ". . . He talked a little more and he got red in the face and he said, 'If you bother my two boys, you will find yourself wading across Lake Washington with a pair of concrete boots.' "

Brewster, when he testified, denied that he had said this.

After he broke with the syndicate and the Teamsters, Elkins and his wife were constantly harassed. There were anonymous phone calls in the middle of the night. One time an unknown voice informed them, "We are just a minute away and we are coming over to break both arms and both legs."

Elkins explained to the Committee how he handled some men who had been bothering his wife when he wasn't at home.

MR. KENNEDY: How did you finally catch them there?

MR. ELKINS: Well, I left like I was going to leave and I doubled back in another car. . . .

MR. KENNEDY: Then, what happened?

MR. ELKINS: Well, I pulled up to the curb, and I talked to them and they left and they didn't come back no more.

How Elkins could just talk to these men and make them go away intrigued Senator McClellan. He asked: "You did what?"

MR. ELKINS: I talked to them. Well, I pointed the shotgun at them and I talked to them, and they didn't come back any more.

MR. KENNEDY: Did you do anything else with them?

MR. ELKINS: Yes; I did. One of them, yes, I treated him a little rough.

MR. KENNEDY: What did you do with him?

MR. ELKINS: Well, I hit him on the head and knocked him around a little bit and put him back in the car and told his buddy that I was going to shoot the next person that came in my yard.

Elkins knew he needed protection. He realized that if he were to tell the story of how the vice operations had started and who was involved he would not be believed. His record was against him. He had to have corroboration.

So he began making tape recordings of his conversations with Maloney, Crosby and others with whom he was involved. These recordings, which he turned over to Wally Turner and Bill Lambert, were played for the Committee during the hearing. They were extremely informative (and in parts unprintable) and proved beyond all question that Elkins was telling the truth.

He told me that during one of the conversations with Maloney he had been using a recording device concealed in his watch. Suddenly the face of the watch dropped off and hung dangling from wires that were attached to the recorder. Maloney became curious. Elkins coolly replied that it was one of those new watches that operate with a battery. He calmly picked up the mechanism, put it back into the watch, and continued with the conversation.

When I had interviewed Clyde Crosby in Portland, he had denied Elkins's entire story; he hardly knew the man personally, he said; and had, of course, been a bitter enemy of his, knowing he was part of the city's underworld. Since Elkins was to be a witness with a police record and Crosby was a respectable witness, I had Jerry Adlerman and Al Calabrese check any data Elkins could give us to corroborate his relationship with the Portland Teamsters official. Calabrese found evidence in hotel, telephone and travel records which established that it was Jim Elkins—not Clyde Crosby—who was telling the truth.

In order to try to impeach Elkins's veracity, Crosby presented the Committee with the unsigned and unsworn statements of two Portland "ladies," who maintained that contrary to his testimony, Elkins had indeed been active in the prostitution racket. We tried to get hold of these "ladies" but somehow they had temporarily dropped out of sight. We traced them to a hotel in Seattle but before we arrived they were rushed away and hidden. Eventually, through Elkins's far-flung contacts and with the help of Arthur Kaplan, then an assistant in the Attorney General's office, we were able to find and subpoena them.

When they arrived in Washington they were frightened. I explained

261

that we were not trying to injure them in any way, and would not go into their own operations except as the Teamsters and the corruption of public officials were involved. After they became convinced of our good faith they agreed to testify. On the stand they unequivocally refuted their charge involving Elkins in prostitution. They had made it, they said, only because a police officer connected with Crosby had told them they would be taken to the Oregon Institute for the Insane if they refused.

One of the girls was taking narcotics and asked me to try to get her admitted to a Federal institution so that she could be treated. This, of course, we did.

William Langley, the District Attorney from Portland, took the Fifth Amendment on all questions. The tape recordings, the strong circumstantial evidence and Jim Elkins's testimony all involved him deeply in the operation of the Portland vice ring.

Langley hardly looked the part, nor did his wife, who accompanied him. He seemed more like a man on his way to his twentieth reunion at an Ivy League college, than a discredited district attorney on his way to the Senate caucus room to take the Fifth Amendment.

When he returned to Portland from our hearings he was convicted of a misdemeanor and removed from office.

The Committee also heard some controversial testimony that involved Mayor Terry Shrunk of Portland. He himself appeared as a witness. Following our hearings he returned home and was indicted on a bribery charge, tried and acquitted.

These stories only touch upon the problem. Evidence developed by the Committee showed that gangsters today control steel companies, laundry and dry-cleaning establishments, frozen food operations, and many other kinds of businesses. Hoodlums living reputable lives in Los Angeles have major vice and gambling holdings in the Midwest. They seek to corrupt and do corrupt public officials to an alarming extent. A man I mentioned earlier, the public prosecutor in Lake County, Indiana, had $310,000 in cash pass through his hands. He refused to explain its source to the Committee. In adjoining Porter County, Indiana, the assistant sheriff was offered $100,000 to let vice rackets operate. The man who offered the bribe, Thomas Morgano, said he was going to control the county "corner to corner"—not even a "fly is going to come in"—and those who opposed him would find themselves dead in the trunk of a car. A major vending company paid mobster Mickey Cohen $10,000 simply to remain "neutral" in a battle over locations for machines in Los Angeles. The leading restaurants in Chicago for the last twenty years have paid gangsters and hoodlums to handle their labor-management relations. The two "mob" attorneys through whom the arrangements were made both took the Fifth Amendment before the Committee. A number of major beer distributing companies have gangsters on their payrolls to handle their labor problems.

There can be no question that these operations are profitable. Our investigation and hearings show that Mickey Cohen spent $275 for his silk lounging pajamas, $25,000 for a specially built bulletproof car and at one time had 300 different suits, 1,500 pairs of socks and 60 pairs of $60 shoes. His tax returns, however, showed a total income of $1,200 in 1956 and $1,500 in 1957. When asked where his money came from, Cohen said he borrowed it from his friends and thus it was not necessary to declare it. Tony Accardo has a twenty-two-room house with an indoor swimming pool, two bowling alleys and a pipe organ; three of his bathrooms have gold-plated fixtures and one has a bathtub that was cut from a solid block of Mexican onyx which cost $10,000. The house is estimated to be worth a half-million dollars.

What steps are we going to take to deal with this problem? A great number of the people whom our Committee proved were involved in these operations are still active. With the Committee out of existence, it would appear that they now have almost nothing to fear. James Squillante and the Gallo brothers are still flourishing in New York, Giancanna and his lieutenant, Rocco Pranno, are still doing business in Chicago.

The methods of our law enforcement agencies have not kept pace with the improved techniques of today's criminals. We are still trying to fight the modern Al Capone with the weapons that we used twenty-five years ago. They simply are not effective. And the result is that within ten years our whole economy will be drastically affected. I think that there are steps that can and should be taken to deal with the problem.

One very effective move would be for each state to set up an agency that would periodically inspect the way law enforcement is being handled in the various localities within its jurisdiction. This has been done in England, and I think it would be most beneficial here. The agency's reports should be made public, so that everyone would know whether his officials were adequately meeting their responsibilities. And each law enforcement officer would know that his work was being subjected to close scrutiny.

In my opinion, however, our first and most urgent need is for a national crime commission. This commission would serve as a central intelligence agency, a clearinghouse to which each of the seventy-odd Federal agencies and the more than ten thousand local law enforcement agencies throughout the country would constantly feed information on the leading gangsters. The commission would pool and correlate all its information on underworld figures and disseminate it to the proper authorities.

Where a general intelligence squad has been in existence, as in Los Angeles, St. Louis and New York, the results have been startlingly good. But Captain Hamilton of the Los Angeles Police Department has said: "No matter how good a job a local intelligence division can do it is still handicapped by inability to exchange information with other similar groups throughout the country. A national clearinghouse for information about the organized underworld would provide us with a weapon to strike a real blow at this nation's organized criminals."

New York's able District Attorney, Frank Hogan, also favors the establishment of a national crime commission, and suggests the possibility of its being modeled after the New York State Crime Commission: "Such a Federal agency could funnel information to local enforcement officers. If the local law enforcement officer receives the information and sits on his hands, the Federal agency could bring pressure to bear by taking its material to the State's Governor to have him remove the lethargic prosecutor if necessary to get action."

But these groups, and others like them, suffer for lack of a nation-wide organization. A national crime commission could alert the law enforcement bodies in the various sections of the country to the movement of gangsters and hoodlums and provide detailed information on their backgrounds. Because some public officials are corrupt, this information would have to be disseminated with care. But if a national crime commission had been in existence, it would have furnished the Los Angeles Police Department detailed information on Johnny Dio when he arrived there several years ago to set up a business. It would have briefed the Miami Police Department on the activities of his brother, Frank Dioguardi, who joined a coin-machine operation in Miami last year. When several of the leading gangsters from Cleveland moved into Miami, law enforcement officials and the Miami Crime Commission would have known about them. There has been an influx of gangsters and hoodlums from the Midwest into the southwestern section of the country, including Arizona. Before the inhabitants of some of the peaceful cities were aware of it, leading underworld figures had acquired motels, bought into race tracks and gained control of some of the most profitable pieces of real estate. The people there had no way of knowing who their new neighbors really were. A national crime commission could have forestalled this.

Only through a nationwide network can we fight the widespread penetration by criminals into our economy. Its members, appointed by the President, should be nationally prominent, of unquestionable integrity, and experienced in exposing crime. It would not be a national police, but a national information service for local police. With such an organization, even a one-telephone sheriff could prevent a hoodlum, well known in New York or Los Angeles, from coming into his community and taking over a local union or business. And where it might be helpful, the commission would hold hearings to expose criminal activity, so that other Federal agencies could take action, or Congress could supplement present legislation.

The point I want to make is this: If we do not on a national scale attack organized criminals with weapons and techniques as effective as their own, they will destroy us.

265

Chapter 13 / "GET REUTHER"

OUR HEARINGS on the long, incredibly bitter UAW-Kohler strike in Sheboygan, Wisconsin, opened in March of 1958. Behind them lay a ten-month struggle within the staff and Committee that almost caused its complete breakup.

I had gone into the investigation with an open mind. I knew about the strike in a general way, of course; I was aware that another Congressional committee had already looked into it and tried unsuccessfully to settle it; and that the National Labor Relations Board had held extensive hearings. But of the illuminating details I knew little, and of firsthand knowledge I had none. Certainly I had no strong convictions about it one way or another. Although I did not see how a third investigation could turn up anything new, there was so much public interest in the matter that early in the life of the Committee we decided to launch our own probe of this much publicized strike.

I first realized that Committee trouble was brewing shortly after the Dave Beck hearings ended, when stories began to appear in the press quoting "unnamed Republican Senators" and "Republican sources" as calling for an investigation of the UAW. (Many of them, I later learned, originated with Senator Mundt.)

Invariably these "sources" commented that they doubted that the Committee would go into the Kohler strike because Walter Reuther was involved, and the Democrats—"especially the Kennedy brothers" —were close to Reuther. This idea was fertilized by publicity initiated by the Teamsters and Jimmy Hoffa, who were anxious to draw the Committee's fire from the Teamsters and direct it at the UAW; away from Hoffa and at Reuther. (It was the same tactic that had been employed a few months earlier, with Cheyfitz pointing a finger at Beck.) The Teamsters were promoting the story that they were under investigation because Reuther was directing the investigation—and me.

A friendly Teamsters Union lawyer admitted to me that the union was circulating a rumor that the investigation of the Teamsters had been planned in a secret meeting between Walter Reuther, Adlai Stevenson and me, in the fall of 1956. Our purpose, it was said, was to discredit the Republicans and destroy Reuther's enemies—notably the Teamsters—within the labor movement. The flaw in this story was that I did not meet or talk to Walter Reuther until a year and a half later, when he was about to be called as a witness before the Committee in the UAW-Kohler hearings. Nevertheless, the idea was planted that Reuther, attempting to rule the labor movement and America, was aiming at his enemies through me.

These propaganda efforts were insidiously successful; and by May, 1957, it seemed to me that the unnamed "reliable sources" must be seeking out every journalist who would listen, for Kennedy-Reuther stories were now appearing weekly in newspapers, and magazines all over the country.

Before these stories had even begun to circulate, however, I had sent Vern Johnson, one of our staff investigators, out to Sheboygan to look into the UAW-Kohler fight and see if he could unearth any information that would warrant our making a full investigation and holding hearings. On May 27, he reported back. There were charges and countercharges by both sides, he said, but he had found nothing new, nothing that would add to the millions of words of testimony taken by the NLRB, or make another probe worth while.

But by this time the stories of a political fix were appearing in the press and causing considerable comment. I went to see Senator McClellan. I told him I felt that a Congressional committee hearing, to be successful, should be able to develop clear-cut points, and it did not

267

seem to me, on the basis of Johnson's report, that a third hearing would accomplish a great deal. However, I said, because of the stories if for no other reason, I thought we should go ahead with it.

Senator McClellan said he was prepared to investigate Reuther, Hoffa, Beck or anybody else; that he felt we had made some progress; that the Committee had a good record. He believed that the evidence of secondary boycotts and violence in the Kohler strike might make for a profitable hearing—if politics could be kept out of it. But he had read the stories in the papers, too. Under the circumstances, he said, he feared a hearing free from politics was virtually impossible. Nevertheless, he felt also because of the public interest we should proceed.

But within three weeks, the problem came to a political head. A major news story broke in *Newsweek* magazine: "Counsel Robert Kennedy has ignored continued demands for investigation of Walter Reuther, GOP members say privately." The Republican members were unhappy, the article continued, and they all agreed that the reason an investigation had not been made was that the Democrats and, specifically, the Kennedys, did not want to embarrass Walter Reuther. The Republicans who made these charges, flying in the face of facts known to them, were all unnamed but "reliable."

This sort of thing could no longer be ignored. At the next public meeting of the Committee with all the Republican members present, my brother called attention to the *Newsweek* article.

He said: "Now I don't have any information that would accord with that and I think that if that is the opinion of the members they should come out and say if they believe the counsel has ignored demands for investigation of Walter Reuther."

Senator Ives spoke up. He stated unequivocally that he had made no such statement to any newsman and that he was perfectly satisfied with the manner in which the investigations were conducted.

Senator Goldwater said that all the members of the Committee, of course, were completely satisfied with the investigations and that he had given out no statement even implying criticism of the Democrats or the counsel.

"So far as this Republican member is concerned, I'm as happy as a squirrel in a little cage," he said.

Senator Mundt said: "I too am perfectly happy and I'm as happy as a South Dakota pheasant in a South Dakota cornfield."

Afterward, a reporter to whom Mundt had made one of his "the-Democrats-and-Kennedys-are-covering-up-for-Reuther" statements asked when the hunting season opened on pheasants in South Dakota.

While Senator Curtis made no comparison between himself and animals or birds, he expressed general happiness and pleasure about the way we were proceeding with the investigations.

This put all the Republican members on record. Senator McClellan called the meeting "a love feast."

I was skeptical, and with reason, for soon the "nonattribution" news stories started again. Happy as everyone claimed to be, they were still saying privately for publication that the Democrats and Kennedys were shielding Walter Reuther. And there was no way we could answer.

The most important factor in the Committee being a success was public confidence. Investigating labor-management affairs was delving into a very sensitive area. If the public became convinced that the Committee was being used for political purposes or was being influenced by political considerations the effectiveness of the Committee would be destroyed. I felt that if the public ever accepted the idea that we were not investigating the UAW or Walter Reuther because he was a Democrat, no matter what other good work the Committee might do, we would be ineffective. I had seen it happen before, and I was determined it should not happen to this Committee. The stories that were being leaked were unfair and untrue but it seemed we had no way to answer them.

There was a way the matter could have been handled to everyone's satisfaction. Some time before this, at Senator Goldwater's request, we had hired an investigator and assistant counsel, Jack McGovern, who had been the minority counsel for the Lobbying Committee. McGovern was a Republican and the only appointment made to the staff because of political considerations.

And so I went back to Senator McClellan to ask that Jack McGovern be placed in charge of the UAW-Kohler investigation. I said public confidence in the work of the Committee was imperative. Because of the stories being circulated I knew I had become personally vulnerable and therefore a possible source of embarrassment to the Committee. While I had had no personal contact with Reuther or even anyone in the UAW up to this point, from what I knew of the UAW-Kohler situation nothing had been uncovered that would "get Reuther" as the Republicans hoped. But because of the "cover-up" stories and the widespread sympathy for Kohler, I knew that if the investigation did not prove Reuther and UAW corrupt, or at least uncover evidence of serious wrongdoing, it would be considered a complete whitewash. It would be said the Committee had failed to expose the union and Reuther not because he was clean, but because he was a Democrat. However, if McGovern conducted the investigation and nothing was revealed the Republican Committee members and the public would be satisfied—or at least so I thought at that time. Senator McClellan accepted the idea.

Subsequently, with the approval of the Republicans, on July 22 McGovern was appointed to handle the UAW-Kohler investigation and all other matters involving Walter Reuther. Senator McClellan assigned to assist him Vern Johnson, the staff member who had been out to Kohler in May. It was understood that as McGovern and Johnson needed more investigators, we would make people available from the staff and the General Accounting Office.

From that July date until December, 1957, I heard nothing from them about how the investigation was going. Ignoring the established *modus operandi,* they addressed not one report, question or request to me personally. I learned later from Johnson that this was deliberate; it seemed that McGovern, even though he was conducting the investigation because of me, feared I would turn all the information I was given over to the UAW! Johnson said also that McGovern had instructed him, for the same reason, to omit certain material from other memoranda that he subsequently did submit to me. I admit that this was highly irritating—but I said nothing at the time. As it later developed, for a while the only persons who received regular reports were the Republican members of the Committee.

The first report Senator McClellan received from McGovern was in October, 1957—some three months after McGovern took over—

270

when he submitted a lengthy memorandum. McClellan gave me a copy to study. By this time I had studied the NLRB reports. We found that McGovern's report consisted largely of verbatim excerpts lifted from the National Labor Relations Board Trial Examiner's hearings. McGovern had taken the NLRB records, extracted the excerpts that were unfavorable to the UAW, and incorporated them in his report to the Chairman and the members of the Committee. Furthermore, there was nothing in his report unfavorable to the Kohler Company—this despite the fact that the NLRB examiner, though criticizing the union for mass picketing, had found that the company had refused to bargain in good faith and had been guilty of a number of unfair labor practices.

I was deeply concerned. If any other investigator had submitted such a report, based on somebody else's work, I would have suggested to Senator McClellan that he be fired. But I was reluctant to move in this case, lest later it might be said that I had tried to take over the investigation; and that the reason it had not been successful was because I had interfered.

At one of our hearings in early November, 1957, seated off by ourselves as someone else was doing the questioning, Senator Goldwater and I had a long conversation and discussed the McGovern report. I told him how dishonest McGovern's report was, and that he would not remain on the Committee staff if he were anybody but a political appointee. Senator Goldwater said that he thought I should take over the UAW-Kohler investigation. I replied that under the circumstances because of the stories originating from the Committee's Republican Senators in the press, I was reluctant to do so. I told him our preliminary investigation had found that the facts were essentially those disclosed in the NLRB report and therefore a new investigation was unlikely to accomplish what he wanted and expected, namely to destroy Walter Reuther. I told him I knew that if the investigations and hearings did not at least seriously tarnish Walter Reuther, there would be a charge of whitewash, and all the Committee's work would be affected.

In the course of our talk Goldwater remarked that he was not interested in calling Reuther before the Committee, or even in investigating Reuther. For that matter, he said, he was not in favor of calling or

271

investigating the UAW-Kohler dispute, either. I was surprised, but those days were full of surprises.

We resolved nothing. I told him that in view of the Republican-inspired press stories, I was not going to interfere unless the Committee asked my opinion. They could run it the way they wanted to.

And still, the cover-up stories continued to appear. It was frustrating, because nothing that I could do or say to put the record straight seemed to have any effect, and because those responsible for the stories publicly denied that they were dissatisfied. They remained "as happy as pheasants in a South Dakota cornfield" or "squirrels in a cage."

Often the stories were completely uninformed. For example, the *Wall Street Journal* carried a piece stating that Senator McClellan was reluctant to go into the UAW-Kohler investigation because it would reflect so adversely on the Democratic Senators from Wisconsin and Michigan that they might be defeated in the next election; McClellan would then lose the chairmanship of the Committee because the Democrats would lose control of Congress. This was poor reporting, if nothing else, because in the coming 1958 elections an incumbent Republican Senator, Potter, was up for election in Michigan, and no matter whether he won or lost, it could not affect the control of the Senate in favor of the Republicans.

There were other reports with more serious implications.

In December, McGovern told a press conference in Detroit that he had uncovered "sensational developments" in his investigation of the United Automobile Workers. Neither Senator McClellan nor I knew any more about these sensational developments than the newspapers reported, and we were disturbed that an investigator on our staff, a full month or more before hearings, should describe any developments in his case in such a manner. It was irresponsible, and reflected not only on McGovern's own work but also on the entire Committee.

As might have been expected, the UAW proclaimed that the union had been smeared. It immediately demanded that the Committee put up or shut up.

The columnists now had new fuel for the editorial fires. McGovern's report, they contended, proved what the "unnamed sources" had been saying all along—we were hiding the facts that we wanted no hearings. A radio commentator reported night after night that the Democrats on the Committee were anxious to hush up the sensational developments and that Robert Kennedy was greatly upset because McGovern's investigation had turned up so much material on Walter Reuther. He said that, in fact, I was so concerned about what would be revealed that I was going to resign and in that way try to stop the hearings.

(Later, this same commentator told his listeners that the Kennedys were so unhappy about this particular investigation that my wife, who customarily attended the hearings, was staying away from the UAW-Kohler hearings. It was true that Ethel stayed away, but not because she was unhappy. She was in the hospital having a baby and could not attend.)

I felt that the time had come when, in good conscience, I could no longer remain inactive.

Over Christmas I discussed the situation with Senator McClellan. We decided that I should go out to Kohler, Wisconsin, and talk with both the company and the union, so that we would know at least what new material had been uncovered and what new evidence might be developed. At this time I still had a relatively open mind about the merits of the dispute, though of course I was impressed with Vern Johnson's support of the NLRB report and by my study of that document.

I notified McGovern and Johnson that I was coming, and on Friday, January 3, 1958, flew out to Milwaukee. There I was met by Carmine Bellino and LaVern Duffy, who were to accompany me to Sheboygan and Kohler Village, some sixty miles from Milwaukee, the site of the plumbing fixture plant. Vern Johnson picked us up at the airport.

I wanted Bellino with me because, as our expert accountant, he was qualified to assess what McGovern and Johnson had found out about the finances of the UAW and the company. I wanted Duffy because of the widespread violence engendered in this dispute; he was the investigator who had handled the Committee's violence cases in Scranton, Pennsylvania, and in Tennessee.

We drove through the outskirts of Milwaukee. A heavy snow covered the ground, the houses were brightly lighted and multicolored bulbs and ornaments dotted many of the Christmas trees on the lawns. It was a bright, cheerful city.

Later that night, we arrived in Sheboygan, sixty miles away—a somber contrast to Milwaukee. Even in the darkness Sheboygan seemed dreary. Perhaps my impression was influenced by the temperature, which was below zero when we arrived, or perhaps by the realization that this place had been the scene of an intensely bitter struggle, the effects of which still hung over it like a shroud, touching everything, affecting everyone.

I went to Mass on Sunday at a church just a few blocks away from our hotel. The sermon was in Lithuanian, all the women wore shawls, and those who came to church had the strong, stern faces of people who have worked hard and who have suffered. The church was peaceful and pleasant, and there was a strong atmosphere of the old world about it. It was not difficult to imagine that I was in a foreign country.

I had the same feeling as I talked with the people. They were nice, cordial, personable, but they had been badly hurt by this industrial war. The four years of labor strife had smashed community relations, separated neighborhoods, turned brother against brother. It was difficult to believe that this was America 1958; that I was in Sheboygan, Wisconsin.

Some ten years before, I had visited Israel and the Arab states when the British were giving up their mandate in Palestine and the war between the Arabs and the Israelis was just beginning. The loathing and hatred between Arab and Jew was an all-consuming thing. It was impossible in those days to talk to any representative of either side without becoming immediately aware that every person on both sides had been caught up in the conflict. Men had lost their reason.

The hatred I had felt on that visit to Palestine was just as livid here. Unless you can see and feel for yourself the agony that has shattered this Wisconsin community, it is difficult to believe that such a concentration of hatred can exist in this country.

Men on both sides of the controversy were still hurling the same profane insults when I arrived in 1958 that they must have exchanged the first day the strike started in 1954. Union leaders still spoke of scabs; management referred to goons. Kohler officials termed union leaders headknockers; UAW officials called management strike-breakers. What the company called mob rule, the union called picketing. It seemed to me almost immediately that the strike was as far from settlement that day as it was when it first started.

I went to visit the Kohler Company first. The plant looked even drabber than the town.

Lyman Conger is the company attorney. He also is the force, the brains and the drive behind the dispute with UAW. His has been an extended relationship with the company. He took us on a tour of this plant where they make bathtubs and other plumbing fixtures.

We went with him through the enamel shop where the temperatures ordinarily range from 100 to 200 degrees, although it was not in operation that day. The UAW was attempting to get a twenty-minute lunch period for the employees who work there on an eight-hour shift. This was to be a matter of discussion in our hearings and I later was to remember this tour. Conger had worked in the enamel shop twenty-six years before. He seemed to feel that there was no reason for the plant or the employees to have changed in that time.

Then we went to one of the main offices where we talked for several hours with Conger and Herbert Kohler. They were a strange pair, these two. Kohler, about sixty, looking plump and jolly, sat in the background, leaving the discussion to Conger. He was the owner, and the plant and the village bore his name. But Conger ran the show.

Conger, thin-faced with a hawk nose, has a high-pitched voice and a deep cleft in his chin, which he kept pulling throughout our interview. His face, his manner and his whole body seemed to tighten up at the mention of the UAW. He made no secret of his deep and abiding hate for the union. It was an all-consuming hate—a thing unpleasant to see.

Conger made no bones about the setup: He was in charge and he was running the company as the company had been run when he was a boy. He would permit no interference by anyone from the outside. Particularly he would countenance no interference by a "left-wing"

275

labor union. It was Mr. Kohler's company and Mr. Kohler or his delegate was going to run it—not Walter Reuther or the UAW. Before giving in on this principle, Conger made it clear, the company would close down.

The next time Hollywood looks for a character actor to play the old company retainer, the caretaker and supervisor of the family plant, for a movie on industrial problems at the turn of the century, I recommend to them Lyman C. Conger.

Even the office where we talked was stage-designed to perfection. It had pasty yellow walls and on one of them hung a picture in a cheap frame. It looked as if it had been bought in a five-and-ten-cent store. We sat on stiff wooden chairs which, like the desk, must have been there for at least thirty years.

I was struck by how small a part Mr. Kohler took in our interview. It seemed as if he were there only because he felt he had to be. As it became evident later when he testified before the Committee, Mr. Kohler knows little about the actual running of the company, or about the seriousness of the issues in dispute between his company and the union. Conger runs the operation for him. Mr. Kohler makes the speeches and undoubtedly is happier that way. But as we left the plant, for some reason I had the feeling that if Herbert Kohler had been more involved, this all might have been settled long ago.

That same afternoon we interviewed the UAW leaders, Allan Graskamp and Donald Rand, in their office on the second floor of a rambling Sheboygan building. We took McGovern and Johnson with us. The office, with its long wooden desks and rows of benches, its walls marked with posters and slogans, looked like the campaign headquarters of some lesser political candidate who knew he couldn't whip city hall.

They were not happy to see us. They were anything but friendly. Our meeting almost broke up in anger before it began.

Rand, a fellow of medium build, with an oval face and rash judgment, began making a speech to us. Our investigation was unfair, he said. We had no business investigating the union in this dispute. Why were we persecuting them? Why didn't we go over to the Kohler Company and get to the real source of trouble.

We hadn't come to hear speeches. We listened to him for a few minutes and then made it clear that we were there to get facts, not a sermon. We were interested in their side if they wanted to give it to us factually, but as far as I was concerned, he could save the speeches for the next union meeting.

Graskamp, whose rugged face showed worry and strain, seemed more reasonable. I told them we would leave them for two hours to think over what sort of helpful information they might give us—then we walked out.

During the afternoon I had to smile remembering the many news stories that cast me as a tool of the UAW. Apparently these men had not read my press clippings.

In spite of the unfortunate beginning we had made, then and later I was impressed with the difference between these officials of the UAW and the men Jimmy Hoffa and Dave Beck surrounded themselves with in the Teamsters Union. It was a striking contrast—one I noted again and again as I came in contact with other UAW officials. These men wore simple clothes, not silk suits and hand-painted ties; sported no great globs of jewelry on their fingers or their shirts; there was no smell of the heavy perfume frequently wafted by the men around Hoffa.

We arrived back at their headquarters at 5:30 P.M. and stayed some four hours talking with them. I told them that from what I knew of their dispute they had made some serious mistakes and that where they were wrong they could expect the Committee to be critical, but that they would always have a chance to give a complete explanation. I assured them that Senator McClellan was a fair man. I urged them to co-operate fully, and promised that if they did they could expect him to be understanding. The best thing they could do, I said, was to come in and tell the truth, and where they had made mistakes, admit them.

And in the course of my studies it became plain to me that mistakes had indeed been made. For instance, in the early days of the strike, the union had formed mass pickets at the plant and with a human blockade had kept workers out. And it had erred in other ways: the record showed some eight hundred instances of violence, threats, telephone calls, 75 per cent of which had been directed against the nonstrikers.

For this the UAW as a union must accept the major share of the responsibility, even though it was not possible then or during the hearing to show that the union had ordered or condoned it. In my estimation, though union officials protested to the contrary, there was no great evidence that they took major steps to try to stop it. In addition, the union, though it did not import gangs of goons as the company charged, did permit some ten or twelve organizers to come in and lend a hand. Of itself, there was nothing wrong with this. However, two or three of these were big hulking men, and the testimony revealed they were under no direct instructions and were permitted by the UAW to do exactly what they wished. The result was that two of them caused considerable trouble and got into serious difficulty.

One of them, a 240-pounder named Albert Vinson, attacked a much smaller man in a bar, knocking him onto the floor and beating him unmercifully. Vinson was ultimately convicted and sent to jail.

Another UAW representative, John Gunaca, together with two other men, beat up an older man and his son after they got into an altercation in a filling station. The older man died some eighteen months later. The doctor's report stated that there was no connection between the beating and his death, but there seems to be no question that he never completely recovered from the brutal and callous beating he received.

During the early part of the strike there were so-called "house parties" or rallies. A group of strikers would gather in front of the house of a nonstriker, chanting and yelling catcalls. These demonstrations were, of course, frightening, particularly to the man's family, and caused extreme bitterness in the community. Often UAW officials were present, proof that the union was not discouraging these activities.

As I talked with the union officials that evening in Sheboygan and later on in Washington, they had something to say in their defense. They pointed out that although there had been some violence where the union was directly involved, there had been no destruction of company property. They admitted the mass picketing but said it was an effort by union members to protect their jobs against scabs; 98 per cent of those who walked the picket line, they said, were strikers, not outsiders. They emphasized that it had been a long, agonizing strike, involving thousands of men, many of whom lost their jobs to non-strikers, and saw their families go hungry as a result. It was a miracle no one had been killed.

These men felt hatred, too. But it was hatred born of anger and frustration—not the insatiable hatred that Conger seemed to feel.

They told of the background of the company and its relationship with its employees and argued that this was also a factor to be considered when assessing fault and blame. The Committee, when it held its hearings, went into this history in some detail.

The Kohler Company is an old, family-owned establishment and its eighty-eight-year history has been marked by bitter and sometimes bloody relations with its employees. Kohler management has long been opposed to unionization, claiming that the company could care for the workers' interests far better than any outside organization—or even better than the workers themselves. Such paternalism was characteristic of big business fifty years ago, but is rare among companies in this modern industrial age.

Kohler Village is an old-fashioned company town, another relic of the nation's industrial past. The company pays most of the village taxes and has the ruling voice in community affairs. Approximately seventeen hundred people live in the Village and 90 per cent of them work for Kohler Company.

Kohler's labor problems date back to 1897, when the company cut the salaries of all its workers by 50 per cent. By way of compensation, they gave each employee who stayed on the job a bathtub.

During the 1934 strike, the company brought in guards (testimony later developed the fact that they wore black shirts and carried guns). Arms and ammunition were stored in the company's offices and truck-loads of company men patrolled the streets. One evening, some of the strikers gathered outside company gates and began throwing rocks at the buildings. They broke windows and damaged other company property. The guards fired tear gas bombs into the crowd but mis-

279

calculated the direction of the wind and the gas drifted back toward the plant. As the strikers continued to throw rocks, the order to open fire on them was given. The blackshirts started shooting and chased the strikers out of Kohler Village. Forty-seven were shot, most of them in the back. Two were killed.

A Catholic priest, Father J. W. Maguire, a member of the Chicago Labor Board, one of those who rushed immediately to the scene, stated: "I have been in many strikes but I never saw such needless and ruthless killing by supporters of the law. . . . You don't have to shoot people in the back when they are running away. I examined a score of wounded and all except two were shot in the back. . . . I am not going behind fences to say what I have to say. There are human rights and property rights, but human lives are more sacred than property rights."

The strike was broken. The employees came back to work on the company's terms.

During the 1930's the management arranged for and financially supported a company union. The firm, still picturing itself as the "father" of its flock of workers, arranged bowling, basketball, baseball, band, chorus, card playing and horseshoe pitching for its workers —but kept salaries comparatively low. Its hiring wage, for example, was anywhere from fifty to eighty cents an hour less than that of its major competitors.

In 1952 Kohler workers decided they wanted their own bargaining agent and voted to affiliate with the UAW. Company officials bristled under this affront. The 1952 contract was the only one they signed with the UAW. When the contract came up for renewal in 1954, the union made new demands, some of which at first were considered drastic, a twenty-cent-an-hour general wage increase, plus ten cents for skilled workers, a union shop, an arbitration clause that would make the decision of the arbitrator binding, more lunchtime or a compensatory allowance, a dues check-off system, and a relaxation of the company's lay-off policies. Kohler turned down every one. Negotiations went on and the union withdrew most of the demands, including the one for the union shop. Still there was no settlement. The union voted to strike.

Within a month of the strike the company had the upper hand. From the first day of the walkout, the company made it clear that it would continue to operate in an effort to break the strike. And amid violence and threats on both sides, after a short time the plant was able to go back into operation.

The union then again modified its demands. But by this time the Kohler Company was back at work with outsiders and nonstrikers. No longer were they interested in settlement, and their sole concession was to offer to raise wages by three cents an hour.

Within a few months the company was winning the battle with ease. It has continued to win. In fact, their business has steadily increased.

Actually the union hierarchy has realized it has been beaten since that first summer of 1954. In a desperate effort to end the strike, it has been willing to concede virtually every point in dispute in return for a face-saving seven-cent-an-hour increase in salaries—and in the opinion of one eminent jurist, who attempted to mediate the dispute, it would accept five cents. But Kohler, as it revealed before the Committee, has no interest in settling or in signing a contract with the UAW.

We had interviews with a number of other witnesses while we were in Sheboygan. McGovern and Johnson told me they would be ready to go into public hearings by February 1, which was less than a month; they said they had done about all on the case they possibly could do.

I was interested to discover what some of the "sensational developments" were, of which they had so enthusiastically informed the press. One, it seemed, involved $100,000, which McGovern had found was missing from the union treasury. Carmine Bellino later studied the union's records and within an hour found the explanation. McGovern had looked for it in the wrong column of expenditures. The $100,000 was accounted for.

Still another investigation that had consumed much of their time centered around huge amounts of knackwurst which the UAW had purchased from one of the Sheboygan shops to feed the strikers. Because so much of this particular kind of meat had been bought,

McGovern and Johnson decided there must be some kind of kickback to union officials. No one would want to eat that much knackwurst.

We looked into it. The explanation was quite simple. The people of Sheboygan of German and Slavic extraction just happen to like and to eat an awful lot of knackwurst.

An executive session of the Committee was scheduled for January 8. All the staff members concerned in this case were to be present.

Prior to the meeting, I went to see Senator Curtis and talked with him for more than an hour about the UAW-Kohler matter. At this particular time I felt that he was more reasonable on the subject than either Mundt or Goldwater. He asked me why we had not launched an all-out investigation of the UAW as we did of the Teamsters. I told him there was no comparison between the complaints received and the evidence available in the two cases, and said that if he had any specific information or any definite complaints, I would send an investigator that very night to look into the matter.

He stopped me cold with the announcement that he understood that all the incoming mail and complaints received by the Committee were examined first by the AFL-CIO. I was hardly able to believe that I had heard him correctly. It seemed impossible to me that a United States Senator and member of this Committee could even suspect such a thing.

I made my position clear. I said I had known little about the UAW before this investigation began, and even less about Walter Reuther, whom I still had never met, but the tactics of the Republicans in the entire matter, including their unfairness about my role in it, were putting me in his camp. Toward the end of our talk he seemed slightly more understanding.

Our executive session on January 8 aroused considerable interest. Reporters and television cameramen gathered in the hallway as we entered the hearing room. There was a fascinated speculation about what would happen behind closed doors when the great issue—the UAW-Kohler strike—came up. Some wondered whether this might be the last meeting of the Committee; whether UAW-Kohler might be the issue on which we would break up.

It was a lengthy meeting and not a pleasant one. My brother im-

mediately made a motion that the UAW-Kohler-Reuther hearings be
the first order of business, and suggested that we schedule them for as
soon after the first week in February as possible. Senators Mundt,
Goldwater and Curtis seemed flustered. We were told that they didn't
think such haste was necessary; they did not want to rush into this
matter; and first we should look into a UAW dispute with an Indiana
firm, the Perfect Circle Company.

Here I spoke up. Both McGovern and Johnson, I reported, had
told me that they would be ready to proceed with the hearings on
the first of February. I pointed out that we had already spent considerable time on investigation.

My brother said he was perfectly willing to go into the UAW-Per-
fect Circle strike[1] if the Committee decided it wanted to. But, he
added, for eight months there had been charges that we had been
dodging the Kohler case, that the Kennedys were against calling
UAW witnesses and Walter Reuther, and he felt we should go ahead
with the hearings immediately. He said he was surprised at the attitude of the Republicans, in view of all the critical press comments
that we had been covering up for Reuther. Again the Republicans dis-
claimed any responsibility for these reports.

I explained to the Committee members that I had been to Kohler
and made an investigation, and that I felt there was little to be brought
out in hearings that was not already general knowledge. However,
because of the public interest, I thought it imperative that we should
get on with the Kohler case and give it a full airing. To make the
record clear and complete, I asked McGovern and Johnson to speak
up then if I had interfered with their work or investigation in any way.
Johnson said I had given every assistance, and McGovern remained
quiet.

But as now became apparent, their investigation had not been
complete by any means. They admitted that they had studied the union
books—but had not audited the company's books. And though they
had gone into the union records over a four- or five-month period, they
did not have any idea whether Vinson, the UAW official involved in

[1] We did later.

283

an assault, had been on the union payroll or whether he received money while in jail.

The Committee directed Carmine Bellino to examine both the union and the company finances at once. It also gave Senator McClellan jurisdiction over the investigation, which was to continue until the hearings opened.

As the investigation went on, it was again brought home to me how McGovern and Johnson had gone about their work. What I learned during the next thirty days was almost unbelievable.

At one point I attempted to pin Johnson down about his interview of Judge Harold F. Murphy of Marinette, Wiconsin, an important witness in the National Labor Relations Board hearings. The judge had been responsible for the Board's investigation; he had ordered the union to end its mass picketing; as an impartial negotiator he had made efforts to settle the strike; he had testified before the Board that the company was completely adamant about signing the contract with the union, and that the reason there had been no settlement—as Conger's own statements revealed—was that the company did not want a settlement. In short, Judge Murphy knew a great deal about this case.

The union was anxious that he testify at our hearings; though he would be critical of the union, he would give the Committee a good idea of who was responsible for prolonging the strike.

I asked Johnson and McGovern several times about Judge Murphy. Johnson told me he had interviewed the Judge but doubted whether he would make a good witness. Since the Judge had played such a major role in the NLRB hearings, I continued to press Johnson about him and finally asked him for a report of his interview. Johnson said he had not yet had a chance to have his notes typed up. Becoming impatient, I called Judge Murphy on the telephone to ask him what he knew about the strike.

He told me that he had gained the distinct impression while acting as mediator that the company felt it had nothing to gain from settling.

When he appeared as a witness he said:

JUDGE MURPHY: . . . it was perfectly obvious that the attitude of the Kohler Co. was that the strike had been won, and that they had

284

the union beaten, and that there was no point in their receding from any position that they had taken.

I am not quoting language. You are asking me now about an impression and how I felt. . . .

MR. KENNEDY: Did they make any statement about teaching the union a lesson?

JUDGE MURPHY: Mr. Conger made that statement at one time.

MR. KENNEDY: What did he tell you?

JUDGE MURPHY: Well, he didn't tell it to me alone. I don't know who was present. But Mr. Conger made this statement along the same line when many people were present: That the strike in 1934 had resulted in twenty years of labor peace, and they expected that this strike would bring about the same result.

At one time, Mr. Conger made the statement that they were going to teach the union a lesson.

At the end of our telephone conversation, I asked him about his previous interview with Mr. Johnson of our staff. He replied that neither Mr. Johnson nor Mr. McGovern had ever interviewed him; in fact, this was the first contact he had had with anyone connected with any branch of the Government since the NLRB hearings.

When a staff member makes a false report, the entire investigation is jeopardized. Since Johnson and McGovern had been in Sheboygan for some six months, and were in control of the investigation, we were depending on them for a great deal of the information. Had it been possible, I would have suggested to Senator McClellan Johnson be released then and there. But as when McGovern had copied the NLRB report, there was nothing I could do. Both men were protected by politics.

Then Bellino discovered that the two had overlooked large sums of money that the company had spent to purchase guns and ammunition shortly before the strike started. They also failed to tell us that company officials held target practice at the plant just before the strike, using targets in the shape of human forms. They failed to mention that the company had spent a great deal of money on spies who not only infiltrated the union but who also investigated an NLRB representative.

I felt that if we put on a hearing and what they had done in this investigation became apparent it would be a fatal blow to the Committee. But what was the alternative? We had to try to check and recheck all their work. It was an unpleasant, trying time.

It was in late December or early January that I first heard about Francis Drury, who was to be one of their key witnesses. The previous May, he had been caught attempting to burglarize the Detroit office of a rival union of the UAW, the Mechanics Educational Society of America. When first arrested, he maintained that he was merely a burglar looking for money and stamps. In view of his past record of some twenty arrests and ten convictions, this story made sense.

However, a short time later Drury changed his tale and said that he had been sent to the MESA office by high UAW officials to burglarize their files. He claimed he had worked for the UAW in former years as a paid goon. His immediate boss had been a man named McCluskey, he said, who sent him out to Kohler to terrorize the nonstrikers. He also claimed that McCluskey had paid him to perform thug-duty for the UAW in other areas.

At about the time of Drury's arrest, Clark Mollenhoff, the Washington reporter, interviewed Jimmy Hoffa in Detroit. Hoffa told him that the corruption in the UAW centered around a man named Drury. He knew this for a fact, he said, because he had made a personal investigation of Drury. He added that the Committee should look into Drury, and his association with the UAW.

This served only to arouse my suspicions of Drury, but McGovern and Johnson now felt that if they could run down the UAW man named McCluskey—the man Drury said employed him to perform goon work—the Kohler investigation would be "busted" wide open.

While they hunted I sent Walter Sheridan out to Detroit to look into the story Drury had told. He discovered that Drury had dropped his regular attorney and that three lawyers close to the Teamsters Union and to Mr. Hoffa had been in touch with him at the time he changed from being a plain burglar to a burglar for the UAW.

One of these attorneys went with McGovern and Johnson to interview Drury in prison. Drury told them he had also done jobs of violence for McCluskey in Louisville, Kentucky, and in St. Louis—for which he had been arrested and jailed in both places.

Although Johnson told Kenny O'Donnell that he had checked

out this story thoroughly and that it was true, O'Donnell made a check of his own with officials in the two cities and discovered that Drury, while he had indeed been jailed in both places, had not been involved in labor violence. He had been jailed for burglarizing stamp machines. Again we had been misinformed.

Then Sheridan telephoned from Detroit and said that he believed Drury was part of a phony scheme to mislead us and that the whole tale about a man named McCluskey was a fake. Nonetheless, we spent the first three weeks of January in a comedy of errors looking for the elusive Mr. McCluskey. First we heard McCluskey was in Florida— we looked for him there. Then we heard McCluskey was in Louisiana —we looked for him there. Finally it began to dawn on even Johnson and McGovern that there was no McCluskey and that an early investigation of Drury and his whole background would have indicated this.

The tip-off and climax came when Johnson wrote a memorandum indicating that a man by the name of Brotz had made the arrangements for McCluskey to bring Drury and the other goons to Kohler in 1954.

Mr. Brotz, we found, had been dead since 1951.

As the time for the hearings grew nearer I was more and more concerned about the "investigations" conducted by McGovern and Johnson. I certainly wanted to do the best possible job of presenting the facts in this case. But the antics of these two men had shaken my confidence in their ability and their sincerity in this investigation. Yet I could not disassociate myself from what they were doing. As chief counsel I was responsible for their actions and for the information that they furnished me to use in hearings.

Only a short while before the UAW-Kohler case was to go into open hearings McGovern called Russell Nixon, a former Harvard professor, to his office and suggested that Nixon give information about the alleged Communist leanings of UAW officials. He also made arrangements to call Julius Emspak for the same purpose.

Nixon released a public statement that McGovern had tried to get him to become an informant for the Committee. Senator Ives was aghast. Why in the world, he wanted to know, were we so foolish as to go to such people for our information? Did we think for a moment that we could trust them? Both Nixon and Emspak have been identified at various times before Congressional committees as followers of the Communist party line.

McGovern said he had taken this action not on his own, but at the direction of Senator Karl Mundt. This was certainly a 180-degree turn from the Karl Mundt of the old days. Now we were going to Communists for help in our investigations. His old hero, Senator McCarthy, must have turned over in his grave.

And still this was not the end of my problems. What had started out as a comedy of errors with the knackwurst trackdown had become first a nuisance and now a serious liability.

On the very eve of our hearings, UAW lawyer Joseph Rauh came to my office. He was angry because, he said, McGovern and Johnson had picked up a certain UAW official at eleven o'clock at night, driven him around and threatened to expose his alleged left-wing leanings if he did not turn informer on Walter Reuther. Rauh said the Committee staff members had threatened and tried to blackmail the man. As chief counsel, what was I going to do about it?

I spoke to McGovern and Johnson. They denied the story. Johnson said he had interviewed the man but that there were no threats. McGovern said he had never even interviewed the man, let alone driven with him in an automobile at that time of night, and that the whole charge was false.

Later, during the course of the hearings, the UAW officials came back to see me and insisted that their man be called as a witness to tell how our investigators had acted. I again went to McGovern. Again he denied that he had done any such thing. I told him the UAW was bringing the man in the next morning at ten-thirty o'clock and were going to demand that he testify. At nine-fifteen the following morning, McGovern came to my office. He told me he had lied. He said it would be very difficult for him if he were forced to admit publicly what he had done.

I told him to get out of my office. I didn't want to have anything more to do with him. When the UAW officials arrived, I told them that McGovern had admitted his fault and that it would be better for the Committee's future work if this matter were not injected into the

UAW-Kohler hearings. The UAW officials agreed, but very reluctantly.

McGovern and Johnson are seemingly intelligent young men who probably would make no particular impression on you if you passed them in the corridor of the Senate Office Building, or if you saw them at lunch in the restaurant of the Carroll Arms Hotel across from our office. Yet the extremes to which they were willing to go—and the extremes to which the politically minded members of the Committee were willing to push them—were a betrayal of our work and our purpose. They were willing to risk a good record of honest accomplishment to "get" the UAW.

As the hearings approached, it was understood that the Committee would hear every witness the Republicans wanted to call. Since this was a labor dispute with charges and countercharges by both sides, McGovern and I agreed that a representative of the company and a representative of the union would appear as the first two witnesses.

We met in executive session to try to work out the details. Everyone sensed that weeks of wrangling were ahead—and it is a fact that before they were over, the hearings stirred up so much bitterness among the members that many questioned whether we could ever work together again. Already the growing resentment was evident.

Jack McGovern had suggested that Lyman Conger be the first witness for the company and that some minor UAW man speak for the union. I agreed that Conger should be the first witness for Kohler, but suggested that Walter Reuther should be first for the UAW. I said that at the end of the hearings, as the testimony was developed, both Conger and Reuther should be recalled.

Immediately the Committee was embroiled in a heated controversy right along party lines over whether Reuther should be the first UAW witness. The four Republicans took the position that anybody but Walter Reuther could appear first for the union. But they did not want him as the first witness. Under no circumstances, they insisted.

Senator McClellan made himself clear. With his innate fairness he pointed out that we were to hear charges and countercharges, and that in order for the Committee to get a general picture of the problem before going into intricate details each side should present its best spokesman first—the union as well as the company. He added that he was not afraid to call Reuther and he could not understand what the Republicans had to fear from letting him appear at any time.

The Republicans said that if Reuther testified first he would steal the show and the rest of the hearings would be an anticlimax. If we insisted, they would walk off the Committee. This was an ultimatum.

After we spent five executive sessions trying to work out this problem, Senator McClellan capitulated and the hearings were scheduled to begin on February 26, 1958—with witnesses to be called in the order decided upon by the Republicans. At the very outset of the hearings the Chairman made a public statement to this effect and said he was not accepting any responsibility for the method and manner in which the case was presented.

Even before we called the first witness, the UAW-Kohler case had been blown into a national issue. With the exception of Senator Ives, the Republicans on the Committee had been certain at first that these hearings would destroy Reuther; they had sold themselves on this idea without making the slightest investigation. But by the time the hearings began they were not quite so sure. I felt they were going to be disappointed. And when it was all over they were disappointed —very.

I had seen Dave Beck and Jimmy Hoffa on the witness stand. For all their incredibly bad records they were bright, articulate witnesses when it came to discussing matters of labor philosophy. The leaders of our big unions don't climb to power without learning what the labor unions are all about. They have ability and drive and know-how, and they can express themselves. That some are corrupt doesn't change the fact that they know more about the operations of their unions than all the members of our Committee and the staff and me put together. However, to go even further and put a union official on the witness stand and debate with him on general subjects in the hope of embarrassing him, without proof of wrongdoing, can be disastrous. I think Senator Mundt and Senator Goldwater both came to learn this lesson at the hands of Walter Reuther.

290

The first witness was Allan Graskamp, president of Local 833, whom I had met in the union office in Sheboygan. He was an unpretentious man, but curiously impressive, with a straightforward, down-to-earth manner. As a witness, he probably made a better introductory impression for the union than the more sophisticated Walter Reuther. He spoke intelligently, in simple, short, easy-to-understand sentences as he described his union's problems with the company. He made no pretenses. He just told the truth.

"When it came time for the strike, the wages themselves were unimportant. It was the dignity of the guy working there; the right to have a union steward bring up a grievance for him; the right to have it discussed . . . the right to have the guy go up there and get an honest settlement if he is entitled to it. That is what the strike is all about."

Never at any time during the five weeks of hearings did Senator Mundt, Senator Goldwater or Senator Curtis ask questions critical of the Kohler Company, or questions that would elicit a reply unfavorable to the company point of view. Apparently it never occurred to them that there were two sides to this controversy. On the other hand, Senator McClellan, Senator Ervin and Senator Kennedy placed questions on both sides of the issue, developing facts that might add something to an objective study.

There were heartbreaking stories on both sides. A mother testified that she had raised her children and educated them through the help of the company that employed her and that she owed more to the Kohler Company than anybody in the world. She knew the strike was wrong.

Nonstriker Dale Oostdyke told of his terrible experience. His brother, who was a striker, had tipped him off the day before the walkout began, and he slipped into the plant. He was caught coming out on his way to a National Guard meeting.

He testified: "One of them [the strikers] jumped on my back and about that time there were at least three or four more there. And one of them kicked me in the back and on the side and two of them picked me up by the arms. One picket was very small and he hit me on the left side of the temple while the other two were holding me. . . ."

291

We heard testimony concerning the men in the enamel plant for whom the union was trying to get a twenty-minute lunch period. I had this exchange with Mr. Conger:

MR. KENNEDY: You say the men put the equipment in the oven, then they can step back and eat their lunch during that period of time. How much time is there before they have to do some more work?

MR. CONGER: Two to five minutes depending on the piece.

MR. KENNEDY: So you feel they can step back from the oven, take off their masks and have their lunch in two to five minutes?

MR. CONGER: Mr. Kennedy, they have been doing it for thirty-six years to my knowledge and I am sure they can do it.

I could not possibly understand the company's attitude. It made me furious, madder really than when witnesses took the Fifth Amendment. We knew what those people were; we expected nothing more from them. But to hear a reputable American businessman, in 1958, matter-of-factly advocate a two- to five-minute luncheon period—well, until then I had believed that that kind of thinking had long since disappeared from the American scene.

During the hearing a question was raised about the temperature in the enamel shop. Union officials said it ran from 100 to 250 degrees Fahrenheit. Conger insisted it ran from 80 to 90 degrees, except in the summer when it sometimes hit 100. I reminded Mr. Conger that he had taken me through the shop in the dead of winter when there was no work going on and that it had been very, very hot.

He snapped: "Well, you didn't have a thermometer."

The company had other policies that I considered completely callous. What possible explanation can there be today for its attitude about married women employees who become pregnant? The union had been trying to get the company to agree to rehire women who had to leave work to have a baby.

The company's feeling was that women should be able to "take care of themselves."

I asked Mr. Kohler about this when he was a witness.

MR. KENNEDY: Can the girl always get her job back within two years? Is that written in the contract?

MR. KOHLER: No, we don't guarantee her job. We try to take her back.

MR. KENNEDY: There is no guarantee of that?

MR. KOHLER: No, sir.

After the first three days of our hearings there was little newspaper coverage or interest until Walter Reuther testified. Maybe that was the reason some months later, after more than a million words of testimony, the New York *Daily News,* which continuously had urged a UAW-Kohler investigation, carried an editorial once again asking when we were going to investigate UAW activities in the Kohler strike in Wisconsin; further, whether the Kennedys were protecting Walter Reuther in that matter.

There was unpleasantness during the hearings as there had been before. Senator Curtis, I thought, had no reason whatever to go into the premarital relationship of a UAW official and his wife. Before they were married, company detectives had followed them to Milwaukee and turned the information that they were living together over to Milwaukee vice squad officers, who raided their apartment. When Senator Curtis aired this information, my brother asked why it was necessary to bring the matter up, since it had nothing to do with the UAW-Kohler strike. Senator Curtis's reply was that they had had their pictures taken and that the photo had been published in the UAW paper; therefore the use of union funds was involved, and he felt the facts should be developed.

When it was brought out that there had been violence during the strike, Senator Goldwater observed that this was a pattern: the UAW had been part of the CIO, and more than thirty people had been killed in CIO strikes. The comment made a news story. What the Senator failed to mention was that the thirty people who had been killed were all strikers. Later on he followed this up by saying that the Communists used violence and it was significant that the CIO used similar tactics. My brother interrupted. He questioned whether there was any more significance in this fact than there was in the fact that we had a brother named Joe and Stalin's first name also was Joe.

More than once I noticed that the GOP members had lists of written questions in front of them. Indications were that they all originated from the same person, for several times, to my amusement, when a Republican arrived late he would read off questions that one of his Republican colleagues had already asked.

UAW Vice President Emil Mazey was a belligerent man who had

grown up in the labor wars, a man who shouted first and thought later. At times, though, his unrestrained conduct was understandable, and once at least I found myself strongly in sympathy with him. Our hearings that day brought out the fact that Conger's company spies had made notes on such things as where strikers bought their food and who visited and worked in the UAW soup kitchen. They noted that children of strikers and nonstrikers were playing together; that the son of a striker flicked his finger in the eye of a nonstriker's child; that a little boy who was the son of a striker retrieved a ball several times from Kohler property where it had been batted; and that one striker had once dressed in a costume of Abraham Lincoln.

At the end of the day, after the activities of the company spies had been thoroughly exposed, Mazey walked up to Conger and glowered: "You are a despicable son of a bitch."

The following day Conger protested Mazey's action, and at once the Committee was in a state of uproar and outrage, with the Committee members taking sides and yelling at each other about who was right and who was wrong.

Some of the witnesses called had never been interviewed, with the result they gave conflicting testimony and proved nothing. On March 24 Senator Goldwater suddenly announced at a Committee meeting that he saw no reason to call Walter Reuther; he did not believe Reuther could add anything, although if he did come he would have some questions to ask him.

I thought Senator McClellan was going to faint at this. After all the charges of cover-up, whitewash and shielding, after months of investigation and weeks of hearings, Reuther's chief antagonist, Senator Goldwater, was suggesting that there was no reason to call him. When the Chairman recovered from his surprise, he said he would not be a party to denying Reuther an opportunity to testify. As far as he was concerned, Reuther would be called as a witness. Reuther appeared. He gave long, detailed answers. He knew his subject—unionism— and was smart enough to admit at the beginning the mistakes that the union made.

Reuther said, looking back over the violence in this strike: "On the question of whether they [the strikers] should have kept people [nonstrikers] out, we have no argument. I think that was an improper activity. The question is, picket lines are not formed in vacuums. . . . I think if I was sitting here today and you said to me would you do that again, I would have made a trip to Wisconsin to see that it did not happen."

Reuther's self-confidence was not appreciated; at one time Senator Curtis asked the Chairman to reprimand him for questioning Senator Goldwater, instead of answering questions himself.

One newsman said, at the end of the hearing, in reference to Reuther's often wordy answers: "I'll bet there's one thing that Mrs. Reuther never says to Walter at night: 'What did you do at the office today, dear?' "

However, he was a smart, confident, articulate witness, and the Republican Senators were no match for him. The reason was he was talking about something he knew far better than any of us—unionism. Once he had admitted the union's mistakes, the general philosophical questions asked of him gave him no concern.

At times, when he talked about his union people in the Kohler strike or about his own personal experiences as a labor leader, he could make the point dramatically. He said: "The Kohler strike was about people . . . the men and women of Local 833 have served notice on the Kohler Company that it is not living in some remote corner of the world far from the mainstream of living."

Again he told us: "I have laid on the floor of my own home in my own blood, and I have had fellows stick a .45 in my stomach and the other fellow say, 'Pull the trigger and let's get it over with.' "

Before the hearing there had been a good deal of discussion about going into Reuther's trip to Russia in 1933 and a famous letter the Reuther brothers allegedly wrote to one Mel Bishop, a friend in America, praising the Communist system.

We located Mel Bishop. He had left the UAW in the late 1940's after becoming closely associated with some of the gangster element in Detroit, and had gone to work for Jimmy Hoffa's Teamsters. Hoffa made him a union official and when we found him, he was with Local No. 612 in Birmingham, Alabama.

In our interview he said the letter had been written by Victor

295

Reuther, not Walter, and that around 1935 he had given it to his then schoolteacher for safekeeping. He said, and later testified under oath, that he had never seen the letter since then. We located the schoolteacher, who was then living in Pennsylvania. She said she had never seen such a letter.

There were approximately five so-called "authentic" copies of the letter in existence, each worded differently. A number of them had been placed in the Congressional Record as "the genuine letter." Because of Bishop's unreliability no one ever raised the question of the letter at the hearing. So even this maneuver was unsuccessful.

Reuther at one point took exception before the Committee to a speech in which Senator Goldwater had been quoted as saying: "Walter Reuther and the UAW are a more dangerous menace than the sputniks or anything that Russia might do."

Senator Mundt defended his Republican colleague. Reuter shouldn't complain. "That would not make you very dangerous. Sputniks are not dangerous. They are weather beeping things going around. There is no warhead in a sputnik. . . ." he said.

MR. REUTHER: Anything the Russians can do I take to mean treachery, immorality, inhumanity, every indecent thing they are capable of.
SENATOR MUNDT: You cannot abominate Communism, Mr. Reuther, any more than I do. I have been working on this problem as long as you have. I just point out that a sputnik is a little old thing flying around without any warhead or dynamite and that doesn't make you dangerous. I don't know how dangerous you are. Maybe you are not at all. A sputnik is not.
MR. REUTHER: You cannot be cute enough to wash this one up.
SENATOR MUNDT: I am just calling your attention to it.

On the matter of finances, Carmine Bellino testified that UAW records were well kept; that a review of Reuther's personal finances showed that he had his records intact for a period of over fifteen years, and that there was no evidence anywhere of misuse or misappropriation of union funds. When Bellino made such a statement, it left no question that the UAW and Reuther were clean in this area.

On Saturday afternoon, March 29, 1958, the last day of the hearing, Senator Mundt told Walter Reuther: "The first issue was the matter of corruption. Certainly, as far as this Senator knows, on the records we have there is no evidence before us of corruption insofar as your activities are concerned."

Senator Goldwater, that same afternoon, as Reuther was finishing his testimony, admitted to me: "You were right. We never should have gotten into this matter. This investigation was not one in which we should have become involved."

It took the Committee several weeks to heal the breach and to re-establish public confidence. Shortly after the hearings were finished, both Johnson and McGovern resigned.

After five long weeks—one of the longest hearings we conducted on any one subject—after eighty witnesses, and more than a million words of testimony, we proved that when a strike is long and violent, it will engender great antagonism. And, of course, everybody knew that before we started.

In 1959 Senator Mundt and Senator Curtis made one more attempt to link Reuther's name with Hoffa's and Beck's in the mind of the public. It was another fiasco.

The public hearings lasted for six days and dealt with an intra-union argument in Toledo, Ohio, during the 1940's which had been publicly aired in 1951. Senator Curtis conducted this hearing. A major point had to do with proving that a UAW official had marched in 1947 in a Labor Day parade with a cap and four stars on his shirt! The hearing did reveal that Richard Gosser, a UAW vice president, had some years before had an interest in a hardware store that sold goods to the union. But he had disposed of this in 1950 after the union made an investigation. The hearing also showed that a former UAW official, Pete Zvara had been guilty of wrongdoing—but had been booted out of the UAW for it.

At times during this hearing, Senator Curtis and I exchanged hot words. I knew we had at least five hundred cases in our files that were more important. This thing was a farce and I said so.

He came up with the perennial charge: I was following the "Walter Reuther line." But no one believed this any more. Even Senator Goldwater appeared disgusted. He said at the time, "I don't like Walter Reuther but this is no way to handle the matter."

297

In summary, I am not saying that Walter Reuther's political philosophy or economic philosophy is correct or should be followed or accepted or that I accept it. What I am saying, however, is the fact that one does not like Reuther or his philosophy does not make him dishonest.

Senators Goldwater, Mundt and Curtis and others in the U.S., because they disagreed with Reuther politically and economically, wanted him and the union investigated. It would follow automatically, they believed, that Reuther would be portrayed just like Beck and Hoffa. Why didn't you do to Reuther what you did to Beck and Hoffa, I have been asked. The reason is very simple and is the answer to this whole question. Reuther and the UAW have made mistakes, as I have pointed out, but as a general proposition the UAW is an honest union and Walter Reuther is an honest union official who attempts to run an honest union. For some people that is unfortunate but nevertheless it is true. Any attempt to equate the UAW with the Teamsters, or Reuther with Hoffa will fail—and in fact, did fail. The sooner this fact of life is accepted in the country, the better off we shall all be.

The final six-day hearing on the UAW was the last public hearing conducted by our Committee. With the passage of the new labor bill, Senator McClellan stated that there would be no more hearings. I resigned my post as chief counsel. However, my problems were not over.

The following day, while I was working on this book at my home, I heard that Senator Goldwater had given a statement to the press accusing me of having run out on the Reuther investigation. More disgusted than angry, I tried to reach him on the telephone and after several attempts succeeded. I reported what I had been told and asked whether he had, in fact, made such a statement.

He said that was not exactly how he had expressed it, though he was not completely satisfied with what had been done in the case. I asked if there was anything further he thought I should do.

"No, no," he protested. "I want to get back to Arizona now. I don't want any more hearings."

"Then why did you say it?" I asked.

"That's politics," he said.

I told him that I didn't consider myself a part of politics; that ours was a bipartisan committee and had tried to run the investigations on nonpolitical lines.

His answer was brief. "You're in politics, Bob, whether you like it or not."

Chapter 14 / COMMITTEES AT WORK

THROUGHOUT THE MONTHS and months of our investigations and hearings my relationship with the members of the Committee was usually good—but it was better with some members than with others, and better at some times than at other times.

For Senator McClellan, the Chairman of the Committee, I had the highest affection and respect. No other Senator could have done the job that he did. He had great patience and was innately fair, criticizing both labor and management wherever he found wrongdoing. I never knew him to pull his punches, and in my long experience with him, never did he ask or tell me not to investigate a particular individual, company or union. He was the most devastating cross-examiner I ever heard, and always commanded the respect not only of his colleagues but of the witnesses. He could enter a hearing room with only a slight knowledge of the details of a case and within a few short minutes grasp exactly what its pertinent points were and how they should be emphasized. I found this to be an extremely rare ability.

I also had the greatest personal admiration and affection for both Senator Ervin of North Carolina and Senator Church of Idaho. Both of them, despite many other duties, worked extremely hard and devoted long hours to the work of the Committee. They too had the ability to get to the core of a situation and they never favored in the slightest way either labor or management. All they were interested in was the truth and they treated all groups alike. I heard Senator Ervin on several occasions destroy a witness by telling an appropriate story which made the point better than an hour-long speech or a day of questioning. He could be particularly devastating when a witness was pompous or overbearing.

Senator McNamara had been a labor official himself and as such probably understood the problems of labor better than anyone else on the Committee. Although he criticized wrongdoing, he felt, particularly after the first year, that the Committee's work was being used to blacken the name of labor as a whole. This was a matter of concern to him as to many others. By the time of the UAW-Kohler hearings, he felt that the Committee had outlived its usefulness. He said so and resigned. I disagreed, because at that time we still had no law dealing with the problems we had uncovered. Later Senator McNamara showed great courage in supporting labor legislation, although it was vigorously opposed by Hoffa, who has considerable political strength in McNamara's state of Michigan. Hoffa afterward marked McNamara as well as my brother for political extinction.

Senator Church joined the Committee when Senator McNamara resigned after the first year. The whole staff was immediately impressed with him, and he gave new life and zest to the Committee. He was absolutely fearless, asking some of the most astute and penetrating questions that I heard put. I envied his articulateness. He was a tremendous addition to the Committee.

Senator Kennedy is my brother. I am highly prejudiced and therefore shall make no comment on him except to say that I think he will make a great President.

Senator Ives was hardworking, sincere, and always most co-operative. His understanding and knowledge of the labor movement made him, apart from anything else, a distinct addition to the Committee. He examined and studied problems objectively and as long as he served on the Committee I never knew him to allow political consideration to influence his decisions. We on the staff missed him sorely when he decided not to return to the Senate in 1959.

Senator McCarthy was already a sick man when the Select Committee was established, and attended only a few of our hearings.

I was personally very fond of Senator Goldwater. He worked extremely hard, was tough, had a sense of humor. He played politics to the hilt and sometimes slightly beyond. He could cut you to ribbons, slit your throat, but always in such a pleasant manner that you would have to like him.

Until the last week of the Committee hearings, Senator Mundt and Senator Curtis never criticized me to my face. However, I knew that they, and particularly Mundt, were sources of the "nonattribution" stories that the Democrats were covering up for Walter Reuther. On one occasion, in an effort to embarrass me, Senator Mundt wrote a letter to an attorney saying he was outraged that I had publicly discussed an investigation without first clearing it with the Committee, and that he was going to suggest disciplinary action against me. The only trouble, as he told me later, was that he had misread the newspaper clipping that had been sent to him; he had thought it was an announcement of an investigation of milk unions; actually it said we were investigating allegations that certain dishonest union officers had "milked union funds." When I pointed out to him that a careful reading of the clipping or a telephone call to my office would have clarified the situation, he was all smiles and compliments.

I did not respect him for the way he played up to Hoffa, Reuther and other witnesses when they were on the stand, yet attacked them viciously when they were not present to defend themselves. Witnesses pleading the Fifth Amendment were sometimes taken over the coals by Senator Mundt but when a witness talked he withheld his criticism.

Senator Capehart, who joined the Committee as a successor to Ives, made no contribution. It seemed to me that in his questioning of a witness he almost invariably sided with those under investigation. It was most peculiar.

He was critical of our work from the beginning. Shortly after he became a member of the Committee he sent his assistant to talk to me. I was asked whether we were observing due process, and whether witnesses were being treated in a way that Senator Capehart would approve. I was courteous, but the assistant's visits suddenly ceased. I subsequently learned why: he had been indicted in New York for tampering with a witness.

Senator Capehart was not the only one whose questions often seemed biased, and apparently not only to me. During the first hearings in 1957, this bias was so obvious that many protesting television viewers bombarded the Committee with phone calls and telegrams. One Senator received two hundred telegrams during a noon-hour recess and another, who evidently received even more, was so angry at the reaction that he wanted the Committee to find out about the $75 "clerk" who directed the TV programming.

The voice of the people had its effect.

Frequently people have said to me: "I've watched some of your hearings on television, and it's obvious that you already know the answers to most of the questions you ask a witness. Why ask the question when you know the answer? Why do you call him at all if you already have the information? Why not simply give your information to the Committee or to the Justice Department?"

These are points that go to the heart of the operation of a Congressional investigating committee.

It is true that in almost every case I did know the answer, or at least knew what it should be if the witness answered truthfully. But if we had not called the witness the alternative would have been for me or a staff member or an expert to testify to information that we had acquired through interviews. Unless we were testifying to material in the records or introducing documents, this would have been completely unfair. Congressional committees that follow such a procedure, particularly when dealing with matters that reflect on a person's character and reputation, are headed for disaster.

A staff member who testified that "X told me Joe Labor Leader makes sweetheart contracts and is misappropriating union funds, and Y told me that Bill Industrialist is paying off" not only could do inconceivable harm but might well fail to convey a sense of the authenticity of his information. Testimony of this nature should be given by the person who has the information at first hand, not by a staff member whose only knowledge is that he was "told it."

Imagine the protests that would have arisen if a staff member had testified at the first hearings that Nathan Shefferman told him he was paying the bills of Dave Beck, or that Robert Scott told him that Jimmy Hoffa used union funds to hide his brother from the police. This would be hearsay of the rankest sort. The Congress would not tolerate it and neither would the public. The criticism that would follow would be completely justified: Let Nathan Shefferman, Dave Beck, Robert Scott, Jimmy Hoffa come in and testify for themselves on such serious matters; let's hear it from them under oath.

Obviously there might be exceptions, circumstances in which this kind of testimony is warranted, as when a witness changes the truthful story that he has told an investigator earlier or when a staff member or some third person can give evidence to corroborate testimony already in the record. But if Congressional committees were to permit hearsay testimony of this kind as a general procedure the result would be absolute havoc. Yet, I have heard this course advocated by a number of very intelligent people, persons who have been outspoken in their criticism of Congressional committees in the past.

The reason I attempted to know as much as possible about what witnesses could and would testify to, and consequently what answers they should give, is that in no other way is an orderly presentation of evidence and testimony possible. It was our job to present the facts so that members of Congress could see clearly the areas in which legislation was necessary. If we had allowed witnesses to come before the Committee with no real idea of what testimony to expect from them, without first interviewing them, studying and checking their information, we should have had utter chaos and confusion, plus many inequities. At best, every hearing would have turned into an endless fishing expedition or a guessing game, a tremendous waste of time. We should never have got anything done.

However, the most important advantage of checking and rechecking testimony is that it lessens tremendously the possibility of damaging an innocent person's reputation. A prospective witness who intended to make a charge against another person had his story checked from every possible angle. On quite a number of occasions, after checking, we did not permit him to testify.

More than once a witness who had information that was easily documented also offered other information that we could not corroborate. If we could prove the truth of a major portion of his testimony, we would, in most instances, permit him to testify about anything within his knowledge. However, if the uncorroborated part could not be supported and was not in context with his other testimony and was of a damaging nature, we would ask him not to go into it. If he did not agree, we would not permit him to testify. On only one occasion, did a witness ignore our admonition.

This was a Texan, who charged that a certain union leader was involved in a murder plot. The rest of his testimony was verified by other witnesses, but on this point it was unsupported. The man whom he accused had never been arrested, let alone convicted, of any crime. In an interview before the Texan took the stand, I told him that we had been unable to document his story on this specific point and, although I was not questioning his word, because of the seriousness of the matter I was not going into it. He agreed, as did his counsel. On the witness stand, however, after finishing his corroborated testimony, he went on to tell of the death threat. I at once explained to the Committee that though we knew of this charge, we had not gone into it because we had not been able to document it. Furthermore, we immediately called the union leader whom he accused, who denied the charge categorically.

As an interesting sequel, at the request of the "accuser," both men took lie detector tests. The "accused" passed; the "accuser's" test was inconclusive.

I might add here that though I do not believe lie detector tests are conclusive, I think they can be very helpful. The machines are used widely throughout the United States by the FBI, the Office of Naval Intelligence, the Secret Service and the police departments of many cities. In my opinion the tests are far more effective when used on a sensitive person than on someone who has a psychological problem that keeps him from distinguishing easily between right and wrong.

In our investigation into the vice rackets in Portland, we had the essential information from one witness, Jim Elkins. Because he was an ex-convict, we spent three months checking and rechecking his story before permitting him to testify in public.

I believe that not merely the *proper* procedure but the *only* procedure for a Congressional investigating committee is to acquire full and complete information on the witnesses and on their testimony. When that work is not done, a committee is heading for troubled waters.

What kind of witnesses should be allowed to testify?

It is usually possible to find a witness who will testify to almost anything about a person who has been active in public life or who has taken a stand on issues; such a man is bound to have made enemies. I think, therefore, that a Congressional committee must, to a considerable degree, take responsibility for the testimony of its witnesses. You cannot put a man—or woman—on the stand, allow him to hurl accusations indiscriminately and, when his testimony is found to be untrue, disown him and accept no responsibility. Of course, a witness may make statements that you could not possibly have anticipated; that happened a number of times before our committee. But at least there should be a painstaking effort to confirm everything you think he will include in his testimony. In my estimation it is not enough merely to permit the person he accuses to come in and answer the charges after they have been made; the charges should be verified and corroborated before the witness is permitted to make them.

I told our investigators when they were hired that we were going to try to establish the same degree of proof in every case that we might need in a court of law. This was our goal. Admittedly, evidence was sometimes placed in the record that would not have been admissible in a court—for instance, hearsay testimony or a witness's opinion. However, our purpose was different from a court's and a latitude of this kind was essential. Our Committee was seeking information to determine legislative needs, and the more information we had, as long as it had been verified, the better the Committee and Congress could do its job. But our broader latitude in receiving testimony made it that much more incumbent on us to verify the evidence presented.

Looking back over the record, I do not know of any witness whose reputation was besmirched by our Committee. An examination of some fourteen million words of testimony shows no instance where the regular staff presented a case that was not fully and factually established and documented. We made mistakes, certainly, but in three years of hearings I can think of no case that the regular staff presented for which the Committee need apologize. However, I know the record would be far different if we had not spent so much time verifying testimony and obtaining documentation.

Much of the criticism of Congressional committees could be avoided by sound investigative work before a case is presented. I was an assistant counsel to the Senate Permanent Subcommittee on Investigations when Senator McCarthy was its chairman. I lasted only six months. With two exceptions, no real research was ever done. Most of the investigations were instituted on the basis of some preconceived notion by the chief counsel or his staff members and not on the basis of any information that had been developed. Cohn and Schine claimed they knew from the outset what was wrong; and they were not going to allow the facts to interfere. Therefore no real spade work that might have destroyed some of their pet theories was ever undertaken. I thought Senator McCarthy made a mistake in allowing the Committee to operate in such a fashion, told him so and resigned.

The House committee investigating Sherman Adams called as a witness John Fox, a former editor of the Boston *Post*. He testified, among other things, that Bernard Goldfine had helped to finance the education of Sherman Adams's children and was paying the rent on Adams's house in Washington, D.C. Some Committee members questioned the accuracy of Fox's testimony at the time of the hearing, but the charges could easily have been checked before Fox testified. However, it was not. Immediately following the hearing, which caused a great sensation, newsmen found that his testimony was completely untrue. The fact that Adams had been so badly maligned aroused the sympathy of a great many people. Unfortunately, as far as others were concerned, the disproof never caught up with the charge.

The antics of staff members as well as the caliber of their work can cause difficulties and undeservedly discredit the work of Congressional committees in general. An investigator's attempt to "bug" the hotel room of Bernard Goldfine caused such a furor that it not only diverted attention from Goldfine's unconscionable conduct but subjected the committee and its staff to severe criticism. They lost much of their effectiveness in the important work they were doing, and Congressional committees generally were hurt. To cite another well-worn but obvious example, Cohn's and Schine's whirlwind "investigating" trip to Europe, and Cohn's efforts to obtain special treatment for Schine when he went into the Army, were major factors in giving Congressional committees a black eye from which they have not yet fully recovered.

I might say here, apropros of the bugging of Goldfine's room, that our Committee staff never used wiretapping equipment or a listening device. With one exception, we never even recorded a conversation without first obtaining the person's permission. The one exception was when a staff member had an interview with a witness who, he believed, intended to try to trap him and later distort the conversation. He wanted a recording for his own protection.

Directing a Congressional investigation, which probes into the intimate affairs of human beings, can be at times an upsetting, even harrowing, experience. Once, for instance, we were looking into the affairs of a businessman who was involved with Jimmy Hoffa, but there was a question whether the Committee would conduct hearings on his activities. I interviewed him in our office in Detroit. After we had finished I told him it would not be necessary for him to testify in public.

He put his head in his hands and burst into tears. His children were graduating from school at that time, and he was overcome with the relief of knowing they were not going to be embarrassed and humiliated.

Many other innocent wives and children were not so lucky. The actions of a particular witness may rob him of sympathy—but his sins should not be visited upon his children. I learned after our hearings on an important man in Chicago that the car pool operated by the mothers of the neighborhood children would no longer stop and pick up his children for school, and that his wife had been ostracized socially.

Unless a man's personal affairs were an intrinsic part of the investigation, we did not get into them at all, for this simple reason: It was none of our business. In every investigation facts about a witness's life are uncovered that are not of public concern, for example a man's extramarital affairs. These matters were kept out of hearings far more than they were brought in, and only where the use of union funds was involved was the subject considered to be any business of the Committee. When a witness was willing to answer questions, I always discussed the matter with his attorney and arranged for his use of union funds to keep a girl friend to be referred to in the hearings as expenditures on behalf of himself or friends, with no other details given.

Sometimes the offer was rejected; occasionally the gratitude was overwhelming. Big burly Mike Singer, Hoffa's representative in Hawaii and Puerto Rico, toured the country with his girl friend at union expense. When told the lady would not have to testify, he rushed at Senator McClellan, threw his arm around him and tried to kiss him. The Chairman was not pleased.

As a general proposition, however, because it is certainly not the U.S. Government's business, we stayed away from the personal lives and habits of our witnesses.

It is never a pleasant task to present such evidence. And it is a terrible thing to see a grown man cry. You feel as if you are intruding on the most personal of all experiences.

What can be done about the abuse of investigating power? Some people who are concerned about these matters have suggested that laws or rules be passed to govern the operation of a committee. Others have suggested the more drastic step of doing away with Congressional committees altogether.

In my estimation, rules and regulations can do very little to cure the major faults that exist in Congressional committees. What rule can you pass to prevent a Congressman or Senator or counsel from asking an unfair question? What regulation can you write to prevent a committee member from yelling at or browbeating a witness? To set up a system under which all questions are cleared with the chairman, as though he were a judge, would not only be too cumbersome but completely unacceptable to individual committee members. Furthermore, the fault with many investigating committees has been their chairman. (In the case of our Committee he was a lifesaver.)

However, there are basic rules that ought to be followed. For instance, every witness should have the right to have counsel whether he appears in executive or open session; he should have full knowledge of the purpose of the hearing and of why he is being called as a witness.

We followed these procedures. Every witness had counsel and at the opening of every new series of hearings, the Chairman, Senator McClellan, made a statement of its purpose. Furthermore, any time a witness or his lawyer wished to know the legislative intent or the pertinency of a question, either the Chairman or I, on his instructions, would explain. This seemed to me not only fair, but almost to be required by the recent decisions of the Supreme Court of the United States.

What about cross-examination?

To a certain extent our Committee permitted it. Under our procedure, and I think it should be followed by all Congressional committees, lawyers for witnesses were allowed to submit questions by way of cross-examination. They were written out and given to the Chairman and then asked by him.

Obviously, a more complete cross-examination would afford witnesses certain protections that they do not have under the present system. But an investigating committee looking into Communism or corruption or racketeering would bog down in interminable delays if unlimited cross-examination by all witnesses' attorneys were permitted. Committee members and lawyers would wrangle endlessly over what were proper and permissible questions, and the committee would become a completely ineffective instrument. Our Committee, during its two and a half years, heard more than fifteen hundred witnesses. If unrestricted cross-examination had been permitted, I doubt if we could have heard one hundred.

Furthermore, we, and I believe most investigating committees, have safeguards for witnesses that do not exist in courts, which at least partly fill the gap. For instance, we permitted any witness to give a detailed statement answering all the charges made against him. In addition, he was permitted to give explanations, challenge the testimony of other witnesses, and question their veracity on the basis of such facts as he might choose to submit. During his testimony, of course, he could answer in detail each question put to him.

Our Committee also allowed a person to take the stand immediately following any derogatory testimony given by some other witness. If later other evidence was developed against him, the same procedure was followed. Thus, he might appear several times over a period of days to refute or explain charges. On occasions, where adverse testimony was going to take several days, we permitted a witness to present his side of the story at the beginning, with the understanding that he would be recalled at the end of the hearing for examination.

If we expected that information reflecting on the integrity of someone not scheduled to appear as a witness would be brought out, he was notified by telegram, letter or telephone, and told that if he wished to testify or file a sworn statement with the Committee he could do so.

These are basic procedures that can and should be followed. However, in the final analysis, if the chairman, members of the committee or the committee's counsel are going to be unfair there is nothing in the way of rules, regulations or laws that can really stop them.

Because the investigative power has been misused, some people, as I have said, have advocated abolishing investigating committees. In view of the commendable record of most such committees, this suggestion is hardly justified. It is the old remedy of shooting a person to cure his cold. The stock exchange and investment banking, Teapot Dome, the five percenters, Alger Hiss, conflict of interests and hundreds of more worth-while investigations have been conducted with dignity and honor. More than this, much of our most important legislation has grown out of the factual basis laid by Congressional investigations.

And the by-products of these investigations have been extremely important.

Justice Douglas in his book *We the Judges* put the situation in its proper perspective:

. . . the investigative function is sometimes turned to publicity purposes with the aim of making political capital out of somebody's misfortune or mistake. But the fact that the power is often abused does not detract from its importance.

The right to ask a question and the right to demand an answer are

311

essential to the democratic processes. I have often thought that without those rights any government would be intolerable. Certainly modern government is so complex and involved that opportunities for machinations within the bureaucracy flourish. Only the pitiless light of publicity can restrain them. That is why the embarrassing question from the Senator or Congressman sitting at the end of the table serves a high function. His right to demand an answer spells in a crucial way the difference between the totalitarian and the democratic regime.

This of course applies wherever there is a concentration of power, whether it be in government, business or labor.

Furthermore, there have been abuses in other areas of public life for which no one has suggested the remedy of abolishment. A policeman, by making an arrest in a small community, may ruin the life of the person charged. The mark is on the man's record, the word has gone out and even if later he is completely cleared, it can be too late. Or a prosecuting attorney can easily have someone indicted on flimsy evidence. The initial scandal may ruin the person's career, even though he may later be found not guilty. A judge can do incalculable harm if he is prejudiced or partial. The Attorney General of the United States has the power to do great harm. So, as a matter of fact, has the President.

And we have had bad policemen and district attorneys and judges, bad Attorney Generals, even bad Presidents. There is no guarantee under our system that a man will always act rightly simply because he is handed a badge or is vested with authority or because he takes office. There is always the danger that power or politics or pressure will corrupt any office, high or low. But because individuals have, on occasion, misused their power, we do not advocate doing away with the offices they hold. I have never heard anyone suggest that we do away with the police force, the district attorney's office or the judicial system, even though we have abuses in those areas every day of the year.

When a Congressional committee abuses its power, the remedy is to point it out and to get rid of those responsible. For this, it seems to me, we have a built-in safeguard in the public press. All Congressional committees' work is subject to public scrutiny, more so really than the work of any other group. If a witness is abused, if an investigation is unfairly or improperly conducted, if Senators or staff members stoop to unethical practices, the press is always present to expose it. The press serves as a sort of safety valve against the violation of civil rights. This is not the ideal, obviously, because often there is a delay in obtaining a cure for the abuses; nevertheless the press, the responsible part, is a potent and powerful safeguard.

This is one of the reasons I am strongly against having committee proceedings in private. (I am discussing here our kind of operation and obviously not matters dealing with national security.) In the first place they do not remain private, for the choice morsels are leaked to the press. Certainly we saw that during the days of the McCarthy Committee and even in our own Committee. I don't remember one executive session where anything of any significance that we discussed did not get out to the press. This can be extremely unfair, for invariably, only one side of a story is leaked. Secondly, I think the public is entitled to know what is going on and should have as full information as is possible. Public knowledge is a major deterrent to abuse.

This is a serious matter. It seems to me that where a public body is dealing with persons' reputations as we were, the press has an obligation and responsibility to remain vigilant.

Of the 1,525 witnesses whose testimony our Committee heard, 343 of them took the Fifth Amendment. Without question, we heard the expression, "I refuse to answer on the grounds that a truthful answer might tend to incriminate me," more than any group or body in the history of the United States.

Why did we call a witness if we knew he was going to take refuge behind the Fifth Amendment? First, we did not know for a fact that a witness would plead the Fifth Amendment until he actually appeared before the Committee and did so. Second—and this sometimes happened—a witness might answer some questions and refuse to answer others. His decision depended on the particular question asked of him. On a number of occasions I was told by a witness's attorney that his client intended to take advantage of the Fifth Amendment, yet when the witness appeared he answered all the questions put to him.

Beyond these practical considerations, I do not feel that a person who pleads the Fifth Amendment should be treated better or even any differently than a person who is willing to come before a committee and answer questions. Why should a person be able to avoid appearing before a Congressional committee and answering possibly embarrassing questions simply by stating, usually through his attorney, that if he appears he will plead the Fifth Amendment? This would be highly unfair to those who are willing to co-operate. If a witness is going to "take the Fifth Amendment," let him take it openly and plainly. He should not be permitted to answer questions by proxy any more than any other witness.

Furthermore, I strongly feel that a witness, in his very refusal to answer questions, is frequently giving important information to Congress and to the public. Dave Beck's invocation of the Fifth Amendment was certainly a shock to the country. His refusal to say whether he had taken $370,000 of the union's money, as much as anything else, showed Congress the need for some kind of Federal control to safeguard union funds.

Some attorneys advise their clients to plead the Fifth Amendment on every question and not to be selective. There is some legal precedent indicating that such advice is well founded. Although I could never be sure until a particular question was asked whether the witness would claim the Fifth Amendment, I could often tell early in the questioning whether I was going to get many answers out of him. When a witness resorted to the Fifth Amendment on every request, I felt he should be interrogated only on matters I would have asked about if he were answering questions. In other words, I questioned him on a point only when the facts had already been established in the record or when I had some definite information to support the question. For instance, if we had a gangster or underworld figure from Chicago or New York who was taking the Fifth Amendment, I would not ask him whether he had been involved in a murder or armed robbery, or had been the gunman for Albert Anastasia, unless I had some specific information that he had been.

I am not claiming that when I questioned a witness I always had positive proof on the subject matter of interrogation. In many instances, where a gangster was concerned, the information came from police files and could not be positively verified. These people not only wouldn't talk to us, they wouldn't and haven't talked to anyone. However, if I had some information to support the question, I believed that I was justified in asking it.

But this is where abuses creep in.

For instance, a witness from the Midwest was pleading the Fifth Amendment on every question when suddenly Senator Curtis asked him what his relationship was with the Governor of Iowa. I knew this was an unfair question at the time, for we had no information that the man even knew the Governor of Iowa or had had any dealings with him. The witness, of course, did not have to plead the Fifth Amendment on that question, but since he was pleading it regularly, once more made no difference to him. In any case, he exercised his privilege and refused to answer on grounds of self-incrimination. And in Iowa, as I had expected, the story was "Gangster Takes Fifth Amendment on Ties with Governor." I immediately put out a statement that we had absolutely no information about any relationship between the Governor and the witness. But the damage had been done. It was low politics and a perversion of the use of the Congressional investigating committee.

Very early in the hearings in 1957, my brother pointed out the unfairness of this kind of procedure, but as late as one of our last hearings in 1959 it was still being practiced. For example, in September of that year a former UAW official who had taken some pay-offs from an employer invoked the Fifth Amendment in answer to all questions. In the course of his interrogation, he was asked by Senator Mundt if he had made kickbacks to Richard Gosser, vice president of the UAW. He took the Fifth Amendment. Robert Manual, an assistant counsel appointed by the Republicans, then asked if Reuther had not instructed him to take the Fifth Amendment, with the implication that it was a cover-up for the UAW. My brother asked if there was any evidence whatever that the witness, Zvara, had kicked back to Richard Gosser. Senator Curtis and Robert Manual had to admit that there was not. My brother showed the unfairness of the questioning by asking Zvara if he had ever kicked back to Robert Manual. Again, on this, Zvara pleaded the Fifth Amendment. Manual also admitted that there

315

was no evidence whatever that Walter Reuther had had any conversations with Zvara in connection with his appearance before the Committee, let alone instructing him to plead the Fifth Amendment.

If my brother had not pointed these things out at the time, the record would have carried a completely unfair implication. As it was, one news story did report that Zvara pleaded the Fifth Amendment on kickbacks to Gosser.

Unquestionably the Fifth Amendment has been misused and, on occasion, abused. Hoffa turned it on and off for his subordinates as he felt it would help him. However, I would not have it changed. It is an important safeguard written into the Bill of Rights of our Constitution at the insistence of James Mason of Virginia. It grew out of the abuses practiced in the Star Chamber days in the reign of the Stuarts, and it is one of the rights that a free people possess against the potential abuses of government. It is part of our heritage, and should not be abandoned. No dictatorships recognize it, and we certainly cannot pay too high a price to protect ourselves from statism of that type. The Fifth Amendment does make the work of law enforcement, grand juries and Congressional committees more difficult, but it does not prevent them from accomplishing their objectives. And after all, it is not the Fifth Amendment that is causing the graft and corruption in the country, or even preventing it from being cleaned up.

What is really needed is not a change in the Fifth Amendment but more vigorous law enforcement, both locally and by the Federal Department of Justice. What is needed is a change in attitude. What is needed is for the people themselves to take a more active interest in their affairs, both locally and nationally. Crime, corruption, delinquency will continue to spread as long as people remain disinterested and lax and apathetic. We could do away with the Fifth Amendment tomorrow and the cancer of corruption would not be checked.

As I have said before, I have far more respect for the person who takes the Fifth Amendment than for those who appear before the Committee and say they cannot remember, who equivocate, rationalize or lie. In my experience, those who exercised the Fifth Amendment privilege and claimed that an answer might tend to incriminate them were, at least, telling the truth.

It has been said that one should not reach any conclusion about the guilt or innocence of a person claiming the Fifth Amendment. In a legal sense, I would agree. But certainly, if testimony is given that a man has violated his trust, misappropriated union funds or made a pay-off to a union official, and he then appears before the Committee and refuses to answer on the grounds of self-incrimination, it is less than human not to reach some conclusion. At the least, the witness's employer or colleagues should begin an immediate investigation into his affairs to determine his fitness to hold his position. Furthermore, although the Fifth Amendment is for the innocent as well as the guilty, I can think of very few witnesses who availed themselves of it who in my estimation were free of wrongdoing. I know of several who took the Fifth Amendment out of fear, but aside from them, for whom I felt immensely sorry, I know of none whom I should like to work for or have work for me—or have anything at all to do with.

Chapter 15 / CONCLUSION

THESE THREE YEARS have had their share of frustrations. One, of course, was the failure of the Teamsters to take action to clean up their own union. From our investigation we knew that many state and local officials were not meeting their responsibilities in the area of law enforcement because of politics, dishonesty or ineptness. Although we exposed improper activities on the part of at least fifteen attorneys and fifty companies and corporations around the country, with the exception of the Bar in the State of Tennessee, no management group or bar association has taken any steps to clean house. The only group that has tried to maintain standards and clean out their corrupt and dishonest elements has been the AFL-CIO. Their efforts should be kept in mind by those who seek to use our investigation to blacken all labor.

The lack of action by the Department of Justice is disappointing. It has lost some of the cases through incompetence. Senator McClellan, who was a witness in the perjury trial of James Cross, president of the Bakers Union, made no secret of the fact that he was highly critical of the way the Government attorneys presented that case.

In New York, where Hoffa was tried for wiretapping, the chief witness for the Government testified that he had met Hoffa in Detroit on July 10, 1953. Three weeks prior to the opening of the trial, Carmine Bellino had given the prosecuting attorney a detailed chro-

318

nology of Hoffa's whereabouts for every day over a period of some three months in 1953. It showed that on July 10, when the witness claimed he had met Hoffa in Detroit, James Hoffa was in Seattle, Washington. Not Detroit. And much to the embarrassment of the prosecutor, Hoffa was able to bring in documentary evidence as well as witnesses to prove it.

Afterward, I asked the U.S. attorney why, with the help of Bellino's memo, he had not been able to get his dates and places straight. He made the astounding admission that he had not read Bellino's memo.

Another case in point, about which I have gone into detail elsewhere, is the Government's handling of the bribery case against Hoffa in Washington, D.C.

Even the Dio case in New York was incompetently managed. District Attorney Hogan was making progress in his investigation linking Dio with the acid blinding of Victor Riesel. Suddenly in the midst of the investigation the Department of Justice stepped in and indicted Dio. They used an obstruction of justice theory—that Riesel was about to appear before a Federal Grand Jury and expose Dio's operations and the acid had been thrown in his eyes to stop him. The case was badly handled. Six days before it was to come to trial, an assistant Federal attorney called me in my office and asked for all the material we had on the paper locals in New York. That made me angry. I asked him if they were putting on a Broadway show or a case. The paper locals material was extremely complicated. If this was important to the presentation against Dio they had come to us too late to review and understand all the material. There was no time for them to grasp even the most rudimentary details of this case. I told him what they were doing was of the greatest importance and it was a disgrace to have the case handled in this way.

In Nashville, Tennessee, the judge who reversed the conviction of Glenn Smith for income tax evasion was highly critical of the poor manner in which the Government handled the case.

Furthermore, many of the cases that we sent to the Justice Department for possible prosecution lay dormant for ten months, a year, and sometimes even longer.

There have been problems, then, in conducting these investigations.

But the long hours of our work, the tediousness, the frustration, the worry have had their compensations.

A number of important labor leaders have been toppled from power as a result of the Committee's revelations—Dave Beck from the Teamsters, James Cross from the Bakers, William Maloney from the Operating Engineers, Klenert and Valente, president and secretary-treasurer, respectively, of the Textile Workers Union. A large number of lesser officers, International vice presidents and local union presidents have lost their jobs.

On the other hand, the major target of the investigation, Jimmy Hoffa, and his chief lieutenants still hold their union positions despite overwhelming evidence of corruption. This also has its compensation, for if Hoffa weren't still president I doubt whether we would have had new Federal legislation. He was the symbol in the minds of members of Congress of what needed to be corrected.

In the long run, the legislation and the awakening of the public are what are important. It is not sufficient to get rid of a Dave Beck or a Jimmy Cross or a Hoffa without passing a law to deal with the problem that has been uncovered. The honest elements of organized labor, the Meanys and Dubinskys, recognize this.

And Hoffa's days are numbered. Because of recent court decisions the Teamster monitors have the power to press for his removal. I believe they will. Even if this does not prove true, a man with Hoffa's power and position, and so corrupt, cannot survive in a democratic society if democracy itself is going to survive. I believe the country, not Hoffa, will triumph.

The investigators themselves can also take a great amount of satisfaction from the knowledge that their work often shook the foundations of a community and even of a state.

Duffy's and McShane's investigation in Tennessee brought about five convictions of important Teamster officials, the impeachment of a judge, and the removal of several public officials from office. It was a No. 1 news story in the state and it caused a tremendous impact.

Bellino's investigation of Dave Beck in Seattle knocked from a position of power a major political figure who, more than any one

320

man, had dominated the state's affairs.

Lee Nulty's investigation of Local 107 of the Teamsters had a tremendous effect on Philadelphia.

Walter Sheridan's investigations in Indianapolis and St. Louis; Langenbacher's investigation in Pontiac, Michigan; Pierre Salinger's investigation in San Francisco; Adlerman's and Calabrese's in Portland; Willse's, Kelly's, May's, Tierney's, Constandy's investigations in New York; Ralph Mills's in Miami; Sinclair's in Gary, Indiana; Kopecky's in Chicago; and the work of others elsewhere had tremendous impact; and I regret that I have not had space to deal with all of them.

More than twenty individuals, labor leaders, management people, gangsters and others directly involved in the investigations have been convicted and sentenced to prison terms as a result of the work of these men.

And as this is written there are other encouraging developments. As a result of the work of the Committee, indictments are pending against some of Mr. Hoffa's closest associates, including international vice president John O'Rourke of New York, international trustee Raymond Cohen of Philadelphia, William Presser of Cleveland, Anthony Provenzano of New Jersey, Mike Singer of Los Angeles, Barney Baker now located in Chicago, Theodore Cozza of Pittsburgh, Vincent Squillante of New York, and Harry Gross of Miami and New York. Cornelius Noonan, an official of the ILA, is under indictment along with Gross in New York.

Maurice Hutcheson, international president of the Carpenters Union, faces a contempt of Congress indictment in Washington.

Whether any of these cases results in conviction, the fact that the Justice Department and state authorities brought some of these matters to the attention of grand juries indicates that positive action has replaced lethargy in the attitude of government toward this important area of corruption.

The labor movement itself has had a drastic overhaul. The Teamsters have been expelled from the AFL-CIO and other unions have been placed under suspension or their officers have been removed.

There is tremendous satisfaction obviously in the fact that Congress has passed legislation that will deal with the abuses we have uncovered. Under the new law labor unions no longer will be able to file false or incomplete reports of their financial and administrative affairs. These matters must now be reported in detail to the Secretary of Labor and no longer may be concealed from union members or the general public.

Union officials no longer will be able to engage in secret conflict-of-interest deals. Management officials no longer can hide anti-union expenditures or make secret payments to labor "consultants," such as Nathan Shefferman, to do their dirty work. All such arrangements must be reported.

When our investigation began one hundred Teamster locals were under trusteeship and some had been for fifteen years—which means it had been that long since rank and file members were allowed to have any voice in running their own local affairs. Provisions of the bill deal with dictatorial trusteeships such as those practiced by the Teamsters and by the Operating Engineers, which kept two local unions shackled for twenty-nine years. The law sets up minimum standards for imposing trusteeships and provides for freeing locals from improper trusteeships.

Fair election procedures and a secret ballot are provided union members under this law. Now Federal and administrative action can be taken to overturn unfair elections, and there must be elections of International officers at least every five years and local officers every three.

The bill also seeks to rid the labor movement of ex-convicts such as many of the unsavory characters Jimmy Hoffa employs in his "palace guard." It blocks ex-convicts from serving as union officers for five years following their release from prison.

It sets up machinery for recovering misappropriated union funds and provides criminal penalties for embezzlement of union money. Under the statute every officer now must be bonded and a labor union may not lend more than $2,000 of its money to a union official.

It prohibits offering or accepting bribes in labor-management relations and provides for criminal prosecution in cases of violence or the threat of violence that might deprive a union member of his rights. The law as passed corrected some obvious weaknesses in the Landrum-Griffin Bill which passed the House of Representatives in 1959. For example, under that bill a broadly drawn section outlawed all union contract provisions designed to protect working men and women from sweatshop competition. Had it been passed into law, racketeers operating run-away sweatshops could have infringed on the rights of honest union workers—and would have been protected by the law.

The House and Senate conferees who developed the new bill made major improvements in the House measure; I am convinced that we have a far better and a fairer bill because of that conference.

Obviously, the law still is not perfect. Just as large corporations, such as General Motors and U.S. Steel have different problems from small retail establishments, so do small and large unions have different problems. Laws regulating business recognize these differences. The newly passed labor law falls with equal weight on all unions, regardless of their strength or economic bargaining position. The restrictions on picketing in the new measure are desirable where a strong union wields its power in a socially irresponsible manner and for all practical purposes forces membership on employees who may or may not wish to join the union. On the other hand, these same restrictions will work to the detriment of small, weak unions whose sole weapon in the face of determined employer resistance to union activity is a peaceful picket line. This provision will have a seriously adverse effect on the development of responsible trade unionism, particularly in the unorganized sectors of the economy. This is most unfortunate. However, I am extremely pleased that a law was passed. For the most part it is a good law and one that is absolutely essential.

The sordid dishonesty uncovered by the McClellan Committee is a reflection on all Americans, for it cuts across all segments of our economic life—labor, management, the law, the press. The new labor bill is a big step forward, but it cannot be considered an end-all; we cannot afford to sit back and with smug satisfaction assume that the job has been done. The revelations of the McClellan Committee were, in my estimation, merely a symptom of a more serious moral illness.

In the fall of 1959, I spoke at one of the country's most respected law schools. The professor in charge of teaching ethics told me the big question up for discussion among his students was whether as a lawyer you could lie to a judge. Evidently, things are not going to improve. I told the professor and said later in my speech that I thought we had all been taught the answer to that question when we were six years old.

And yet two children, eight and twelve year old, were corrupted during the course of the TV quiz programs, and many older people who were approached also accepted the crooked arrangement.

For our nation to survive in the period of heightened international competition, we must reaffirm some of the basic values of our fore-bears, values that are deeply rooted in the history of our country and in its rise to a position of strength and respect in the community of nations.

The tyrant, the bully, the corrupter and corrupted are figures of shame. The labor leaders who became thieves, who cheated those whose trust they had accepted, brought dishonor on a vital and largely honest labor movement. The businessmen who succumbed to the temptation to make a deal in order to gain an advantage over their competitors perverted the moral concepts of a free American economic system.

Neither the labor movement nor our economic system can stand this paralyzing corruption. Premier Khrushchev has said that we are a dying house, a decadent society. That he says it does not make it true. But that corruption, dishonesty and softness, physical and moral, have become widespread in this country there can be no doubt.

The great events of our nation's past were forged by men of tough-ness, men who risked their security and their futures for freedom and for an ideal. The foot soldiers at Valley Forge, the men who marched up Cemetery Hill and those who stood by their guns at the summit, the men who conquered the West, the Marines who fought at Belleau Woods and at Tarawa did not measure their sacrifices in terms of self-reward. And because of what they and countless others like them achieved, we are now a powerful and prosperous country.

But have the comforts we have bought, the successes we have won, the speeches that we make on national holidays extolling American bravery and generosity so undermined our strength of character that we are now unprepared to deal with the problems that face us? The records of the McClellan Committee are studded with disturbing signs that we are not prepared. Dangerous changes are taking place in the moral fiber of American society.

These are uncertain times for the United States. People say, But what can we do? We must all begin to take a greater interest in our national affairs and let our legislators know where we stand on the important issues that arise. We must take new interest in the running of our communities, the operations of our schools, and in such important matters as the physical, mental and spiritual fitness of our children. A recent survey shows that, even in democratic unions, less than 12 per cent of the membership attend the meetings with any regularity. The men to whom the unions belong must take a role in the running of them. And certainly an ethical practices code such as the AFL-CIO has adopted should be introduced by management groups such as the Chamber of Commerce and the National Association of Manufacturers.

It seems to me imperative that we reinstill in ourselves the toughness and idealism that guided the nation in the past. The paramount interest in self, in material wealth, in security must be replaced by an actual, not just a vocal, interest in our country, by a spirit of adventure, a will to fight what is evil, and a desire to serve. It is up to us as citizens to take the initiative as it has been taken before in our history, to reach out boldly but with honesty to do the things that need to be done.

To meet the challenge of our times, so that we can later look back upon this era not as one of which we need be ashamed but as a turning point on the way to a better America, we must first defeat the enemy within.

APPENDIX

(This information derives from police records, court records and sworn testimony before the Committee.)

WILLIAM BUFALINO of Detroit was set up in the juke-box business by some of the biggest gangsters in the city. Subsequently Hoffa made him head of juke-box Local 985 which, according to testimony before the Committee, was often operated as nothing more than an enforcement arm run for the benefit of certain preferred employers. Bufalino's local also has jurisdiction over car washers in the Detroit area, who often work under contracts calling for only $20 to $30 for a seventy-hour week.

HENRY DE ROMA, twice convicted on a narcotics charge and once for murder, is a trustee of Local 805 in New York City, in charge of preserving union funds.

SHORTY FELDMAN was Hoffa's chief lieutenant in Philadelphia. He has been arrested fifteen times and convicted four times, and served a term for burglary in Sing Sing. Feldman brought together Hoffa and Raymond Cohen, secretary-treasurer of the largest local in Philadelphia. Cohen has been convicted himself and the Committee found that eighteen of his officers, business agents and organizers had police records. It also showed that more than $400,000 of Cohen's local union funds had been misused. Even after he took the Fifth Amendment before the Committee, he was made an International trustee of the Teamsters Electrical Union, elected on Hoffa's slate at the 1957 Miami convention.

327

JOHN FILIPOFF took the Fifth Amendment before the Committee on the use of strong-arm methods in an election and a conflict-of-interest business transaction. Hoffa afterward made him organizing director of a major drive on the West Coast.

DAVE FRECHETTE was a Hoffa lieutenant in Florida. Secretary-treasurer of Teamster Local 290, he exploited the segregationist feeling in the area to whip into line the recalcitrant owners of house-building firms.

ABE GORDON, vice president of Local 805, was a close friend of Hoffa. His local was used often as the headquarters of Johnny Dioguardi and other underworld figures. Gordon spent $85,000 of union welfare funds to buy from his cousin a piece of property that was worth only $25,000. Afterward the property was renovated by nonunion help and used frequently as a private resort by Gordon and his family.

MILTON HOLT, secretary-treasurer of Local 805, was convicted in 1954 of helping certain favored employers to gain monopoly control of the distribution of coin machines; in 1959 he was convicted of perjury. In 1958 and 1959 he received loans of more than $243,000 from an employer, some unsecured and interest free.

FRANK MATULA, identified as a "cartage enforcer" in Los Angeles for favored employers, is a convicted perjurer. Hoffa appointed him one of the International Union's three trustees to guard the union's funds.

JOHN TIMOTHY O'BRIEN of Chicago was elected an International vice president on Hoffa's slate. From his own Local 710 in Chicago, over a six-year period, he received a salary of $471,000, more than $90,000 in 1956 alone.

TONY PROVENZANO is president of Local 560 in New Jersey, and in 1959 was elected president of Joint Council 73. He has underworld connections and was identified before our Committee as taking pay-offs from a number of employers. He is expected to succeed John Conlin, who is first vice president of the International Union in New Jersey. Conlin, also close to Hoffa, was identified before the Committee as also being involved in pay-offs.

MIKE SINGER, a Hoffa representative, tried to place a monopoly control of the grease business in Los Angeles in the hands of favored employers. He was indicted by a Federal Grand Jury.

ZIGMONT (ZIGGY) SNYDER received a twenty- to thirty-year sentence for armed robbery and has been arrested four other times on the same charge. An officer of Hoffa's home Local 299 in Detroit, he had charge of the docks. He also incorporated the Great Lakes Cargo Handling Company to direct the loading and unloading of waterfront cargo in Detroit. Ziggy Snyder, union official, didn't bother to solicit membership among the employees of Ziggy Snyder, businessman. The company employed nonunion labor exclusively.

Ziggy Snyder, businessman, formed another company in Detroit called the Fort Wayne Manor Auto Wash, established with the assistance of Teamster official Larry Campbell. Again he employed nonunion labor, who worked under sweatshop conditions. Before the Commitee, Snyder took the Fifth Amendment. Another Teamster official convicted of sodomy caused labor trouble for businessmen in order to get customers for Snyder's nonunion car wash business.

JACK THOMPSON, an officer in Local 332 in Flint, Michigan, has a record of fourteen arrests and five convictions, including a conviction for armed robbery and arson.

GUS ZAPAS stated that he had been arrested so many times (forty-five) that he could not get a job in Chicago. He went to Indianapolis and became an official in the Indiana Conference of Teamsters. He had no legitimate source of income for at least a year prior to this job.

INDEX

ACF Wrigley Grocery chain, Detroit, 221
AFL-CIO, 42, 72, 84, 102, 125, 161, 196, 210, 212, 213, 218, 228, 318, 321
A & P Stores, 223-225
Abass, Ahmed, 115
Abrams, George, 138
Accardo, Tony, 84, 247, 263
Acropolis, John, 242, 243
Adams, Sherman, 307
Adelizzi, Joseph L., 157, 158-159
Adelstein, Bernard, 242, 243-246
Adonis, Joe, 89, 244
Afro-American, 57
Akros Dynamics case, 179, 228
Alderman, Jerome, 116, 173-174, 233, 261, 321
Allen, Frank J., 66
Alo, Jimmy, 90
Amalfitano, John, 250
American Legion, 219
American Weekly, The, 231, 232, 233, 234
Anastasia, Albert, 6, 49, 76, 244, 245, 314
Anchor Motor Freight Lines, Cleveland, 155
Anheuser-Busch Co., St. Louis, 26, 225
Anonymous letters, to McClellan Committee, 183

Anslinger, Harry J., 177
Apalachin, meeting at, 62, 239-240, 241
Army-McCarthy hearings, 176
Associated Transport Co., 26, 321

Baker, Barney, 48, 52, 60, 88-91, 123, 131, 136, 182, 183, 321
Baker, Mollie, 90, 183
Bakery and Confectionery Workers Union, 190-196, 218, 220, 229, 318, 320
Balkwill, Howard, 94, 95-96, 97-98
Ball, Bob, 58
Bar associations, 228, 230, 318
Barbara, Joseph, 239-240
Barbera, Anthony, 137
Barker, Albert, 193
Bassett, Sam, 9, 11-12, 18
Batalias, Peter, 199
Beck, Dave, 3-16, 17-35, 41-42, 50, 59, 72, 77, 78, 80, 91, 92, 106, 119, 123-125, 129, 130, 151, 157, 166, 181, 183, 203, 214, 218, 225, 268, 277, 297, 298, 304, 314, 320, 321
Beck, Dave, Jr., 26, 41-42
Bell, Henry, 240-242
Bellino, Carmine, 3-4, 7, 10-11, 15, 17, 20, 25, 33, 47, 49, 52, 81, 86, 93, 95, 96, 97, 99, 101-103, 104, 111, 113, 173, 187, 273, 281, 284, 285, 296, 318-319, 320

Other DA CAPO titles of interest